NOMADS
at the Crossroads

NOMADS
at the Crossroads

Editor

O.P. Goyal

ISHA BOOKS
DELHI-110 033

Nomads : at the Crossroads

Rs. 880

ISBN: 81-8205-149-5

Published in 2005 in India by
Isha Books, D-43, Prithviraj Road,
Adarsh Nagar, Delhi-110 033

Laser Typesetting at : Shree Vaishnavi Creations, Delhi
Printed at : Chawla Offset Press, Delhi

Contents

Preface

The word 'nomad' is derived from the Greek word for pasture – nomos. The term nomadic is now a common metaphor for aimless wandering. In fact the movement of traditional nomadic peoples is far from haphazard: it is both predetermined and systematic. Most nomads live in marginal areas like deserts, steppes and tundra, where mobility becomes a logical and efficient strategy for harvesting scarce resources spread unevenly across wide territories.

The main livelihood of nomads is herding. They keep the productivity and survival of their herds through extensive yet cyclic wandering in areas where there are not enough resources to remain in one place permanently. They have special ways of adapting to the arid and unreliable climatic conditions. They have a strong and viable social system and community organization which enhanced their self-reliance and survival capacities to meet their needs, even at times of disaster such as drought. Children of pastoral nomads go without modern education, but not without education at all. They receive traditional education that is oriented to their ways of making a living and which contains the cultural and societal values of society.

Nomadism as a way of life was a logical, valid and productive mode of existence. Pastoral nomads proved to be resistant to external forces. Their land, culture, lifestyle could not be overrun by modern civilization. As the world economy is changing drastically, and pastoral nomads everywhere are facing the impact. They have been at the mercy of shifting commodity prices, tariff regulation, and trading patterns over which they have little or no control. As the monetized economy expanded to engulf the pastoral nomads, they have become more and more dependent on goods from settled communities, and their sensitivity to macro change is increasing.

The book contains intersting portraits of the life and livelihood of the various nomadic groups of the world. From marriage to religion, from animal husbandry to popular justice, all aspects of the culture and daily life of nomads are elaborately described. It also provides authentic information about the existing patterns of nomadic settlements and the challenges confronted by nomads from modern reforms.

Editor

1

Introduction

The word 'nomad' is derived from the Greek word for pasture – nomos. The term nomadic is now a common metaphor for aimless wandering. In fact the movement of traditional nomadic peoples is far from haphazard: it is both predetermined and systematic. Most nomads live in marginal areas like deserts, steppes and tundra, where mobility becomes a logical and efficient strategy for harvesting scarce resources spread unevenly across wide territories.

There are three main groups of nomads:

Pastoralists

Pastoral nomads move with their households in search of pasture for their animals. There are an estimated 30-40 million of them in the world. Livestock is central to their livelihood and the basis of their culture. Their movement is seasonal, linked to rainfall and the availability of good forage for their animals.

Goat herders in the Peruvian Andes graze their animals on richer grasses at lower altitudes during the wet season, then move to higher altitudes during the dry season.

Of the 60,000 Sami in Scandinavia only 6,000 are still nomadic. They may migrate with their reindeer up to 300 kilometres from sheltered forests in the winter to coastal grasslands in the summer.

Hunter-gatherers

Groups like the San of the Kalahari Desert, the Inuit of the Canadian Arctic, native people of the Amazonian rainforest and various hill tribes of Southeast Asia are nomadic in that they move in search of particular animals to hunt or foodstuffs to gather. These hunting cultures are now disappearing or changing under the influence of modern consumer society and the cash economy.

Traders and Craftworkers

Other groups may have nomadic lifestyles although they are neither pastoralists nor hunter-gatherers. In the West the best known of these are the Rom or Gypsies, sometimes known as Travellers.

Originally from northern India, the Rom moved north-west about 1,000 years ago and scattered across Europe, working as petty traders, musicians, farm workers and day-labourers.

Sea Nomads

The Sama Bajo are a small group of sea-faring nomadic people who've lived and fished near southeastern Sulawesi in Indonesia for more than five centuries. They live in temporary villages built on sand-banks or on beaches or at sea as boat-dwellers. They sometimes experience a reverse form of sea-sickness if they spend too long on land.

For the Sama Bajo the sea is a combination of *tambah* (medicine), *batam banang* (home), *lalang* (road), *alu'intah* (food) and *seha* (friend). It's also home to their ancestral god *Umba Made Lau*. Major rituals centre on the water. After a child is born the umbilical cord and afterbirth are thrown into the sea. According to Sama shaman Sandro Nduseng this ensures that 'their spiritual brothers and ancestors will protect and watch them throughout their life'.

Today the Sama Bajo are under severe threat. Large areas of coral have been pillaged for limestone; the reefs on which they rely for fish are dying. At the same time Japanese and Taiwanese trawlers are scooping up the remaining fish and destroying the ocean floor with their nets. In addition Australia has prohibited 'outsiders' from fishing for shark fin and sea cucumber (traditional Sama Baja foods) within its exclusive 200-mile economic zone.

Plains Indians

Plains Indians are nomads. Nomads means they are always moving from place to place looking for food. Nomads have to carry everything they own with them every time they move. Before they had horses, the Indians would have to carry everything on foot or use dogs to carry things. They used dogs with packs like saddlebags and with travois to carry stuff.

In a very short time Plains Indians learned to be expert riders. Along with hunting they learned to use the horses to make war and go on raids. They could go much farther than they ever could on foot and arrive rested and able to fight. The tribes who learned how to use horses first and fast had a huge advantage over other tribes. They quickly pushed other tribes out of their former territories and expanded their territories. Tribes like the Comanche and Cheyenne who had horses and knew how to use them first pushed other tribes like the Apache, Wichita and Tonkawa south and west off the plains. The Apache who now live in New Mexico and in Old Mexico used to live way up in the Texas panhandle and north of Texas. Bands of Comanche warriors on horseback were powerful and feared by everyone – Indians and Europeans.

African Nomads

Over the centuries, many semi-nomadic and nomadic cultures have inhabited the desert environments which stretch across the African continent. Pastoral peoples continue to live in these harsh habitats. Their inventive architectural responses reflect timeless, sophisticated thought processes and involve cultural strategies:

— Spatial mobility is the key to their viability;

— Women are the primary producers, owners and users of the domicile;

— The architectural process unfolds in the context of marriage ritual.

The Fulani people of West Africa are the largest nomadic group in the world. As a people group they actually contain a large number of people from diverse groups who were conquered and became a part of the Fulani through the spread of Islam. The original Fulani however are of the North African or middle eastern origin and have lighter skin, thinner lips, and straighter hair. They are known as "white people" to many Africans. The first group of people in West Africa to convert to Islam through jihads, or holy wars, they were able to take over much of West Africa and establish themselves not only as a religious force but also as a political and economical force. The Fulani are a very proud people, they are the missionaries of Islam and ended up conquering much of West Africa.

The Fulani are primarily nomadic herders and traders. Through their nomadic lifestyle, they established numerous trade routes in West Africa. Many times the Fulani go to local marketers and interact with the people there getting news and spreading it through much of West Africa. The most important object in Fulani society is cattle, and there are many names, traditions, and taboos concerning cattle.

The number of cows a person owns is a sign of his wealth. This has caused significant conflict in recent months between the Fulani and other ethnic groups. The reason for this is that the cows will many times go into the fields and eat the grain of local farmers. With increasing numbers of other transportation being used the Fulani are at risk of losing their identity as nomads and are being forced to settle in farms and villages. This sometimes creates other problems, because the Fulani are very proud people of their unique culture and used to ruling over the other people.

Another difference between the Fulani and other African people is that the Fulani have a huge respect for beauty. Beauty is considered very important and one of the ways this is shown is through tattoos that are put all over the body. A distinguishing feature of a Fulani can be their lips, which are many times a blackish color from the use of Henna or tattooing done on the mouth. Being brave and feariess are very important for the Fulani as is seen by their numerous weapons. One tradition is that when 2 boys reach coming of age they two boys hit each other with their staffs not showing any pain but instead laughing. Many have died in these ceremonies which are now against the law in many countries but continue to be practiced.

The Fulani normally raise large amounts of cattle and have therefore settled in large plain areas of Mali, Niger, Burkina Faso and Guinea. The Fulani hold to a strict caste system. The 4 caste subdivisions are the nobility, merchants, blacksmiths, and descendents of slaves of wealthy Fulani

Tuareg People

For a thousand years, the nomadic Tuareg people have roamed the sands of the eastern and central Sahara Desert. But today, many find themselves caught between economics and a desire for their old ways. And as economics wins out, many are settling in the ancient desert trading post of Timbuktu. Known as Blue Men because of their indigo robes, these camel-herding nomads pretty much held their own against the 20th century — until its last three decades. Starting in the 1970s, droughts have forced many from their desert homes. In 1990 a rebellion by an autonomy-seeking group of Tuareg from the northwestern African nation of Mali forced many others to flee. More than 165,000 settled in refugee camps in neighboring countries, waiting for peace.

By 1996, calm had returned to Mali, but a drought has continued. Many Blue Men have lost their animals to it. Others lost their animals during the upheaval. These animals — camels, cows, goats and sheep — are the key to their nomadic life. They provide these nomads with milk, cheese, meat and transportation. Their camels enable them to transport salt bars in a 17-day caravan from Taudenni in northern Mali south to Timbuktu. And if a person needs money, he sells an animal.

For a thousand years, the nomadic Tuareg people have roamed the sands of the eastern and central Sahara Desert. But today, many find themselves caught between economics and a desire for their old ways. And as economics wins out, many are settling in the ancient desert trading post of Timbuktu. Known as Blue Men because of their indigo robes, these camel-herding nomads pretty much held their own against the 20th century — until its last three decades. Starting in the 1970s, droughts have forced many from their desert homes. In 1990 a rebellion by an autonomy-seeking group of Tuareg from the northwestern African nation of Mali forced many others to flee. More than 165,000 settled in refugee camps in neighboring countries, waiting for peace.

By 1996, calm had returned to Mali, but a drought has continued. Many Blue Men have lost their animals to it. Others lost their animals during the upheaval. These animals — camels, cows, goats and sheep — are the key to their nomadic life. They provide these nomads with milk, cheese, meat and transportation. Their camels enable them to transport salt bars in a 17-day caravan from Taudenni in northern Mali south to Timbuktu. And if a person needs money, he sells an animal.

Upon leaving the refugee camps, their herds decimated, many fell back on the sedentary lifestyle learned there and headed for Timbuktu in search of work. Some earn money as tourist guides. Others by giving tourists camel rides into the desert. Still others selling tourists trinkets. Some have gone into goat herding or agriculture. And some exist on aid from the government and the United Nations.

Many yearn to return to their nomadic ways, but economics holds them to Timbuktu. Others who desire a nomad's lifestyle feel it's more important for their children to get a school education, and so they stay on in Timbuktu. When their children finish school, they will not know the desert ways, and they, too, will stay on. Some Tuareg have been able to return to their traditional life, following trade routes deep into the Sahara with their camel caravans and making their homes around desert oases. Their desert lifestyle is not an easy one. Daytime temperatures can reach 120 degrees F (49 degrees C), so they travel by night, navigating by the stars. Sand storms shift the landscape and pepper exposed skin and eyes. They face a constant search for water.

Their home is a tent. When visitors come, they layout carpets and cushions, and drink mint tea. Both men and women wear flowing blue robes and elaborate silver jewelry. The men wear turbans and veils while the women go unveiled and decorate their eyes with kohl. Women enjoy respect and freedom as well as descent and inheritance through the female line. Traditionally, these people have had a feudal society. It consisted of a relatively small number of noble families — organized into tribes — a large number of vassals and a lower class of black serfs. While nominally Moslem, the Blue Men h1ave also held on to many of their pre-Islamic rites and customs.

A Berber people with a population of about one million, the Blue Men are no strangers to Timbuktu. They attacked the town in the 15th century and have ruled there several times since. Many more times they have terrorized it. For centuries these tall, fiercely independent warrior people made the Sahara their sanctuary. Only caravans willing to pay the price of passage were allowed to move. Even the Arabs, who conquered so much of Africa, Asia and even Europe, were unable to impose their will on these nomads. That's why the Arabs called them "Tuareg" — the "abandoned of God." While the French colonial powers drew lines in the sand to create Mali, Mauritania, Niger and Algeria, the Blue Men continued to freely wander across them.

Some Tuareg, not having enough animals to resume the old nomadic ways, have taken a sort of middle ground — they have settled in oases not too distant from Timbuktu. The closest one to town is about 20 miles away, a five-hour camel commute. There the government teaches them to tend vegetable gardens, growing tomatoes, carrots and cabbages. But it's not a popular activity.

The settlement's chief lost 50 camels, goats and sheep in a month-long trek out of Mali in 1991. He now has a few animals but not enough to survive on. Like most of the village's Blue Men, he makes the five-hour trip to Timbuktu once a week to swap leather sandals, silver jewelry, leather bags and daggers for salt and other commodities. The chief says he is happy to be back from the refugee camp, but adds that without his animals he is worse off now. Like numerous other settled Tuareg, the chief says his prayer is that he will be able to again build up his herd and bring back the old days.

Himba

The friendly Himba tribe are descendants of a group of Herero herders who fled into the remote northwest after been evacuated by the Nama. Both ethnic groups speak the same language. The Himba are rustic people. They primarily herd and breed cattle and goats and lead a nomadic lifestyle. These nomads travel with their herds to different watering places, depending on the time of year.The Himba have resisted change and adhere to their traditions and cultural heritage which is rich, unique and immersed with meaning, significance and harmony.

The Himba were coerced into being hunter-gatherers after they were impoverished by Nama cattle raiders in the mid to late 1800's. Consequently, they were called the Tjimba, derived from the word meaning aardvark - 'the animal that digs for its food.' Many of the tribe members fled to Angola where they were called Ovahimba, meaning 'beggars'. A new leader with the name Vita (meaning war) emerged. After the First World War he relocated his people in Kaokoland, since the area was now under South African, and not German rule. Today, they live their pastoralist lives without much interference. Gradually, they have had to merge traditional ways with Western values.

The Himba have a number of charming rituals. Perhaps the most interesting is that of the ritual fire, the okoruwo. The fire guarantees contact between the living and the dead, which is essential for harmonious living and keeping the ancestors happy. It is kept alive until the death of the headman. Subsequently, his hut and the fire are destroyed. His family dance in mourning all through the night and before his ritual burial, everyone says to him. 'Karepo nawa', meaning stay well. Afterwards, a fresh mopane tree stump is lit from the cinders of the old fire and spiritual peace returns to the people.

The beautiful Himba women are renowned for their intricate hairstyles and traditional jewellery. Their stunning features, beautiful jewellery and clothes, along with their noble, proud bearing of the Ovahimba have caught the attention of visitors from far and wide. It is truly an honor to visit these last nomads of Africa. Since Himba men and woman wear few clothes besides a loin cloth or goat skinned mini-skirt, they cover their bodies with red ochre and fat to protect their skin from the sun and to give their appearance a rich red colour. The proud Himba women take quite a few hours for beauty care every morning. The entire body is massaged with a cream, which consists of rancid butterfat and ochre powder. The fragrant resin of the Omuzumba bush is added as well. The cream lends the body an intense reddish shine, which is consistent to the Himba ideal of beauty.

Himba women have a distinctive plaited hairstyle and headdress. Young Himba girl's ondato (plaited hair) is usually divided into two to four plaits. When they approach puberty their plaits are brought forward over their eyes. The hair at the base of the neck gets shaved sometimes. Young women's hairstyles change from the prepubescent hairstyle to that of a mature woman who wears many thick plaits and also wears the erembe (post-pubescent headdress). Adolescents and young Himba boys also wear the ondato. Men almost ready for marriage wear ozonya (two parallel plaits running from the top of the head to the back of the neck.) However, married Himba men comb out their hair and wear turbans.

The Himba jewellery is made from iron or shell, and as a result of their unique designs have become very popular amongst western visitors. Clothes, hairstyle and jewellery are all of particular significance to the Himba and are part of their tradition and culture. Even newborn babies are festooned with pearl necklaces. When the children are a little older, beaten copper bangle shells are worn.

Himba dwellings maintain their ancestral style of domed or conical huts made from palm leaves, mud and cattle dung. The Herero, on the other side, build larger structures with a peaked roof and a rectangular door. During the course of a year the family will relocate from one home to another in search of grazing for the animals. Therefore, is it important not to take anything from a Himba hut, even if it seems deserted.

Hunger and Famine

Famine has struck parts of Africa several times during the 20th century. While graphic media coverage has helped to raise international awareness of African famines since the 1970s, it has done less well at explaining why famines persist, how they occur, and how they differ from the equally (if not more) serious problem of chronic hunger. An adequate discussion of both problems must begin by addressing common misconceptions. Further, one must consider the broader political-economic and ecological reasons why so many African peoples are still vulnerable to deprivation, despite the numerous "coping strategies" they have long employed in order to survive in harsh and unpredictable environments.

According to the United Nations Food and Agricultural Organization (FAO), the average African consumes 2300 kcal/day, significantly less than the global average of 2700 kcal/day. Recent FAO figures estimate that 316 million Africans, or approximately 35 percent of the continent's total population, is chronically undernourished. Although hunger in Africa is hardly a new phenomenon, it now occurs in a world that has more than enough food to feed all its citizens. Moreover, while Africa's population is growing rapidly, it still has ample fertile land for growing food. Hunger, therefore, reflects not absolute food scarcity but rather people's lack of access to resources—whether at the individual, household, community, or national level—that are needed to produce or purchase adequate food supplies.

The reasons people cannot obtain enough food are, of course, rooted in several different historical patterns of inequality. These patterns include the inequalities between Africa and its former colonizers or contemporary financiers, and between Africa's rich and poor. It also includes inequality between members of the same households, where food and the resources needed to obtain it (such as land and income) are often unevenly distributed between men and women, old and young. Whatever the reasons for food deprivation, when the result is malnutrition (defined as a deficiency of protein or vitamins, as opposed to undernutrition, referring simply to caloric lack) it can do lasting damage, increasing susceptibility to diseases such as malaria, rickets, anemia, pellagra, and perhaps acquired immune deficiency syndrome (AIDS). Malnourished children suffer stunted growth and, often, learning problems. Malnourished adults have less energy to work. Over the long term, inadequate nourishment can cast communities into a vicious cycle of sickness, underproduction, and poverty.

Famine is commonly defined as "acute starvation associated with a sharp increase in mortality." This seemingly straightforward definition, however, avoids the much more complicated question of why people reach the point of starvation. Contrary to popular media coverage of the issue, famine in Africa is not an abrupt event, nor an immediate, inevitable outcome of drought or other climatic misfortunes. Rather, research on the history of famine shows that several factors typically contribute to a society's or region's vulnerability to starvation, and that some of the causes of famine have changed significantly over the past century.

As with hunger, a few basic facts about famine may be laid down. First, it is mostly children who die, followed by men; women's greater biological stamina makes them most likely to survive prolonged food deprivation. Second, the primary cause of death is not starvation itself, but diseases such as diarrheal infection and malaria. Third, famine not only increases mortality rates but also decreases fertility—and thus birthrates. Fourth, famine is typically rural, because for Africa's leaders (precolonial, colonial, and independent) food security in politically influential cities has almost always taken priority over rural areas. Fifth, the reported mortality rates from contemporary African famines are notoriously inaccurate, due partly to the difficulties of collecting such information, but also to international agencies' tendency to exaggerate figures in order to emphasize need for donor support.

A final point is that famine typically strikes only after people have exhausted a range of strategies intended to compensate for unpredictable climatic, economic, or political downturns. It is the nature and effectiveness of these "coping strategies" that have been most transformed by the environmental, demographic, and political-economic changes of the past century.

For example, rural communities in arid and semiarid regions have long cultivated drought-resistant crops such as millet, sorghum, and cassava, in an attempt to produce enough surplus to last several months of dry weather. Although this remains a desirable strategy for many rural dwellers, environmental degradation in some areas has reduced yields. Of greater impact has been the need to produce cash crops such as cotton, a change that leads farmers to depend more and more on markets for basic food supplies. When drought leads to crop failure, farmers may have little or no money to buy food—just at the moment that grain prices are skyrocketing. Under such conditions rural dwellers might seek income elsewhere: through wage labor, for example, or the sale of household assets such as family heirlooms, furniture, or livestock. Such strategies are unlikely to work, however, in severely impoverished regions; selling assets can also increase vulnerability to future famine, if it leaves a household without draft animals or transport.

Cultivating far-ranging social relations is also a time-honored "coping strategy." When famine threatens, rural dwellers often ask their urban relatives for money, food, employment, or temporary foster care of children. Entire families may also migrate, either to cities, neighboring countries, or, if necessary, relief camps. Abandoning home and field, however, tends to be a last-ditch strategy; by the time people migrate they may have already severely cut back on their daily food intake.

Africa's nomadic pastoralists have been among the hardest hit by 20th-century famines. Historically, they have survived in austere environments by migrating seasonally between grazing lands and developing commercial and patronage relationships with farming communities. In the past several decades, however, new obstacles, such as national borders, fenced-off land, and expanding agricultural settlements, have increasingly restricted seasonal movements. In turn, this has provoked conflicts between nomads and surrounding communities, as well as between nomads and the national governments that control food aid. Since the 1960s, declining rainfall in arid regions, such as the Sahel, has also restricted nomads' migratory range.

As the experience of many nomads indicates, the descent into famine depends a great deal on politics. During the colonial period, improved infrastructures and agricultural technologies should have improved food security, but colonial governments' high taxes, crop requisitions, forced-labor policies, and overall lack of accountability all increased vulnerability to famine in many regions. In the French colony of Haute-Volta (now Burkina Faso), for example, rural households that were forced to grow cotton suffered severe famine after rains failed and world commodity markets collapsed in 1930.

That many independent African governments have proven as unaccountable as their predecessors explains, in part, why famine still occurs in the late 20th century; war is another major reason . Some famines have followed governments' failure to respond to warning signs—such as the Zimbabwean famine during the drought of 1991-1992, for example—while others have resulted from draconian government efforts to control and extract revenue from rural populations. The Ethiopian famine of the mid-1980s, for example, was caused not only by drought but also by burdensome government crop requisitions and massive forced relocation schemes in the country's northern regions. In such instances, the lack of basic democratic institutions made it possible for famine's warning signs to go unheeded, both within and beyond the country in question. As the economist Amartya Sen has noted, ". . . in the terrible history of famines in the world, it is hard to find a case in which famine has occurred in a country with a free press and an active opposition within a democratic system."

Some of the worst contemporary African famines have resulted from wartime sieges. During the 1967-1970 Nigerian civil war, the federal government of Nigeria blocked all food shipments to Biafra, leading to widespread starvation. In 1993, siege brought famine to parts of war-torn Angola. And in Sudan's long-running civil war, the northern-based government has used its control over food shipments to weaken insurgency groups in the south.

Despite their seemingly apolitical humanitarian appeal, international food aid agencies invariably complicate the political picture. Sometimes food relief lets negligent governments off the hook; sometimes it even sustains repressive regimes. Ethiopia again offers a prime example. In the late 1970s and 1980s, the military regime of Haile Mariam Mengistu received huge quantities of food aid to fight a famine it had helped create. Yet 90 percent of international aid supplied Mengistu's followers, while only 10 percent reached equally famine-stricken rebels. The famine thereby strengthened Mengistu's grip on the country.

One the other hand, some countries that experienced dire famine as recently as the mid-1980s have made substantive gains in food security, despite the chronic threat of drought. Burkina Faso is one example; Eritrea is another. In both cases, concrete measures such as soil and water conservation programs on the village level have helped increase agricultural productivity in drought-prone areas, though they have not ended dependence on imported food aid. But past famines have also made food security a potent political issue, one that these countries' leaders cannot easily ignore. Success in combating hunger and famine in Africa will ultimately depend partly on technical advances, partly on sustained economic growth, but also on the recognition, both in Africa and abroad, that food security is a basic right.

Nomads use Animals

Animal mythology and symbolism permeate all aspects of nomadic society. Animals provide milk, meat and blood for food; hides, hair, wool, horn and bone for clothing, shelter and tools; and dung for fuel and fertilizer. Nomads also use animals for transport, freight carriage and traction (milling, threshing and ploughing).

— The Bedouin of Saudi Arabia have a special

vocabulary to describe their camels. The Arabic word for camel (*jamal*) comes from the same root as the word for beautiful (*jamil*).

— In Somali, the word *raadraa* which means 'to track down animals' is now used to describe modern research. The word *layis* which means 'to tame a young camel' is also the term given to exercises in a student work book.

— Mongols use different words to describe the age, colour and size of horses. The word *saaral* is used for a white horse, *ke'er* for a bay and *je'ered* for a reddish-brown steed.

Today, game animals are still valued as intermediaries between the human world and the divine. The Cree in northern Canada believe that if people take more game than they need or lack respect for the hunted, the tacit pact joining the animal and human communities will be broken. Geese flying overhead and ducks fluttering in marshes have a moral link to the people who hunt them. So hunters retrieve their prey not in victory but in a spirit of thanks. Far from seeing themselves in a fight for survival with creatures of the wild, they feel bonds of sympathy for the species they stalk. Northern peoples like the Inuit or Chukchee identify with the whale, polar bear and caribou. Africans like the Okiek and the San identify with the bushbuck and the giraffe. Hunters see themselves and the world around them through the eyes of the animal.

Nineteenth-century anthropologists thought that early cultures believed themselves to be descendants of animals and thus to be bears, otters or eagles. A 'totemic' species was worshipped as a god, revered as an ancestor and classified as kin. Those who shared a totem were considered bound by blood to defend and avenge each another, to avoid intermarriage and to mutually 'respect' the species by refraining from harming or eating totemic animals as well as protecting them.

Today, most specialists share the view of noted French anthropologist Claude Lévi-Strauss. He suggests that we should see totemic systems not as a primitive stage of religion, but as a common tendency of all human beings to classify the social world in natural terms. Among the Iroquois in North America there are Bear, Eagle and Turtle Clans. The Maasai in East Africa have red, white, blue and striped 'cattle clans'.

In a modern world plagued by environmental destruction and loss of biodiversity we are rediscovering knowledge held by indigenous peoples regarding the natural world. Nomadic hunters have to be behavioural ecologists, and herders must know animal science and range ecology. Lapps, for example, know when and where reindeer will seek lichen under winter snow; Inuit know where seals lie, how long they stay under water and which ripples betray their presence. The Turkana in northern Kenya bring their camels, cattle, goats and sheep to the Rift Valley Floor during the wet season. Then in the dry season the cattle and sheep are moved to the cooler mountains while camels and goats browse the remaining lowland shrubs.

No-one knows why people undertook to domesticate grazing animals 10,000 years ago. Killing some animals for meat would have done little to advance the domestication of other live animals and milking was adopted long after more docile domestic animals had appeared. So why were animals domesticated if it meant lots of hard work without any immediate benefits? It may well be that the answers lie in a perceived affinity with animals, along with a 'passion' to embrace and control them.

Pastoral people in particular have an intense interest in domestic livestock. Usually one animal is culturally dominant – it is crucial for subsistence and also used as a yardstick for measuring wealth. Whether yak, llama or cow, the dominant animal is both a medium of exchange and an object of emotional interest and symbolic elaboration.

Moreover, pastoralists internalize the image of their dominant animal. The animal becomes part of a herder's inner sense of self and a lens through which the world is perceived and understood. Pastoral communities everywhere make their ultimate gift to god by sacrificing their most prized animal.

The Nuer of the Sudan take their names from their favourite oxen and cows and draw parallels from their herds to define their own social relations and talk about community life. The gift of cattle from the groom to a wife's family, usually called 'bridewealth', establishes links between the two families that expand over time as the cattle reproduce and are in turn given to others. Today, with the coming of a market economy, Nuer separate their herd into 'cattle of women' and 'cattle of money', since it would be 'polluting' were the former sold or the latter given for marriage.

Maasai sometimes use special names with partners, calling one another 'my bull' or 'my heifer' or 'my cow'. For the Maasai, too, the words for colours, patterns and shapes come from their herds. It is not that terms to describe animals are then used to label colours and patterns, but rather that the system of colours and patterns and shapes are drawn from livestock. There is no 'red' per se, only the redness of a particular type of cow, no 'striped' per se, only a streaked pattern found on particular animals. Thus the world of nature – the patterns of clouds in the sky, the form of rocks, the texture of landscape, the shape of human limbs – are all expressed in the idiom of the animal.

Many pastoralists consider their link with domestic animals to be God-given. They emphasize their reliance on herd animals by prohibiting the hunting or eating of wild animals. Most herders usually consume milk products as staple foods but any wanton eating of meat is prohibited. Milk can be eaten fresh or sour or as butter. Meat is usually only sacrificed in special rituals and blessings – holiest when roasted or used in the distilled form of fat. Only on special Islamic feasts are camels sacrificed by Bedouin, Tuareg or Somali nomads.

There is no cruelty, but rather an attitude towards the victim akin to gratitude. The sacrificial animal should be holy, a perfect specimen – a strong, patient castrate rather than an irascible bull. At its death, its spirit establishes a link between a community and divinity, a state of grace. Whoever eats the flesh becomes one with the group, assuming its obligations and prerogatives. The animal serves to unify the group, joining it to God and advancing its members to another stage of life. It is sometimes claimed that the pastoralists' attitude to their livestock is religious rather than economic, since they prefer to accumulate animals rather than sell or slaughter them.

In fact it is more complex than that – economic logic is coupled with a strong cultural bond. We now realize that there is a good reason to build up herd numbers as a hedge against drought and as a store of 'capital'. Anyone who draws on 'capital' by routinely slaughtering animals and eating meat rather than relying on 'interest' by drinking milk is seen as a wastrel and a fool.

Nomads treasure few possessions. But they deeply value kin and livestock. Periodically moving house and home, they rely most directly for their survival and well-being on one another and on their domestic animals. Pastoralism demands intimate knowledge of animals, but it also demands dedicated effort and continuous labour. Like most occupations, it is best performed as an avocation, a love which is continuously rewarding rather than occasionally profitable. When herders praise cattle in song, or dream of camels, this enhances the necessary but mundane functions of husbandry. But more than that – it's a clear example of the symbolic importance of animals to their lives.

Everyone is linked with nomadism somehow, if only because ger and apartment dwellers alike have at least some relatives out in the steppe whom they visit regularly. For Mongols, the very core of their national identity is intricately intertwined, indeed inseparable, from that of nomadism.

In the suburbs around Ulaan Baatar, families own a small number of animals, relying on their relatives in the steppe for most of their food. Although some of them work in town they still consider their life closely akin to the 'pure' steppe livelihood. They live in gers as their forbears have always done and there is, above all, 'open air' all around. Ulaan Baatar shows links to the pastoralist lifestyle everywhere. Herders often ride through the central square on horseback in front of the imposing cement buildings of the former communist Government.

The inhabitants of Ulaan Baatar's ger districts display a remarkable ingenuity in adapting their lifestyle to the city. Unable to afford to buy or to make the traditional felt roof, many families have erected a second roof over their gers to protect the valuable felt from rain. Some have gone as far as building cement gers, while others actually spend half the year in the steppe and half living outside Ulaan Baatar.

The urban ger is a tangible cultural symbol which helps to maintain the resilience of the Mongol identity. In the tent cities, people have managed to integrate TVs, fridges, and in some cases computer terminals, into the symbolic space inside their gers – and hence into their way of life. Nomadism is often said to be at odds with modernity, yet the dynamic pragmatism of nomads in Ulaan Baatar shows that traditional lifestyles are not completely incompatible with the pluralistic vision of sustainable cities.

Cattle as Capital

Almost all English words for money come from the world of pastoral nomads. *Cattle, chattel* and *capital* come from the same root. Pecuniary comes from the Latin word for cattle, *pecus*.

Conflict between Settled Societies and Nomads

The conflict between settled societies and nomads is as old as Cain and Abel. But now it threatens to destroy nomadic societies. Wayne Ellwood explores the accelerating antagonism and suggests that we would do better to preserve our differences.

The Great Wall of China is one of history's boldest and clearest symbols of a frontier. Erected over 2,000 years ago this colossal piece of engineering snakes hundreds of miles across the undulating plains of China's Northwest. Gazing towards the horizon from the walkway on top of the wall the grassy steppes seem to stretch on forever, to the rugged mountains of Mongolia and beyond to the endless Siberian taiga. When it was built the Great Wall symbolized the outer edge of civilization, a clear demarcation between the nomadic bands of barbarians beyond and the first unified Chinese Empire.

One Chinese Imperial Secretary, fearful of invasion by the warlike Mongols, described the nomadic horsemen as wild animals: 'In their breasts beat the hearts of beasts,' he wrote. 'From the most ancient time they have never been regarded as part of humanity.'

Today the Great Wall is a relic of history and an obligatory stop for foreign tourists on package tours. Buses disgorge swarms of visitors from New Jersey and Tokyo while industrious hawkers pitch postcards of Genghis Khan and bottles of Coca-Cola. The Mongol land north of the Wall (known as Inner Mongolia to distinguish it from the Republic of Mongolia) is now controlled by China. The nomads are still there, but they are a threat no longer.

The Chinese have discovered a way of keeping them in their place. Since 1949, when the Communists took control, millions of Han Chinese, with government encouragement, have flooded onto the steppes – with the result that Mongols are now a minority in their own country. There are 20 million Chinese in Inner Mongolia and barely four million Mongols. Thousands of acres of former pasture have been turned into irrigated farmland and leased to outsiders, disrupting centuries-old migration routes in the process.

Traditionally, Mongols are pastoral nomads: that means they move their animals in a predictable pattern according to the seasons and the availability of forage. In the summer they travel to high ground where rain is heavier and grasses more luxuriant; in the harsh winter, when temperatures may drop to minus 40°C, they retreat to sheltered valleys.

This mobility is absolutely critical to Mongol culture – as it is to all nomads. But like governments the world over, the Chinese are suspicious of this central core of nomadism, this incomprehensible, alien urge to move. So they've set out to do something else about it. With the introduction of post-Maoist economic reforms herders no longer have customary rights to land. Instead they have to bid to win grazing rights to specific parcels, called kulums (enclosures). In return the Mongol owners are obliged to erect a house and dig a well. These ranches are big, often 20 or 30 square kilometres, but they are rarely vast enough to have both good summer and winter pastures.

What this means is that the Mongols have little choice but to plant crops to use as forage for their stock over the scarce winter months. Beijing has also demanded that the herders abandon their subsistence approach (essentially producing for themselves, selling animals when and if they need to) and enter the modern market economy – a shift which has led to much larger herds. With more animals the nomads now find themselves both cut off from their traditional migratory routes *and* increasingly hemmed in by expanding agriculture. The result? Serious over-grazing, soil compaction and, inevitably, advancing desertification.

Elsewhere this process of making nomads settle down (what is sometimes referred to as 'sedenterization') has been carried out with force. When Stalin imposed collectivization (making nomads into ranchers) on Kazakh herders in the 1930s, as many as half the population are estimated to have died fighting the change. Forty years later in Somalia forced settlement, influenced by the Soviet collectivist model, proved disastrous. After the drought of 1974 Somali planners attempted to move 120,000 camel herders from the north into four villages on the Indian Ocean coast. The goal was to train them to be fishermen and small farmers, not an easy task in a region where pastoralism is considered nothing less than a divine calling and camels are fussed over and loved like children. No points for guessing the scheme was a flop.

The desire to control nomads politically and to incorporate them into national (ie non-nomadic) culture has always been strong. By their very nature nomads rub nation states up the wrong way. They don't fit neatly into national boundaries and they tend to look and behave differently from majority populations. In post-colonial states run by bureaucrats wedded to the modernist vision of national progress, nomads are seen as distinctly 'unmodern' – an embarrassment, rather than productive members of society.

Whether we're talking about small bands of nomadic hunters in the Amazon Basin, Inuit hunters in the Canadian Arctic or nomadic pastoralists in East Africa, there is strong pressure from governments everywhere to make nomads stay put. The reasons are varied, sometimes benevolent, usually patronizing. They need to be brought together for their own good, government officials claim – so they can be educated, taxed and given proper health care, electricity and roads.

'We want, as a democratic government, to give all citizens the modern services that a state should give its citizens,' the Israeli advisor on Arab affairs said in 1978 in an effort to justify settlement of Bedouin nomads. The same rationale was widely shared by African countries like the Sudan, home to nearly three million nomadic herders from various tribal groups. Efforts began to 'modernize' the livestock sector 30 years ago. One of the first goals of the (mainly Arab) Government in Khartoum was to settle the (mainly Black) nomads in the south. In the soothing words of a Government report of the time: 'sedenterization... is a means of improving the economic and social conditions of those communities... to integrate them into the life of the nation and to enable them to contribute fully to national progress.'

If not for their own good, then nomads must be settled for the good of the nation. State planners claim that wandering pastoralists are inefficient and that they are ignorant of modern animal husbandry. Their irrational tendency to increase herd numbers threatens to turn delicate rangeland into unproductive wasteland.

These assertions are bolstered by a theory known as the 'tragedy of the commons', a rationale which has shaped government and aid-agency attitudes to nomadic herders for the last three decades. Briefly the theory says this: lands held in common, rather than privately-owned, will inevitably suffer environmental degradation since it is in each nomad's interest to maximize returns by adding more animals to the family herd.

The logical solution following from this analysis is for common lands to be controlled by the state or put into the hands of private owners. And that is just what's happening in African countries like Kenya and Tanzania, where nomads are being dispossessed in their thousands.

In Kenya the Maasai have lost more than 1,000 square miles of grazing land over the past century. And the process is accelerating. In the early 1970s the Government launched its 'Group Ranches' scheme to register large chunks of savannah to particular Maasai communities. This was to be the first step towards private ownership of all Maasai common lands. It was devastatingly effective. Before long more educated or influential Maasai used their guile to hive off huge portions of land within the group territory. As one nomad complained bitterly: 'We said all of us should be given equal pieces of land. But the chairman took a bigger portion than all the other people... My piece is small, only 60 hectares, while the chairman has 320 hectares.'

This soon sparked a desperate free-for-all as ordinary herders saw they would be left with nothing if they did not claim land themselves. Eventually the ranches were subdivided with the majority of Maasai receiving plots too small to support their herds. Unable to make a living the nomads soon sold their small plots: today 40 per cent of some Group Ranches has been sold off to speculators.

In addition, thousands of hectares of Maasai pasture have been creamed off by corrupt officials and local bigwigs. In his travels through Maasailand in 1992 British journalist George Monbiot found communities who had lost nearly all their land to outsiders. In some places, he wrote: 'The entire savannah had been divided among politicians and their friends. Some of the best land belonged to President Moi; the second best to George Saitoti, the Vice-President and the inferior places to their colleagues.'

To the south, in Tanzania, a quarter of a million nomads have had lands snatched by sharp-eyed entrepreneurs and massive state-run farming projects. On the Hanang plains near Arusha the Barabaig people, semi-nomadic cattle herders, have lost more than 40,000 hectares to a mammoth wheat-growing project funded by Canadian Government aid dollars. In some cases the dispossession has been violent: pastoralists have been beaten and their homes torched by Government workers clearing the land in advance of the towering Canadian-supplied tractors. Evidence is already mounting that mechanized mono-cropping of wheat is eroding the land at a rapid rate.

The view that common ownership causes nomads to abuse the land is rooted in ignorance. In fact countless examples show that pastoral peoples traditionally had sophisticated systems to manage common resources. And this makes sense. The land is all that nomads have – to degrade it or treat it foolishly would be tantamount to suicide. The Barabaig, for example, have complex layers of control involving the community, clans and individual households. Access to pasture and water is rigidly controlled to avoid over-grazing and serious sanctions are levied on those who abuse customary rules.

In Niger, FulBe pastoralists elect a traditional manager called a Ruga to regulate herders' use of natural resources. The Ruga decides which migration routes should be used according to local conditions and what animals should use which pastures. He also sets the times at which herds migrate and settles any conflicts which may arise between nomads and farmers along the way. If there are conflicts between nomads the Ruga alone decides on an appropriate punishment, including banishment from the community if necessary. When nomadic herders 'own' the land in common they make the laws regulating its use – and they make sure that everyone obeys them for the good of the community. The real tragedy occurs when lands are enclosed and environmental stewardship is replaced by intensive use for short-term profit.

Nomadic hunters share this same approach: living in symbiosis with the natural world, taking no more than they need and respecting the limits of the land. For example, Cree hunters in northern Quebec consider the animals they kill chashimikonow – a 'gift' from God. They believe they must not kill too much and only what is given. As a way of showing their seamless connection to nature they burn a piece of meat after the hunt, so the smoke is dispersed in the wind as a sign of respect to the animal spirits.

Violent clashes

Now, as age-old cultures are deprived of their lands, their mobility is rapidly changing. The damage is emerging everywhere. A classic example is the national park system in Africa. Under the guise of 'conservation' both hunter-gatherers and pastoralists are excluded – often by force – from forests and grasslands they have used for thousands of years. As local communities no longer 'own' the land they have little incentive to 'manage' it in a traditional, sustainable manner. The result is increased poaching and violent clashes between conservationists and nomads.

In Waza National Park in Cameroon villagers were moved outside the park fence and can be jailed or fined if found on their former territory. With no stake of their own in the wildlife local people now act as guides for Nigerian poachers with high-powered rifles who slaughter any animal that happens to wander into range. The attitudes and practices of nomadic peoples toward the environment differ profoundly from the values of modern industrial society. It is by now a cliché (but no less compelling) to suggest that tribal peoples feel a mysterious spiritual link to the natural world – a fundamental bond which the rest of us, chained to our houses and property, have lost.

This may go some way towards explaining the deep-rooted ambivalence that settled cultures everywhere seem to feel for nomads. We admire them for their perceived independence as we resent them for an imagined freedom which has always escaped our grasp. In their disdain for national borders and distrust of centralized authority nomads exhibit a healthy scepticism of power – a scepticism we would do well to heed.

Nomadic peoples tend to be politically egalitarian: their mobility gives them a safety valve. Like the Maku hunters of the Northwest Amazon most nomads bristle at the abuse of power by tribal leaders. If one Maku gets too bossy the others will simply pack up and leave. In his meditation on Australian Aborigines, *The Songlines*, Bruce Chatwin wrote that 'psychiatrists, politicians, tyrants are forever assuring us that the wandering life is an aberrant form of behaviour; a neurosis; a form of unfulfilled sexual longing; a sickness which, in the interests of civilization, must be suppressed.'

In Europe, Gypsies have been reviled as vagrants and thieves for generations. A quarter of a million perished in Nazi concentration camps during the Second World War. And the hate continues – in February this year a Gypsy community in eastern Austria was attacked and four men were killed. The Gypsies were warned to 'go back to India'. They've lived in the area for more than 600 years.

It is their 'wandering life' that makes nomads unique. Whether hunters or herders they display an uncanny resourcefulness and flexibility in their ability to survive on some of the most marginal lands on earth. Their elusive mobility enables them to adapt, and sometimes to prosper, in harsh and unpredictable environments. Reason enough for us to support their struggle to maintain their distinct way of life – on their own terms. But if we are really to accept our common links with nomads – and challenge our deep-seated prejudices – we're going to have to confront a more basic and perhaps more primal fear.

Threat to Movement

Nomadic peoples face many threats today, but the most serious is the attempt to stop them moving around.

— Over the last 40 years the Raika camel nomads in Rajasthan, India, have lost access to half of the common lands previously used as pasture.

— In Kenya, Government attempts to bring traditional Maasai lands under private title have ended up removing large areas of land from grazing. In some cases nearly half the land is now in the hands of non-Maasai.

— In Inner Mongolia much of the best grazing land has been turned over to irrigated farming. With privatization nomads have to contract for the right to graze traditional lands. More and more are becoming semi-nomadic and even sedentary ranchers.

Survival Strategies

— *Mobility:* Because nomads live in areas of climatic extremes they've had to be flexible and opportunistic. Mobility allows them to profit from widely-dispersed resources whose availability varies from year to year.

— *Mixed Economies*: Pastoral nomads raise several kinds of animals: usually one large prestigious species and several smaller animals like goats and sheep. Disease or drought affects each species differently, thus increasing the nomads' chances of survival. They also combine animal raising with small-scale farming, fishing, petty trading or migrant labour. And though nomads are subsistence-oriented, they have strong commercial skills, trading or selling animal hides, milk and meat in exchange for grain, tea and modern consumer goods.

— *Tribal Sharing*: Most nomadic peoples are organized into tribes or clans which have a customary claim over a specific territory. Tribal elders control who has access to common property like water, pasture, game or wild foodstuffs. Outsiders have to ask permission if they want to use resources on land which traditionally belongs to another group. Strong tribal identities are also one way pastoral nomads have of banding together to defend their livestock against theft by their neighbours.

Americans see themselves as a society literally on the move. David Watson looks at how this nomadic urge was born and explores its impact on both the land and the people. Movement and migration, always a large part of the human experience, have taken on a dramatically different character since early modern times. The rapid pace, enormous dimensions and universal permanence of movement have become characteristic of what is now a global urban-industrial civilization. The European invasion of America essentially financed the emergence of capitalism. In the process, old cultures were entirely uprooted, indigenous peoples slaughtered and displaced and whole regions pillaged.

It was the *un*-settling of Europe, social critic Lewis Mumford once remarked, that brought about the settlement of America. Those who came here were themselves uprooted, detribalized people. Settlement was itself vastly unsettling, what writer Frederick Turner called 'a spiritual story...of a civilization that had substituted history for myth as a way of understanding life'.

Turner recalls finding himself in the Black Hills of South Dakota, the sacred Paha Sapa of the Lakota Sioux. In a sudden flash he recognized how utterly estranged he was from the place, how it could never have the same deep meaning for him as for the Lakota – not because of the amount of time they have been there but for the way they have lived there.

According to Turner, the West's turn from cyclic myth to an obsession with linear time (and hence with geographic expansion to fulfil its history) underlies the frenzied outward movement of Western society in general and American civilization in particular. The archaic myth of traditional peoples, which we might visualize as a circle, was transformed into a new mystique of history: a single line, an ever-receding horizon. This turn toward history banished the sacred from nature, making the Europeans 'alienated sojourners' whose only outlet was 'the restless drive onward'. Such spiritual repression inevitably brought colossal levels of violence towards the world they encountered. The westward wanderers' testimonies of 'lavish and exhaustless' abundance, says Turner, were also narratives 'of waste, destruction, and frantic despoliation'.

Frontier redemption

Ambivalence toward the land set the tragic conditions of the American experience. The sentimental idea of paradise – a lush, abundant garden – had its corollary in the image of an immense threatening wilderness. Incapable of loving the land for what it was, the invaders had to 'improve' it, pulverizing and reconstituting everything in their path. That acute observer of early American society, Alexis de Tocqueville, likened their advance to a march: 'turning the course of rivers, peopling solitudes and subduing nature'.

De Tocqueville noted the tendency of early nineteenth century Americans to abandon a homestead before even finishing the roof. The settler typically was sustained by the idea that the frontier – a middle ground between corrupt civilization and chaotic wilderness – would bring redemption. Of course, the utopian urge for movement and change also reflected a profound desire for a stable home and roots. Furthermore, connected as they were to the American commitment to markets, these desires were paradoxical. The market system, based as it is on abstract economic exchange, is inherently destabilizing and must ultimately undermine any roots that have been set down. Thus each frontier was eventually exhausted and abandoned by the same forces which caused it to be settled in the first place.

Sacred circle

Looking honestly at the movements of indigenous peoples, we would mostly see a peregrination based on a profound awareness of and ability to live with the land, not against it. Traditional nomads move in a kind of sacred circle, or perhaps an ellipse; in their stories and migrations they return to the source and centre of the world.

In contrast, today's restless 'nomad' moves along a line, following a receding horizon, wrecking and abandoning along the way, never at home, always scheming the next move across shifting, breaking ice. Or maybe the movement is a circle, but it now goes from nowhere to nowhere, around and around like the subway line or the circulation of money. One thinks of De Tocqueville's prescient comment that in America life was 'always changing, but it is monotonous, because all these changes are alike'.

2

Pro and Anti Gypsism

The Gypsy peoples originate from Sind region now in Pakistan. Their Rom language is close to the older forms of Indian languages. The three tribes of Rom, Sinti, and Kale probably left India after a succession of campaigns in Sind through the C11, initially spending time in Armenia and Persia, then moving into the Byzantine Empire after the Seljuk Turk attacks on Armenia. Within the Byzantine Empire they dispersed into the Balkans reaching Wallachia (1385) and Moldavia (1370) ahead of this area falling to the Ottoman Turks. Other groups also moved through India to Gujarat and south of Delhi. Gypsy populations can still be found along all these migration routes.

When entering west Europe they initially had letters of protection from the King of Hungary. This privileged situation did not last long as amazement at their way of life commonly led to hostilities. The Gypsy way of life still leads to hostilities from the people of their host nations. Europeans regard "private property" as sacrosanct, whereas gypsies do not have a word for "possess", which gives rise to two incompatible ways of life and a continual problem of gypsies being regarded as "thieves" from the European's view.

In each host nation gypsies appear to take on the religion, names and language of their hosts, but within the *Rom* they maintain their *Rom* language, names, music, customs and Indian looks. This tight community has meant that after some six hundred years there is still a large population of gypsies not integrated or assimilated with Romanians.

From the time of their arrival in Romania Gypsies were the slaves of the landowners, only to be emancipated in 1851. While in Romania some of the Gypsies took to speaking a version of Romanian called Bayesh which can be heard in some of the songs of Gypsy groups recorded in Hungary. Nowadays about 40% of the Gypsies still speak Romany and many can still be seen travelling in lines of carts along the roads of Romania. The majority live in the towns and villages, some fully integrated into villages, some in large ornate houses standing out from the Romanians, but others in small buildings on scraps of lands on the villages edges.

Gypsies have existed as an oppressed people for a variety of reasons. Perhaps the most significant of these originated in the time and circumstances of arrival in Europe, but a number of other factors complicate the picture as well. Because of the nature of their entry into Europe, Gypsies arrived as a scattered nation of people united by language, culture and origin, but at the same time lacking any of the means by which other populations bound by the same factors assert and defend their identity.

Gypsies had no political or military strength, and no geographical territory with which they could identify. Nor had they a history, or a religion, or a language which was familiar to those around them. Association with the Islamic threat, their dark skin, and the various means of livelihood which exploited the superstitious nature of the Medieval Europeans, all helped instill a negative image of the Gypsy in the Western tradition.

When a group lacks the conventional means of redressing wrongs done to it, it will make the most of what is available; the fear of Gypsy magic was called upon as a means of reprisal some years ago in Florida, for example: a mother whose child was the victim of a hit-and-run accident "vowed to cast a Gypsy curse extending over three generations on the driver and his family if he does not come forward and pay the child's hospital bill." Such incidents help only to reinforce the stereotype from which they ultimately derive.

In addition to these external factors, internal factors have also helped keep the barriers firm. To a greater or lesser extent all Gypsy groups have inherited from India concepts of pollution and cleanliness, and these form a powerful basis for maintaining social distance from non-Gypsies. These beliefs extend into many areas of daily life, regulating involvement with food and its preparation, animals, personal hygiene, and interaction with others, both Gypsy and non-Gypsy. Among some groups, these concepts are vaguely defined; among others, the *Vlax* in particular, they are deep-rooted and pervasive. It is because of these cultural beliefs that Gypsies have discouraged familiarity with non-Gypsies who, by their manner of living, fall automatically into an unclean category, and are therefore able to pollute by association.

The earliest accounts of Gypsies unanimously agreed that Gypsies had no religious or cultural beliefs; some more modern treatments, while admitting that these exist, maintain that they have all been adopted from outside. It is understandable that writers such as [John] Hoyland, [James] Crabb and others came to such conclusions-they were permitted no such information by the Gypsies they were so ardently trying to civilize.

This reserve has had other, further-reaching effects; not often being able to obtain information at first hand about the true nature of Romani life, novelists have embellished their prose with fantasies of their own, and in doing so created in the last century the literary figure with which the Gypsy is today most often associated: a composite Gypsy, wearing Spanish flamenco dancer's dress, traveling in an English Gypsy caravan, playing Hungarian Gypsy music.

The first American account to discuss Gypsies at any length appeared in the Christian Enquirer for September 29th, 1855; American readers were given a picture which must have helped set the stage for what followed:

> The Gipsies ... are an idle, miserable race, a curse to the countries they inhabit, and a terror to the farmer through whose lands they stroll. They seem utterly destitute of conscience, and boast of dishonesty as if it were a heavenly virtue ... Laws have been passed in several countries to banish them, and great cruelties sometimes practiced to enforce these laws ... So deeply rooted are sin and vagrancy in the hearts of this miserable race, that neither penal laws nor bitter persecution can drive it out. They are not beyond the power of the Gospel, however, nor yet beyond the mercy of the Redeemer.

Attitudes towards the Gypsy today are mixed; while negative characteristics, usually theft or baby-stealing, often provide the rationale in fiction for introducing Gypsies into the plot, other, more positive characteristics also find a place. One such is the supposedly unfettered nature of Gypsy life, an outlet for the Victorian reader who no doubt longed for simpler, pre-Industrial Revolution times. But however Gypsies are defined and presented by the dominant culture, such definition and presentation denies

Gypsies their real identity, and this is ultimately a kind of oppression.

The notion of an "outlet" has been discussed by [Werner] Cohn, who believes that Gypsies "persist because they, or groups like them, are needed in our culture," in other words, there exists a need for an avenue of escape, for whatever reason, and Gypsies, or more accurately the fictional image of Gypsies, are useful in providing this. [David] Sibley, quoted in the introduction, goes further and sees the denial of the real Gypsy identity as one means by which the dominant society can maintain its own parameters. Quoting from [Kai] Erikson, Ronald Takaki has also elaborated upon this notion of parameter-maintenance by keeping non-members in their place:

> Deviant forms of behavior, by marking the outer edges of group life, give the inner structure its special character and thus supply the framework within which the people of the group develop an orderly sense of their own cultural identity ... one of the surest ways to confirm an identity, for communities as well as for individuals, is to find some way of measuring what one is not.

Yet another rationale is provided by [William] Kephart, who explains anti-Gypsyism in terms of Gypsies being seen as a countercultural population, a group of people actually working against the values of the majority:

> American Gypsies, too, continue to face prejudice and discrimination ... Some observers contend that it is a matter of ethnic prejudice, similar to that experienced by blacks, Chicanos and other minorities. However, it is also possible that the Rom are perceived as a counterculture ... If people perceive of Gypsies as a counterculture, then unfortunately for all

concerned, prejudice and discrimination might be looked upon as justifiable retaliation.

The Rom least well-equipped to retaliate against such social pressures are those best represented in the American Gypsy community: the Vlax, most of whose history in Europe has been one of enslavement. Existing for centuries in a society which provided all of what little material possessions they had, and which allowed them no involvement in any kind of decision-making, their modern descendants still look to the establishment as a source of support rather than as something to be worked with for the long-term good.

British and Hungarian Gypsies, subject to more assimilative pressures in their countries of origin, for better or for worse have learned to melt more effectively into the larger society, and have a much higher proportion of "professional" occupations represented among them in the United States. An exception among the Vlax are some of the *Machvaya* and other Rom of Serbian origin, a number of whom have also acquired mainstream occupations as well as high status within the Vlax community. It is likely that this is also due to assimilative factors. After abolition, those fleeing from Rumania westwards into Bosnia, Croatia and Serbia fared very differently from those who went eastwards into Russia.

In Serbia, the leveling power of Turkish rule, exerted for successive ages, had the effect of elevating the Gypsies somewhat toward the social status of the other *rayahs*. Here, therefore, although they are still an inferior caste, and not allowed to exercise the rights and powers of citizenship, the Gypsies are perhaps less widely separated from the peasantry around them than anywhere else in Europe. They fought bravely with their Serbian neighbors against the Turks, and as smiths, farriers, and dealers in live stock, have many of them earned a comfortable livelihood, and proved themselves respectable members of society.

It cannot be denied that the fuel for much of the discrimination against Gypsies in contemporary America is provided by the media. It requires very little effort on the part of those writing for the popular press, whether as journalism or fictional literature, to consult the existing sources and come up with material of their own without ever approaching Gypsy agencies themselves for their information. Almost all of the thousands of works relating to Gypsies have been written by non-Gypsies, and it is probably true that most of those have based their creations on the works of other non-Gypsies without ever checking their facts at first hand.

Despite the enormous responsibility that journalists have in transmitting information to the public, with very few exceptions the media continue grossly to misrepresent Gypsies and to perpetuate negative, and often defamatory, stereotypes. It has become so commonplace for the press to define Gypsies, an ethnic people, solely by behavioral criteria, that Gypsies themselves will frequently deny their identity:

> A Houston builder and Gypsy ... now doesn't tell anyone he's a Gypsy because he says it would ruin his business. "I'm not ashamed of it," he says, "but you've got to understand the effect it could have."

It is also true that, because of the widespread enforcement of laws over the past centuries which have forbidden Gypsies to stop anywhere, and consequently to attend school, Romani cultures have developed as non literate cultures. Even in countries with long-settled Gypsy populations and today the majority of the world's Gypsies are not nomadic-a way of life which does not include literacy as a primary skill continues to be perpetuated. As a result, the kinds of organized approaches made to television stations, congressmen, newspaper editors and the like which other minorities have used to bring their point of view before the public, have simply not been within reach.

Lacking access to lawyers, and other establishment means of seeking redress, Gypsies have not, until recently, been able even to take the first step towards challenging media misrepresentation. A situation exists today in which those who write for the popular press feel quite at liberty to say the most outrageous things about Gypsies, while they would be aghast if they were ever expected to put their names to the same kind of article about, say, Italians or Jews or African-Americans.

Non-Gypsy populations receive most of their knowledge of Gypsies from works of fiction and from the media, rather than from Gypsies themselves. Journalists and novelists for years have had completely free reign to exploit their fantasies in print, comfortable in the knowledge that no one would be likely to challenge them-and certainly that no Gypsy ever would.

A traditional, fictional image of the Gypsy, of non-Gypsy origin, has emerged and has become so deeply entrenched in the popular mind that the real thing remains unseen. From an urban perspective, "real" Gypsies-that is, those conforming to the romantic myth-are a rural people; from a rural perspective, "real" Gypsies no longer exist; they are a part of a vanished folk culture. We might compare Brody's description of the "real" Eskimo as conceived by the white community in the Canadian North: "the tough, smiling, naive, ultimately irrational soul who, animal-like, is deeply attracted to roaming the open spaces of the limitless tundra and ice." Again, the mythical individual is removed from the dominant society and merges with nature.

In Britain and France, Romani Gypsies in dirty roadside sites are condemned as unsanitary squatters who give the "real Gypsies" a bad name. The romantics defend the "true Romany" and write of their "purity of blood," perceiving a clear distinction between the Borrowvian ideal and what they see in real life. Others are less charitable: a letter to the press from an angry citizen in England complained that "they are very much detested and feared... even the true gypsy glamourised by George Borrow was never liked".

In the United States and Canada, the average citizen is likely to think that there are no Gypsies in those countries at all. They never see the campfires and waggons they associate with Gypsies, or the violin-toting individuals sporting earrings, embroidered vests and tambourines. Books and articles have been written which refer to Gypsies as "hidden" or "invisible" Americans, and Gypsies make good use of this fictional image as a shield between themselves and outside society, even giving it back if it is in their interests to do so.

Over a century ago, Walter Simson despaired at the widespread false perception which existed of the Gypsy, and at their exaggerated image as "wanderers":

The popular idea of a Gipsy, at the present day, is very erroneous as to its extent and meaning. The nomadic Gipsies constitute but a portion of the race, and a very small portion of.

Little has changed in the intervening century. Judith Okely, in a recently-published work on the British Traveller population shows how "Outsiders have projected onto Gypsies their own repressed fantasies and longings for disorder," and makes the point that "Gypsies do not travel about aimlessly, as either the romantics or the anti-Gypsy suggest." Much is made of this, as well as of stealing and promiscuity, in sustaining the stereotype. Stealing in particular is seen as a Gypsy trait; specialists such as Lombroso or Terry Getsay have even implied that it is a genetic characteristic.

Certainly some Gypsies steal, just as some Eskimos or Berbers or Englishmen steal; others don't. It is social behavior, and it is not transmitted biologically. To believe that such a thing is possible reflects not only prejudice, but an ignorance of scientific fact. Problems which exist today are the result of a continuum of circumstances going back for centuries. Few could argue that there has not been moral justification for subsistence stealing in the past, or that in some places it continues to be necessary, although this is not likely to be taken into consideration in a court of law.

Historically, stealing has meant survival, and there are many shopkeepers throughout Europe even today, who will not serve Gypsies. There are homeowners, too, who will refuse to give Gypsies as much as a glass of water. Given the choice between seeing one's family starve, or else stealing, the latter is going to be the likelier option, whether one is a Gypsy or not. But the public doesn't seem to be interested in Gypsies who don't steal; perhaps it spoils the image it has created.

There are a number of cases on file in the archives of the Romani Union, of crimes such as shoplifting being perpetrated by people reported as Gypsies, but who in fact turn out not to be Gypsies at all. The label is freely applied by police reporters on the basis of behavior assumed to be typical of ethnic Gypsies-which of course it is, if the model sought is the Gypsy of fictional literature. It is to the credit of the Saint Paul Chief of Police that he apologized publicly in 1985 for thus misapplying the word in the news bulletins issued by his department.

There are hundreds of thousands of Gypsies in the United States who deplore the illegal activities of those who make the news, and who make a clear distinction between themselves and *"le Rom kaj coren,"* i.e. Gypsies who steal, and there are hundreds of thousands who try to make a decent and honest living in the face of adversity. Gypsy priests and ministers don't ever seem to generate media interest.

History has shown time and time again that oppressor nations either attribute their own techniques of domination to the people they dominate, or else reinterpret their oppressive acts in what they perceive to be a positive way. Shifting blame onto the victim is a self-exonerating response well known in psychiatric circles. John Hoyland writes that "from such Gipsies who had families" in Maria Theresa's Hungary, "the children should be taken away by force; removed from their parents, relations, and intercourse with the Gipsey race." One child, "a girl fourteen years old, was forced to be carried off in her bridal state. She tore her hair for grief and rage, and was quite beside herself with agitation." Heinrich Grellmann recommended that taking Gypsies' children be used as a means of coercion:

The Gipseys, in common with uncivilized people, entertain unbounded love for their children. This excessive fondness for their children is, however, attended with one advantage: when they are indebted to any person, which is frequently the case in Hungary and Transylvania, the creditor seizes a child, and by that means obtains a settlement of his demand, as the Gipsey will immediately exert every method to discharge the debt, and procure the release of his darling offspring.

In the introduction to the new edition of her book *Gypsies. The Hidden Americans*, Anne Sutherland tells of a communication from the Chief of Police of one northern city who, having read the first edition of her book, expressed gratitude at having learned of such close family feeling amongst the Rom because he could now use it, by exerting pressure upon Gypsy children, to keep their parents in line.

"Wandering" or "roaming" is another commonly-repeated attribute, and are words which frequently find a place in accounts about Gypsies. Yet the words imply aimlessness, as though Gypsy lives have no purpose or direction; they are often qualified by words like "carefree." The harsh conditions of life on the road are never dealt with, and the day-to-day responsibility of feeding a family and keeping it clothed and warm is trivialized out of existence.

Gypsies in western Europe have traditionally been kept on the move because of laws which have given them no alternative. Means of livelihood have been developed which are adapted to this kind of life, and have subsequently become part of the stereotype. Individuals not conforming to these-who include a growing number of those involved in the Romani civil and political rights movement-are not infrequently denied their Gypsy identity by sociologists and others whose investment in them depends upon their remaining passive and traditional.

A Gypsy in a horse drawn wooden caravan is ideal; in a motorized trailer, not quite so authentic; in a house, he's a total disappointment; as journalist Ira Berkow said in a 1975 feature story, "Gypsies are, shockingly, also becoming home owners!" Gypsy women have for long been represented as sexual temptresses, and Gypsy men as a sexual threat to non-Gypsy women, in both song and story. The Impressions' *Gypsy Woman* has been recorded by a dozen artists since it was first released in 1961, and tells of the singer's watching the girl, longing to kiss and hold her as "all through the caravan, she was dancing with all the men" in the "campfire light"; Gypsy Davy is a traditional ballad about a lady who left her mansion and her husband to go off with a Gypsy; Lawrence's novel *The Virgin and the Gypsy* is a typical literary work along the same lines. And yet it was the European slaveowners who took Gypsy women at their will and used them, while calling them "whores," and it was the European slaveowners who castrated their male slaves to protect their own women from their servants' lust.

Werner Cohn may be right when he argues that non-Gypsies need a Gypsy image to project their fantasies onto; an example of this appeared in the Sunday supplement of one Boston newspaper in August, 1986. Describing a Romani family in that city, the writer stated on the first page of her article that from their appearance, ". . . they could be Spanish, or French, or Italian, or Irish," but by the second page she had already begun to be carried away by the lure of the stereotype:

They are glitter and gold, decked out in bright babushka of legend. They are exotic women in colorful skirts, dancing in sensual swirls. They are dark men with smoldering eyes. They are carefree spirits playing the tambourine. The entire image is crowned with a halo of mystique, shrouded in a cloak of mystery. And there is some truth to all of it.

The Victorian preoccupation with the "purity" of the noble savage is understandable in the light of those times, and the attitudes of 19th century "Gypsy buffs" whom Dougherty says "tended to be either superficial sentimentalists or genteel snobs looking for a feudal relic to coddle and patronize," must be interpreted with that in mind. But it is a singular characteristic among some of the contemporary students of Gypsies that the same attitudes persist. Where these people could do more than any other outsiders to help the Romani cause, they stubbornly refuse to disturb their anthropologists' and folklorists' perception of the Gypsy. We may compare 19th century statements made by such specialists with those made in the 20th century: Alexander Paspati maintained that "it is in the tent that the Gypsy must be studied, and not in the villages of the bastardized sedentary Gypsies," and [Richard] Pischel believed that "the Gypsy ceases to be a Gypsy as soon as he is domiciled and follows some trade."

Werner Cohn, believes that: The Gypsies have no leaders, no executive committees, no nationalist movement ... I know of no authenticated case of genuine Gypsy allegiance to political or religious causes.

The most recent denial of the nationalist movement has come from yet another member of the Gypsy Lore Society, Jiti Lipa:

> To be exact, there is no one Gypsy culture nor one Gypsy language ... If in the process of looking for native assistants and for training them [the Gypsilorist finds that] literary talents should appear, so much the better ... In reality, however, it is mere toying, a waste of energy and material means which are not abundant for Gypsy studies. While a missing attribute is being artificially contrived, which is supposed to make the Gypsies an ethnic minority in the conventional sense in the eyes of wishful thinkers and bureaucrats, irreplaceable values of Gypsy culture are being lost in our time.

These attitudes on the part of the non-Gypsy population, whether academic or popular, are a direct result of centuries of oppression, an oppression which has denied Gypsies the wherewithal to make their voices heard and to challenge discriminatory laws and widespread negative media stereotyping. Other persecuted peoples have begun to redress the wrongs being perpetrated against them; there are now no laws operating against

American Indians or African-Americans in this country, nor are they maligned and misrepresented in the press.

Gypsies use their language and core-culture as a kind of moveable country; wherever they have gone, ethnic identity has usually been maintained despite fragmentation and, until recently, a lack of international cohesiveness. Whether the three branches of Gypsy ... prove to belong to one migratory stock or not, it is clear that the Western Romani people were united linguistically and culturally at the time of entry into Europe. Whatever factors divided the contemporary populations, and they are not inconsiderable, they are overwhelmingly the result of involvement with the non-Gypsy, and are directly relatable to the oppression here described. If Romani Gypsies are to regain that unity, the causes and nature of the oppression which destroyed it have to be understood and challenged.

In Britain, traditionally, Gypsies have had very little reason to be interested in or concerned with politics. For hundreds of years they have travelled the country performing menial tasks, taking and often begging whatever employment they could find, fighting the elements, bigotry and mistrust, often being hounded and harassed from county to county by the constabulary pursuing outdated and archaic laws, very often I may add with much more vigour than was necessary. Many a poor Gypsy family went hungry for the day due to a well aimed police regulation boot being aimed at a pot suspended from a kettle iron over an open fire containing the whole days food supply for a family.

It is generally accepted that Gypsies arrived in Europe around the 14th century. Almost from the time they arrived, right up to the present day, they have been despised and persecuted. No people on Earth have such a history of persecution and hatred directed at them for such a prolonged period of time and for no reason. Fear though is often triggered with a fascination. Countless painters, musicians and writers have had their imagination stirred, and some of the public had their heads turned by romantic notions about Gypsy weddings and blood brotherhood, scenes of passion to the sound of violins, moonlight, mystery, magic, fortune telling and secret powers. Then there is the disenchanted view of the landowners and gamekeepers who find their coverts raided and their land fouled and littered. Somewhere between these two extremes the Gypsies exist. A people who in the course of their history have preserved and sometimes acquired beliefs, customs and traditions which are paralleled in many cultures.

A people who's history is preserved in oral traditions and legends, for being nomadic the Gypsies have not left behind archaeological evidence of settlement or cultivation, and because of their history of illiteracy no written documentation of any note. But other documentation is available in various archives and this much is known, that by 1471 the first anti-Gypsy laws had been passed in Lucerne, and by 1637 anti-Gypsy laws had spread via Brandenburgh, Spain, Germany, Holland, Portugal, England, Denmark, France, Flanders, Scotland, Bohemia, Poland, Lithuania and Sweden to encompass the whole of Europe.

The punishment that these laws demanded was varied and vicious. Flogging, torture, branding, mutilation, hanging, shooting, being hunted like animals for sport, bounties being put on their heads and hunted as vermin, the list is endless, the misery incalculable. In England in 1554 Queen Elizabeth I imposed the death penalty, not only for the crime of being a Gypsy, but for anyone in their fellowship and company. Gypsy Liaison Officers were a scarce commodity in those days. Scotland continued to enforce such legislation right through to the 18th century, and indeed much Scottish anti-Gypsy law was on the statute book up until 1906.

In 1994 a Conservative government in England is still passing anti-Gypsy laws, threatening to destroy homes, confiscate property, split up families, provoke needless confrontations, traumatise innocent children caught in the middle of it all, a stark similarity to Germany in the late 30's and early 40's don't you think? This, under a back to basics banner in 1994, the Year of the Family, in democratic England, by a government more dedicated to legalising buggery with sixteen year old boys, than providing conditions for Travellers to live within the law, following the only way of life they and their ancestors have known.

We now have ethnic cleansing by legislation, far more subtle and far more dangerous than ethnic cleansing by violence. That can be fought against, you can see your enemy, fight your enemy, crush your enemy. There is no such recourse with cleansing by legislation, unjust laws and legislation are something different. You may despise them, you may disobey them, you may argue against them, but you cannot destroy them, cannot crush them. They are always there and your way of life is always in peril, constantly under threat.

Once on the statute books, history has shown they will not readily be repealed, if anything they will be reinforced by reforms. Too many species on this planet have become extinct and too many species today are on the endangered list. Are the Gypsies now to be added to it? In this country, and quite rightly too, there are laws to protect the birds of the air, the flowers of the field and the majority of our natural wildlife, with penalties ranging from heavy fines to imprisonment, yet there is not one law to protect the Gypsy.

British justice, we are told, is the envy of the world. The British sense of fair play is legendary. They will lay down their lives in defence of the underprivileged and oppressed. How and where these myths originated is a mystery, and how they have lasted and endured is an even greater mystery. The British Empire was one of the greatest the world has ever seen. Taken by the sword, and held down by oppression and exploitation. How many poor souls perished through torture, slavery and trying to defend their freedom, is anybody's guess. Millions is a conservative estimate. These atrocities were not only confined to foreign shores either.

Politics played no great part in the Gypsies' life. That is rapidly changing. The Gypsy is beginning to realise that it is not the man in the street, not the man in the blue uniform, that is his enemy. It is the pin-striped suited politician stomping through the corridors of Whitehall in jackboot fashion, calling each other honourable and not knowing the meaning of the word, that is his true enemy. It is ironic that the laws now being framed, that this government claims are for the benefit of the Gypsies, are so Machiavellian in their structure. Misleading information oozes from this government like puss from an ulcer, whilst beneath the skin the problem festers on, untreated.

Certain segments of society have always from time to time had Draconic laws aimed at them resulting in bloodshed, misery and torment. Witches, Heretics and Jews spring readily to mind. All have one thing in common, the laws are now repealed and the persecution is a thing of the past. The Gypsies stand alone, unique, as the only segment of society whereby such laws have not been repealed. In fact, today the laws are being strengthened and made even more insidious. Leave or be hounded to death. Every country in Europe has attempted this legislation at least once against the Gypsies. Britain is now falling in line with that maxim once again.

Gypsies in the Early Twenthieth Century

Two dominant stereotypes of the Gypsies which prevailed in early twentieth century Britain and indeed still exist today. Firstly, there was an antipathetic stereotype, through which nomads were portrayed as an idle, dirty, and criminal people. It was often claimed that they posed a threat to the women and children of sedentary society or that they harboured disease and were responsible for carrying it from place to place. Such images of Gypsies have been circulating throughout Europe for centuries. However, it is significant that during the nineteenth century this stereotype increasingly assumed the form a scientific theory of heredity. It was suggested that the psychology, the behaviour and the moral character of Gypsies were determined by their biological inheritance.

The idea that such characteristics were biologically determined was popular in scientific circles throughout the nineteenth and into the twentieth century. However, despite a broad acceptance that the alleged negative traits of the Gypsy were determined by nature, there were those who believed they could be raised from their existing level through compulsory education and missionary work. The second stereotype was of a romantic Gypsy figure. This image evolved with the rise of the Romantic Movement during the nineteenth century.

In the work of romantics the Gypsy was portrayed as an exotic and picturesque figure who had remained in harmony with nature, and stayed independent from the advancing industrial society. The romantic stereotype of the Gypsy was particularly prevalent in the work of artists, poets and novelists. Like the negative stereotype, this image was also able to draw authority from the biological theories of race being developed in the work of scientists. The argument was put forward that the Gypsies were a primitive race who had remained close to nature and remained incapable of advancement.

In 1888 a group of scholars attached to romantic images of the wanderer formed the Gypsy Lore Society. To members of this society the wandering life of the Gypsy represented the last romance left on earth and they bitterly resented any attempt of legislators to interfere with it. These two stereotypes came to exist as a coherent rather than contradictory body of thought and both played an important role in shaping the debate over the need for the education of the Gypsies.

The presence of contradictory stereotypes, which were able to exist as a coherent body of thought, was not unique to the Gypsies. A similar situation can be seen in the case of the Jews who stood accused as being both communist and capitalist conspirators. In the case of the Jews, the two stereotypes were complementary insofar as they formed part of the broader stereotype of a Jewish conspiracy to dominate.

In the case of the Gypsies, the contradictory stereotypes were reconciled through the argument that a race of genuine romantic Gypsies had once existed but that they had become increasingly scarce. The argument was put forward that through a process of racial intermixing with the sedentary population, these romantic wanderers had degenerated and had largely been replaced by a new race of half-breeds. It was claimed that the half-bred Gypsies had all the characteristics of the antipathetic stereotype and none of the qualities of their romantic ancestors.

Members of the Gypsy Lore Society claimed that the Gypsies with whom they were concerned were the 'true' Gypsies. Many actually went as far as to draw up criteria that they claimed enabled them to determine an honourable 'true' Gypsy from a half-breed of inferior blood. Both negative and romantic stereotypes of the Gypsies were employed throughout the debate over the passage of the 1908 Children's Act. The idea that the Gypsies were undergoing a process of racial degeneration came to shape the arguments of both supporters and opponents of the Bill, both in parliament and in the public arena.

The 1908 Children's Act

When the Children's Bill was first introduced into parliament, the clause that related to the education of nomadic children attracted little attention and was able to pass through its first two readings in the Commons unaltered. Clause 118 of the original draft of the Bill held that an offence had been committed:

If a person habitually wanders from place to place and takes with him any child above the age of five. . . unless he can prove that the child is totally exempt from school attendance or that the child is not by being so taken with him prevented from receiving elementary education.

The penalties for the offence of preventing a child receiving an education through wandering were to be harsh.

The guardian of the child could be apprehended without a warrant and fined up to twenty shillings if found guilty, while the child was to be sent to an industrial school. The sentiment behind Clause 118 of the Children's Bill was paternalistic rather than repressive. However, the Bill also represented a desire to bring about the assimilation of nomadic people and was based on the long-standing argument that the surest means to put a stop to the nomadic life was to work with the children of wanderers.

The hope was that if children could be prevented from following in the misguided ways of their parents then within one or perhaps two generations the problem of the wandering peoples would be resolved without resorting to more openly repressive legislation. The Children's Bill soon gained the support of those who favoured the assimilation of nomadic groups. For example, it was supported by the Education Committee of the Free Church of Scotland, which had campaigned for assimilationist legislation since 1896. The Scottish Chief Constables Club also voiced support for the proposals, and expressed a hope that they would enable the children of all wanderers to be committed to industrial schools. The bill also attracted influential support in England including that of Robert Parr, the director of the National Society for the Prevention of Cruelty to Children (NSPCC), and a number of influential Surrey landowners.

The Bill also had its opponents. Clause 118 came to the attention of members of the Gypsy Lore Society provoking a hysterical reaction amid fears that the children of the Romanies were to be rounded up and swept into industrial schools. The Gypsy Lore Society engaged in a letter writing campaign to members of the House of Lords, the House of Commons and both the local and national press.

Both those who campaigned in favour of the bill and those who opposed it drew upon the romantic and antipathetic stereotypes of wanderers and the idea that they were undergoing a process of degeneration in support of their causes. Not surprisingly, those who hoped that the measures contained in the Children's Bill could be used to secure the assimilation of the wanderers drew upon negative images of the Gypsies in order to win support. For example, representatives of the Education Committee of the Free Church of Scotland argued that immorality was rife among the nomadic people and that their children were subjected to evil influences of the worst character. Those who adopted such arguments claimed that education was vital if the Gypsies were to be raised above their existing state and successfully assimilated into the sedentary population. However, there was also a clear desire among those who supported the Bill to avoid being regarded as taking a repressive stance towards the Gypsy of the romantic stereotype.

Indeed, two of the Surrey landowners, Lord Clifford and Lord Farrer, both claimed to have great sympathy with the so-called 'genuine' Gypsies who, said Farrer, carried some flavour of a more attractive life into an unromantic age. Despite such claims, the notion of the degenerating Gypsy was employed as a means to justify the legislation. It was claimed that it was not the romantic Gypsies of the old kind who caused a problem for society and required education and ultimately assimilation. The argument was put forward that these old-fashioned Gypsies were rapidly dying out and therefore the measures would only affect the troublesome half-breeds. This argument was useful in that it enabled supporters of the legislation to advocate assimilation without evoking sympathies for romantic wanderers.

Notions of racial degeneration also characterised the arguments of those who opposed the legislation. The Gypsy Lore Society considered that the measures were assimilationist and pledged to do what they could to safeguard the freedom of the Gypsies. Yet, such was the attachment of members of the society to the romantic stereotype that instead of arguing against the measures on practical grounds members employed notions of a nomadic hierarchy and argued that the small group of 'true' Gypsies should be exempt from the legislation. In the case of the so-called 'true' Gypsies, the secretary of the society, Scott Macfie claimed that education would spoil their romantic way of life. However initially members of the society accepted that for lesser half-breed Gypsies some kind of legislation could be justified.

Macfie wrote: As for the half-breeds and tramps, I know them of course and - equally of course dislike them. . . They live in the country as they would live in a town.

slum, and it could come as no great hardship to force them back to their natural environment. The consistent use of racial arguments by opponents of the clause outside parliament soon seeped into the debates within. When the House of Lords debated the Bill in November 1908, Earl Russell who had come to represent the views of the Gypsy Lore Society in the House took a distinctly racial line in arguing the case of the Gypsies that, he claimed, differed from that of other vagrants. His argument revolved around the idea that the measures would be particularly harsh on the 'pure-blooded gypsy' who was unlikely to have any settled relatives with whom to leave children while they attended school. This line of argument had an interesting affect on members of the House.

Even those who most vehemently supported the Bill felt compelled to profess '. . . a certain sympathy with the genuine gypsies who carry into this unromantic age some flavour of a more attractive life than that which is led by many people in this country'. However, it would seem that the arguments of Scott Macfie and other members of the Gypsy Lore Society as to the degeneration of the Gypsies provided the perfect means through which to excuse the harsher aspects of the legislation.

The justification of Clause 118 in its original form was, in the words of Lord Farrer that: 'They were not the gypsies of the old kind. . . ' as '. . . there were extremely few of the old gypsies left'. The Home Office and Board of Education, both of which supported the Bill, recognised that it would be absolutely impossible to draw racial distinctions between nomads for legislative purposes. As it became clear that the Home Office would not accept an exemption clause for pure Gypsies, the position of the Gypsy Lore Society changed. Macfie claimed that it was better to avoid educating all groups, on the grounds that in the case of the so-called half-breeds and tramps education might make them worse thieves and beggars than they were already.

Perhaps surprisingly, some sections of the press began to express hostility towards what they perceived to be the suppression of a romantic way of life. The Manchester Guardian referred to the 'rosy-faced children in the Gipsy tents' and wrote of the 'horror of the idea of. forcing them into the slum dwelling population'. In one article the idea of sending the children of nomads to industrial schools was actually compared to forcing Huguenot children into Catholic convents. The Home Office considered that public opinion would not tolerate the large-scale removal of Gypsy children into industrial schools. Therefore advocates of the Bill were persuaded to agree to the inclusion of an amendment to Clause 118 exempting the Children of travellers, between the times of the year when they took to the road for reasons of trade. Those who had looked to the Children's Act as a means to facilitate the assimilation of the nomads by forcing their children into industrial schools soon began to complain that the amendment to Clause 118 rendered it ineffective in meeting this end.

Particular dissatisfaction was expressed by both the Education Committee of the Scottish churches and the Surrey landowners who continued to campaign for the exemption clause to be removed over the following years. Outside the work of the Gypsy Lore Society, the desire for the preservation of the romantic way of life of the true Gypsies, was never really more than a theoretical adherence to the belief that there were or had been a group of respectable 'pure' Gypsies. The claim that there had at one time been a respectable race of nomads was often used as a means to justify the assimilation of the so-called half-breeds or pseudo-Gypsies, on the grounds that they had degenerated very far from their respectable roots.

Local Authorities and the Working of the 1908 Act

At the local level it would seem that the introduction of the 1908 Children's Act met with a mixed reception. In some quarters it was clearly welcomed as an additional means through which to secure the eviction of Gypsies from the locality. Such an interpretation of the clause seems perhaps surprising given the fact that many of the most ardent supporters of the Bill as it had passed through parliament had hoped that it would be a useful means through. which to encourage the Gypsies to settle, at least for the winter months. However, although the settlement of the Gypsies was widely considered to be desirable in theory, at the local level the concern was more short term.

There was a long tradition of harassment of the Gypsies by the police and local authorities both of whose preferred method for dealing with the group was to drive them out of their locality as quickly as possible. Such action continued after the passage of the Children's Act and in November 1909 The Sanitary Record and Journal of Sanitary and Municipal Engineering actually advised Sanitary Inspectors of local councils that the Children's Act could be used to drive Gypsies from the area. It was suggested that sanitary inspectors could request that the local school attendance officer pay a visit to the camp to ascertain whether the Act was being complied with and that this would usually result in '. . . a general "treck" on the following day'.

The actions of the police and local authorities in using the legislation against the Gypsies were frequently motivated by a desire to deter the Gypsies from remaining in the area rather than a desire to ensure that the children were receiving an education. Indeed, these authorities often did more to prevent the children attending school than ensure compliance with the legislation. In 1912 a Surrey school attendance officer complained that:

> The principal result of police action in this district is undoubtedly the constant migration of all van dwellers from place to place. They are not allowed to settle and their stay in one place is usually so short as to make it impractical to secure their children's attendance at school.

The ability of the police to use the legislation as a means of removing the Gypsies through threat of prosecution was strengthened by the fact that in many areas the schools refused to admit Gypsy children. In 1910 a sub-committee appointed by the Surrey Education Committee to consider the school attendance of Gypsy children found that school managers throughout the county were making it a policy not to accept the children of travellers and were of the opinion that '. . . their physical and moral condition renders them unfit to associate with. other children'. In one instance the head teacher of a Surrey school had issued a notice stating that:

> Pending the decision of the County Education Authority the children of Travellers cannot be admitted to this school by order of the managers. In this instance the schoolmaster claimed to have been authorised to take this action by the Surrey Education Committee.

It would seem that many local authorities had hoped that under the 1908 Children's Act, the Gypsy children could be committed to industrial schools en masse and that within a generation Gypsies would have been removed from British roads. However, the treasury was unwilling to meet the cost of the committal of Gypsies to industrial schools. Rather it believed responsibility lay with the Local Education Authorities (LEA). The Local Education Authorities were likewise disinclined to carry the cost. Indeed, in some cases even after the courts had ordered the committal of a Gypsy child to such a school, the local authority would refuse to pay on the grounds that they were not responsible for wanderers who could not be considered bona-fide residents of the locality.

Throughout the 1920s and 1930s the debate over whom was to pay for the education of Gypsy children in industrial schools, raged within the County Councils Association and the Association of Municipal Corporations. Although the unwillingness of the education authorities to meet the cost of an industrial school education appears to be a surprising reprieve for the Gypsy children, in 1909 the Scottish NSPCC voiced concerns that the failure to send Gypsy children to industrial schools when ordered by the courts led to their being sent to the workhouse after the prosecution of their guardian. It would seem that in some instances this was indeed the case.

George Gladwin, for example, was prosecuted for failing to send his children to school at Horsham Police Court in 1912. Though the defendant said that he had no idea of the Act being in force. and was willing to comply with it in future, if only he could find somewhere to camp, his two children were committed to the workhouse. Just as the supporters and opponents of the Children's Act had drawn upon the notion that the Gypsies were undergoing a process of racial degeneration in their arguments, local authorities drew upon such ideas as a means to justify their treatment of the Gypsies.

In 1914 the Surrey and Hampshire Education Authorities made a deputation to the Board of Education on Gypsy children. The LEAs were anxious to dispel the idea that they were not doing their best to secure the education of the Gypsy children. The chairman of the Surrey Authority argued that there were a small number of 'genuine gipsies' and that these were of a superior class, their children were clean and no objection was raised to their attendance at the village school. However, in terms which are now familiar, he went on to stress that '. . . the genuine gipsy. . . is comparatively rare' and that with regards to the rest of the nomadic population, they were verminous and their school attendance was so short that they could not possibly profit from it.

There are few clues as to how the Gypsy children fared in school once they had been admitted. School textbooks were inevitably middle class in origin during the early twentieth century and no doubt served to alienate Gypsy children as they alienated a large sector of the working class with illustrations of white-collar workers and large children's toys. Yet there is further evidence of problems that were encountered more exclusively by Gypsy children.

The first Annual Report of the West Sussex Medical Inspection of Schools found that Gypsy children were often excluded from school within a short space of time, as they were 'not appreciated by their teachers'. School teachers often complained that the children were both physically and mentally below the normal standard and in many areas it would seem that the answer was believed to be grading Gypsy children as old as twelve along with 'the "babies" class of five year olds'.

In the early 1940s Mr Stillmann of the Hampshire Education Authority. sought the opinions of local headmasters on the presence of the Gypsy children in their schools and reported his findings to the Board of Education. The following comments are typical of the report:

> The headmaster of Alton Senior Council School informed me that he did not find the gipsy children mixed well with other children because of their ragged clothes and dirty persons. Their educational attainment and intelligence was

> very low indeed, and many of them could neither read nor write. Having considered the reports made to him by various headmasters in the county Stillmann claimed that the '...intelligence of the gipsy child is below that of the normal child' and that they required extra supervision owing to their being extremely cunning.

In many schools it would appear that the assumptions of teachers left them convinced that the Gypsy children should be instructed separately from those of local residents. In 1914 it was found that in most schools around the New Forest in Hampshire, which had taken in Gypsy children, the nomads were seated at separate desks from the other children set apart from the rest of the class. There can be little doubt that Gypsy children were aware of the preconceptions of their teachers.

The autobiography of Silvester Gordon Boswell draws on his experience of antipathy from both teachers and pupils alike: If the schoolmaster said "what standard were you in last school?" and we answered: "Standard Three!" it was "Put him in standard two, teacher they're not hear for long". In the playground children gave a voice to the assumptions of their teachers and Boswell recalls that 'we were called dunces, and we had a fight first day and everyday alike'. Similarly, the autobiography of Manfri Wood testifies to the awareness of Gypsy children of the opinions of their teachers. Wood recalls that, 'the teachers humiliated us like a lot of monkeys in the zoo - just because we were Gypsies and a little different from the rest'.

The 1936 Committee on Vagrancy in Scotland, which investigated the position of nomadic children in Scottish schools, found evidence that supports the testimonies of Boswell and Wood. The report concluded that: The conditions attending school are sometimes hard and unjust, and prejudice against the tinker and his offspring dies hard. Children, it is to be feared, feel their position keenly. J. Macpherson, Deputy Chief Constable of Perth and Kinrose reported that in his experience nomadic children were made to feel like lepers and were sensitive enough to realise that they were not wanted, if not detested.

Thus even when the government did introduce legislation, which it hoped might encourage the gradual and voluntary settlement of the Gypsies, the way in which the legislation was interpreted by police, local authorities and school managers in the localities, often conflicted with these long-term aspirations. Even where there was support for the Children's Act as a means to secure the assimilation of the Gypsies, there was often a contradiction between the theoretical desire to assimilate and the reality of hostility towards settling the wanderers into the neighbourhood, or school. In practice even those who complained most persistently about the presence of Gypsies and the wandering way of life, supported assimilation in theory, only as long as it would take place in another locality. This is a familiar theme in the history of minority groups.

The debate over the 1908 Children's Act goes a long way towards illustrating the problems faced by itinerant minorities in Britain both during the early twentieth century and in the present day. The two contradictory stereotypes of the Gypsies have proven resilient and politicians and local authorities continue to justify the harassment of travellers through the argument that they are not the genuine Romanies but pseudo Gypsies.

Although responses to Gypsies in twentieth century Britain have been profoundly affected by racial stereotypes, successive governments have been able to avoid offering them the protection afforded to other. minorities by refusing to recognise them as an ethnic minority but rather as a group who masquerade as such. Furthermore, the attempts of government to introduce legislation even when paternalistic or humanitarian in sentiment can leave the Gypsies extremely vulnerable. Despite the long-term aims of the government the 1908 Children's Act armed the local authorities with an offensive weapon with which to harass the travellers.

3

Nomads: Anytime, Anywhere

Nomads live in a disconnected world much of the time as they travel between their office, home, airport, hotel, automobile, branch office, bedroom, etc. Thus they must take the disconnected state as a "usual" one, instead of an "exceptional" one. To be disconnected is not a failure mode, as is the current view. Rather, it is a common mode.

As nomads, they own computers and communication devices that they carry about with in their travels. Moreover, even without carrying portable computers or communications, there are many people who travel to numerous locations in their business and personal lives, and who require access to computers and communications when they arrive at their destinations.

Nomadism: Evolution of World System

Social evolution among pastoral nomads has not been well conceptualised. A cyclical movement among pastoral cultures has predominated over the development of complexity. Nomads have many times united into large political formations and created great empires that have subsequently disintegrated. The "xenocratic" empires of nomads represent the upper limits of complexity reached by pastoral societies. Central Asian steppe nomads did not barrier determined by the rigid ecological conditions of the arid steppe environment. This view of nomadic societies is shared by the majority of nomadologists of different countries.

Regarding the problem of general evolution, there are three levels of cultural integration of pastoral nomads are revealed, falling into an order of increasing political complexity as follows:

1. acephalous segmentary clan and tribal formations;
2. 'secondary' tribe and chiefdom;
3. nomadic empires and 'quasi- imperial' pastoral polities of smaller sizes.

A changeover from one level to another could occur in either direction. It is the critical peculiarity of nomadic social evolution that transformation of the political systems did not correlate with other criteria of social complexity. The political system of nomads could easily evolve from the acephalous level to more complicated organizations of power and vice versa, but such formal indicators as increase in population density, complex technologies, increase in structural differentiation and functional specialization did not occur. When transforming from tribal pastoral systems to nomadic empires only a growth in the total population (due to the addition of conquered populations) takes place. The political system becomes more complex and the total number of hierarchical levels increases.

From the viewpoint of anthropological theories of social evolution, the key problem is whether or not the nomads could create their own statehood? How should the nomadic empires be classified in anthropological theories of evolution? These questions are currently discussed by researchers of different countries and, especially, by Marxist anthropologists. It should be noted that for the Marxist theory of historical progress, nomadism has become a stumbling block similar to the 'Asiatic mode of production. How could unchanging or cyclical nomadic societies be interpreted within a framework of the common march of the production modes?

A unilinear Marxist theory of social progress assumed, primordially, changes from lowest economical forms to the highest ones. However, the economic 'basis' of pastoral societies has remained unchanged: the similarities among the modern Masai and Arabs with the ancient Hsiung-nu is very great. Thus, nomadism drops out of a unilinear Marxist dialectic of history. On the other hand, if the economic 'basis' of society did not change, then the 'superstructure' should be unchanged. But the 'superstructure' of the pastoral nomads varied greatly.

The nomads created giant steppe empires, which later disintegrated to separate Khanates or acephalous lineage societies and all of this contradicts the principles of a unilinear Marxist theory of historical evolution. The advocates of the concept of nomadic feudalism and the Engels/ Stalin scheme of five modes of production emphasized the difference in economical and cultural development between nomads and agrarian civilizations, thereby overestimating the level of the economic 'basis' of pastoralism. In these theoretical schemes, many facts were falsified and fitted to the Procrustean bed of the dogmatic Marxism of the Soviet Union. So, the erroneous division into 'early' (pre-feudal and slave- owning societies in ancient Eurasia) and 'late' (medieval feudal) nomads has arisen.

Advocates of the concept of the pre- class development of nomads subjected the concept of 'nomad feudalism' to criticism. As 'true' Marxists, they concentrated on the development level of the economic 'basis' of pastoralists. If the 'basis' of ancient nomads was not a class one, then the 'basis' of the later pastoralists must not be based on class either. On the other hand, primitive 'superstructure' should be adjusted to primitive 'basis'. Therefore, nomads in this approach to social evolution have only approached the late primitive (pre-class, pre-feudal etc.) stage. For example, analysis of the samples from the Ethnographic Atlas of George Murdock indicates that almost all ethnohistorical known nomads have not approached the state level and nor have they had class stratification. But the conclusion relative to the pre-state nature of all nomads led to underestimating the development level of the 'superstructure' for a number of pastoral societies - the great steppe empires.

At present there are two popular groups of theories explaining the origin and essence of the early state. The conflict or control theories show the origin of statehood and its internal nature in the context of the relations between exploitation, class struggle, war and interethnic predominance. The integrative theories were largely oriented to explaining the phenomenon of the state as a higher stage of economic and public integration.

However the majority of nomadic empires cannot be unambiguously interpreted as either chiefdoms or states from the viewpoint of either the conflict or the integrationist approaches. The similarity of the steppe empires to true states clearly manifests itself in relations with the outer world only (military-hierarchical structure of the nomadic society to confiscate prestigious goods from adjacent societies and international sovereignty.

With respect to internal relations the 'state- like' empires of nomads (apart from some quite explainable exceptions) were based on non- forcible (consensual and gift- exchange) relations and they existed at the expense of the external sources without establishment of taxation on the live stockbreeders. All basic economic processes in the stockbreeding society were realized within the limits of individual households. For this reason, there was no need for specialized bureaucratic machinery engaged in the administration-distribution activities. On the other hand, all social contradictions were solved within the framework of traditional institutions of maintenance of internal political stability.

A strong pressure upon nomads could cause a decampment or use of retaliatory violence because each free nomad was a warrior at the same time. In the nomadic empires, the main sign of statehood was absent. According to many current theories of the state, the main distinction between statehood and pre-state forms lies in the fact that a chiefdom's ruler has only consensual power i. e. , in essence authority, whereas, in the state, the government can apply sanctions with the use of legitimated force. The power character of the rulers of the steppe empires was mainly consensual and prevented a monopoly of legal organs. The Shan- yu, Khan or Khagan was primarily a redistributor, and his power was provided by personal abilities and ability to obtain prestige goods from the outside and to redistribute them among subjects.

It is beyond question that this political system cannot be considered as a true state. However, this is not to say that the nomadic administration structure was primitive. The complex societies that Gordon Childe called civilization could appear without the bureaucratic organization of administration. The extensive investigations by specialists in the field of ancient history show that the Greek polis was not a true state. Statehood, with its intrinsic bureaucracy, appears fairly late - in the epoch of post- Alexandrian Hellenistic states and in the Roman Empire.

The nomadic empires, as super complex chiefdoms, provide a real prototype of a particular kind of early state.

The population of typical complex chiefdoms is usually estimated in tens of thousands of people and they are typically ethnically homogenous. But the population of a multi- national super complex chiefdom of nomads may have hundreds of thousands of people, or more. Some of the nomadic confederacies of Central Asia have had as many as one and half million pastoral nomads. And their territory was several orders greater than areas needed for simple and complex chiefdoms. Nomads need a great area of land for pastures!

From the viewpoint of neighbouring agricultural civilizations (developed preindustrial states), such nomadic societies have sometimes been perceived as independent subjects of international political relations and, quite often, as equal in status to the agrarian empires. These chiefdoms had a complex system of titles of chiefs and functionaries, held diplomatic correspondence with neighbouring countries, contracted dynastic marriages with agricultural states, neighbouring nomadic empires and 'quasi-imperial' polities of nomads.

With regard to their settlement systems and urban constructions the nomadic societies had more than temporary camps. Already the Hsiung-nu began to erect fortified settlements, while the 'headquarters' of the empires of the Uighur and the Mongols were true towns. The construction of splendid burial- vaults and funeral temples for representatives of the steppe elite were monumental achievements. In several super complex chiefdoms the elite attempted to introduce written records, while there is a temptation to call some of the nomadic empires true states. This is supported by the existence of a system of laws , as well as legal organs of power, written clerical work and efforts to introduce taxation under Ogodei.

Multilinear Evolution of Nomadic Empires

The empire is one of the forms of the state. Specific

signs of empires are: (1) the presence of large territories; and (2) the presence of a "metropolis" of the empire and peripheral subsystems dependent on the metropolis. The fundamental difference between the nomadic empires was that their "centers" were highly developed only in the military aspect, while they were less developed than the exploited or conquered territories in socio-economic complexity and other attributes of civilization. They were actually "peripheries" in themselves. In this case, the nomadic empire can be defined as nomadic society organized on the military-hierarchical principle, occupying a quite large space and exploiting the nearby territories, as a rule, by external forms of exploitation (robbery, war and indemnity, extortion of "presents," non-equivalent trade and tribute).

One can identify the following attributes of nomadic empires: (1) multistage hierarchical character of the social organization penetrated at all levels by tribal and super-tribal genealogical ties; (2) dualistic organization (into 'wings') or triadic organization (into the 'wings' and centre) as the principle of administrative division of the empire; (3) military-hierarchical character of the social organization of the centre of the empire, more often, on the 'decimal principle'; (4) coachman service (yam) as a specific way of organizing the administrative infrastructure; (5) a specific system of power inheritance (empire as the property of the whole khan clan, the institution of co-government - 'kuriltai') ; and (6) specific character of relations with the agricultural world.

It is necessary to distinguish the classical steppe nomadic empires from (1) the similarly mixed agricultural/ pastoral empires in which the nomadic element played a great role (the Arabian caliphates, the states of Seljuks, Dunai and Volga Bulgaria, the Ottoman Empire) and (2) the 'quasi-imperial' nomadic state formations which were smaller than empires. Nomadic empires were organized in the form of 'imperial confederations'. The confederations had an autocratic and state-like look from the outside. They were created to bring the surplus products of agrarian peasants to the steppe nomads. Their inner structure was consultative and tribal in form.

The stability of steppe empires directly depended on the ability of the imperial confederation to extract silk, agricultural products, handicraft articles and delicate jewels from the settled territories. As these products could not be produced under conditions of a stockbreeding economy, obtaining them by use of force and extortion was the priority task of the ruler of nomadic society. By becoming the sole intermediary between China and the Steppe, the ruler of a nomadic society endeavoured to control the redistribution of plunder obtained from China and, thereby to strengthen his own power. This organized accumulation allowed him to maintain the existence of an empire that could not have existed on the basis of the extensive pastoral economy.

The chiefs of the tribes that made up a steppe empire were incorporated into a military hierarchy of the 'hundreds' and 'thousands.' However, their internal policy was to a certain degree independent of the policy of the centre. This peculiarity has been thoroughly analysed by Thomas Barfield using the example of the Hsiung- nu Empire. A certain degree of autonomy of the pastoral tribes was promoted by the following factors: (1) economic independence made them potentially independent of the centre; (2) basic sources of power (predatory wars, redistribution of tribute and other external subsidies, external trade) were quite unstable and involved relations outside the steppe world; (3) general armament restricted the possibility of political pressure upon tribes; (4) for the tribal groupings displeased by a policy of a Khan, the opportunity of moving to new places, desertion under the protection of the agricultural civilization or revolt with the aim of overthrowing the disagreeable ruler were feasible alternatives.

A mechanism connecting the 'government' of the steppe empire and pastoral tribes was the institution of the gift economy. By manipulating gifts and distributing them among comrades- in- arms and tribal chiefs, the ruler of the steppe empire strengthened his potential influence and prestige as the 'generous khan'. Simultaneously, he bound the persons receiving gifts by the 'liability' of the return gift. Tribal chiefs receiving gifts might, on the one hand, satisfy their personal appetites and might on the other hand, strengthen their intratribal status by a distribution of gifts to fellow tribesmen or by organizing ceremonial feasts. In addition to receiving a gift from the ruler, the tribal chief felt as if he also received some part of the ruler's supernatural charisma and that contributed additionally to rise of his own prestige.

The integration of tribes into the imperial confederation was also achieved by inclusion in the genealogical kindred of different stockbreeding groups, diverse collective arrangements and ceremonies. A certain role in the institutionalization of the power of the rulers of nomadic societies was played by their performance of the functions of a sacred intermediary between the society and Heaven (Tenggeri). Subject to the religious conceptions of nomads, a ruler of a steppe society (Shan-yu, Khaghan, Khan) personified the society's center and; in virtue of his divine abilities, performed rituals that were thought to provide prosperity and stability to the society. These functions were deemed to be of colossal importance for the society. Therefore, in the case of natural stress or disease and loss of livestock, an unlucky Khan could weaken or lose his charisma. The unlucky Khan or chief could be replaced in some nomadic societies or even killed. But ideology was never a predominant variable in power among the nomads.

The life of the steppe society was filled with real alarms and dangers that required quick action from the leader. The power of rulers of the steppe empires of Central Asia was mainly based on their ability to extract external surplus product. The most interesting and novel feature of the steppe empires was their dual structure. From outside they appeared to be despotic aggressive state-like societies because they were formed to extract surplus product from outside the steppe. But from with in the nomadic empires remained based on the tribal relations with out the establishment of taxation and exploitation of the stockbreeders. The force of power of the steppe society's ruler was, as a rule, based on his ability to redistribute earnings of trade, tribute and raids from neighbouring countries. From the viewpoint of multilinear evolution the steppe empires were rather different from other early states as well as from most complex chiefdoms.

Nomadic Civilization

In 1934 Toynbee suggested that pastoral nomads could constitute a special form of solidified civilization. It is beyond question that pastoral nomadism is a special world that stands in opposition to the world of agrarian civilizations. But nomadic civilization is a metaphor rather than a scientific definition. If the culture of nomads is defined as a civilization then why not also the "civilizations" of hunter- gatherers or horticulturalists? In other words, all types of human cultures could be characterized as civilizations.

Nomadism is something other than civilization. Its prosperity occurred during the very long period from the First millennium BCE to the middle of the Second millennium CE. During this period a number of settled-agricultural civilizations appeared and collapsed. The same fate was met for many nomadic societies during the period of nomadic steppe empires. It is not likely that the nomads thought of themselves as a unified cultural group standing in opposition to other nations and civilizations.

Hyksos and Hsiung-nu, medieval Arabian and Mongolian Kereyid, Nuer from Sudan and reindeer-breeder from Arctic have been assigned not only to different ethnic groups, but belonged to different cultural communities. Of course some pastoral nomadic societies could contribute to the core of an emergent civilization (e. g. Arabians), while others could play the role of "barbarian" periphery of an agrarian civilization while others could appear beyond the civilizational process prior to the beginning of modern Western colonialism. It is more accurate to tell about the separate large nomadic patterns rather than to try to erect a large general category based on the notion of pastoral nomadic civilization.

Nomadic Mode of Production

The theory of the nomadic mode of production has emerged in Marxist anthropology. The nomadic mode of production is conceived as a technological mode of production rather than a social one. It is thus compared with hunting, fishing, and agriculture rather than with primitive, Asiatic, feudal and other social modes of production. On the basis of one technological mode of production, different social modes of production could exist. The model of the nomadic mode of production is a too generalized pattern. All possible political formations of nomadic societies fall into the framework of this unified model. But African Nuers live in the separate lineages and are only united by very complicated genealogical ties.

The same social organization was probably characteristic of ancient Ukhians roaming from place to place on the Inner Mongolia steppe. Tuaregs, Kalmyks and

Kazakhs had a developed inner property and social stratification. They were consolidated in tribal confederations that included several tens of thousands of people. Hsiung- nu, Turks, and Mongols organized steppe empires that included many hundreds of thousands (even up to million and more) nomads. The differences in the complexity of social political system between Nuers and Ukhuans, on the one hand, and Hsiung-nu and Mongols, on the other, are considerable.

Russian social science has, in recent decades, devoted a lot of attention to producing a synthesis between the theories of social stages and civilizational approaches. It is fundamentally impossible to do this completely on the basis of orthodox Marxism. At the same time, another powerful theoretical line has emerged—the world- systems approach. Within this framework the methodological synthesis between the evolutionary approach to history (from the lineage reciprocity mini-systems to the capitalist world- system based on the commodity- money relations) and the perspective of history as a totality of different large regional systems (e. g. world-empires, world- economies) has been successfully combined.

Dynamics of Nomadic Societies

In accordance with the world-systems approach, the main unit of development is a great system which includes groups of polities rather than a single country. In this group, the 'center' (core) is identified, which exploits a 'periphery'. The core has a higher level of technology and production and more complex internal structure and gets maximum profit. The core societies pump out the resources of the periphery, organizefinancial and trade flows, and arrange the economic space of the system . I.Wallerstein identifies three modes of production:

(1) mini-systems based on reciprocation,

(2) redistributive world-empires,

(3) capitalist world-system (world-economy) based on the commodity and money relations.

The world-empires exist to exact tributes and taxes from provinces and captured colonies that are redistributed by the bureaucratic government. The distinctive feature of world-empires is administrative centralization and the predominance of the polity over the economy, according to Wallerstein. However, such an approach to the evolution of preindustrial systems is incomplete. It is necessary to note two important circumstances.

First, in addition to the hierarchical world-empires, there were also peer-polity systems. Ancient Greece and medieval Europe served as examples of the coexistence of multi-polity systems. Andrey Korotayev has shown that the West was no exception. In ancient Arabia, several centers and peripheral systems have coexisted in what he calls a 'multipolity'. Therefore, in the preindustrial period, a division of labour between separate elements of regional systems could be performed on the basis of different models of interaction.

Secondly, it is necessary to clarify how many such models and preindustrial modes of production there could, in principle, be? Two models of interaction are known: redistributive "World- empires" and polycentric "World-economies". As to the modes of production, it is more complex. Fursov has created a solid social philosophical theory in which all the main present- day theories were synthesized. In this opinion, living labour manifests itself in two forms -individual and collective. The more developed is production, the more independent is collective labour.

Redistribution only affected the external sources of the empire's income: plunder, tribute, trading duties and gifts. The nomads, in a given situation, took the part of 'class- society' and 'state- society', rising as a building over the settled- agrarian foundation. For this, the nomad elite performed the functions of bureaucracy and commanders, while the ordinary pastoralists were the soldiers of expansion and repressions. Such a society might be called xenocratic.

The concept of semiperiphery was introduced by Wallerstein to designate the intermediate zone between the center and periphery. The semiperiphery is exploited by the core but itself exploits a periphery as well as being an important stabilizing element in the world division of labour. I. Wallerstein argues that the three tiered structure is characteristic of many organizations. The intermediate tier provides flexibility and elasticity of the whole system (e. g. centrist parties, middle classes, etc.). The concept of the semiperiphery was developed mainly to describe processes in the present- day capitalist world- system.

In the preindustrial period, some functions of the semiperiphery could be performed by the trading city-states of ancient times and the middle ages. Marcher states that conquered core regions to form larger empires were often also originally located in semiperipheral regions (e. g. Akkad in Mesopotamia, Macedonia, Rome). The Central Asian steppe empires of nomads were also the militarist "satellites" of agrarian civilizations as this process was guratively pictured by O. Lattimore -"barbarism is a result of civilization." However, the nomads also performed important intermediary functions between distant core regions. Similar to seafarers, they provided the connections for flows of goods, finances, technological and cultural information and epidemic diseases between the islands of the settled economy and urban civilization.

However, it would be an error to consider the nomadic empires as representing the semiperiphery. The semiperiphery is often exploited by the core, whereas the nomadic empires were never exploited by agrarian civilizations. Any society of the semiperiphery aspires to technological and production growth. The mobile mode of life of pastoral nomads did not provide the opportunity to make great accumulations and their society was based on the gift economy. All plunder was distributed by the rulers of the steppe empires between the tribal chiefs and stockbreeders and consumed during mass festive occasions. The nomadic societies were doomed to remain peripheral.

There is a close temporal relationship between the prosperity of the agrarian core state and the power of the nomadic empires. It was most usually the case that the steppe empires arose and were sustained during periods in which the imperial agrarian state was also strong and prosperous. In Inner Asia this correlation is especially clear for here there are many areas of pasture that made possible the formation of a large steppe empire from tribes and chiefdoms. The Han dynasty and Hsiung- nu Empire arose during the same decade. The Turkish Khaganate arose just as China was united under the power of the dynasties of Sui and, later, T'ang. And, in contrast, the periods of crisis in the fourth, fifth and tenth centuries in China led to political entropy in the steppe areas.

The concept of T.Barfield is more complex. He not only established a syn-chrony between the growth and decline of the nomadic empires and similar processes in China, but noted also that the conquest of China was, as a rule, a business of the Manchurian people. The breakdown of centralized power in China and on the steppes released the forest- dwelling tribes in Manchuria from pressure from both of these adjacent powers. Manchuria's people established their state formations and conquered the agricultural areas on the South when both of their neighbouring competitors were weak. The Khitan, Jurchen, and Manchu succeeded in conquest. In Barfield's opinion, a cyclical process of synchronous state formation among the peoples of China and Central Asia was repeated three times over a period of two thousand years.

The theories of Tamura and Barfield complement each other. The relations among migrations and crises of agrarian empires and the activities of nomads is evident. The first global demographic crisis of our millennium occurred at nearly the same time in different parts of Eurasia. It was not only a coincidence that this was also the epoch of the 'great migration of peoples'. Contrary to popular opinion the nomads did not at all desire to conquer the agrarian territories. In order to rule an agrarian society, the nomads would necessarily have to give up their nomadism and their horses. This they were ill disposed to do. It was only during periods of crisis and collapse of the settled societies that the steppe nomads were forced to enter into closer relations with the farmers and townspeople.

The Mongolian storm of the thirteenth century coincided with a new period of moistening in Mongolia and the steppes of Eastern Europe and with a demographic and economic upturn in all parts of the Old World. This brought the culmination of the history of preindustrial empires. The Mongols merged a chain of international trade into the united complex of land and sea routes. For the first time, all the great regional cores.

On the steppe, similar to fantastic mirages, there arose gigantic cities-centers of political power, transit trade, multinational culture and ideology . From this time, political and economical changes in some parts of the world began to play a much greater part in the history of distant other parts of the world. The existence of the first Eurasian- wide empire did not last long. The plague, the ejection of the Mongols from China and the decline of the Golden Horde became the most important links of the chain of events that conditioned its downfall.

Demographers mark the serious crisis in all its main sub-centers in the period of 1350 -1450. At the beginning of fifteenth century, the first Eurasia-wide empire disintegrated. Tamerlane's desperate efforts to restore the transcontinental trade met, in the end, with failure. The Ming resumed the traditional policy of opposing the nomads that resulted in the regeneration of an older policy of the Mongols to remotely exploit China. In the emerging Europe- centered capitalist world-system, the nomads were allotted quite another position. Machine technology, rearms and new sources of energy changed the balance of power to their disadvantage. Since that time, the steppe hinterland has ceased to play an important role in the dynamics of world-system processes.

4

Romani Customs

Romani customs and traditions are as diverse as the number of Roma nations and the countries they inhabit. Generally, there remains a fine cultural thread which holds the Roma people together, no matter where they may be.

Struggle for Identity

Roma as a world population and about numbers. One estimate of 40 million was proposed, which pleased everybody, but when it came to what the total was for America, the generally acknowledged figure of about 1 million was challenged on the grounds that not everybody really qualified, because a good many of those people called *Gypsies* were not actually Roma but *Bayash*-a cover-term for the various non-Romani-speaking American groups, including the *Romanichals*, the *Bashalde*, and the *Romungre*, besides the actual *Bayash* themselves.

The understanding of the Gypsy identity among the non-Roma is vague, which usually results in prejudice. There are many reasons for that: the association of Roma with the Islamic takeover of parts of the Christian world; color prejudice, specifically the association of darkness with sin; the exclusionary nature of Romani culture, which does not encourage intimacy with non-Roma and creates suspicion on the part of those excluded; fortune-telling, which inspired fear but had to be relied upon as a means of livelihood in response to legislation curtailing Romani movement and choice of occupation; the unchallenged function of the "gypsies" as a population upon which mainstream notions of immorality and lawlessness can be projected and thereby serve to define that mainstream's own boundaries; the fact that Roma have no territorial, military, political, or economic strength and are therefore easily targetable as scapegoats because they cannot retaliate; and the fact that the "gypsy" persona has an-again unchallenged-ongoing function as a symbol of a simpler, freer time, a representation that is becoming more and more attractive in an increasingly complex and regimented world.

Various of these factors have combined over the centuries and in different places to become part of the fabric of the Western world view. People who never met a Gypsy in their lives are nevertheless able to provide a fairly detailed picture of how they think Gypsies look and how they live. Their mental image, partly negative and partly romantic but mostly inaccurate, stems from a Romani identity that has become so institutionalized in Western tradition that it has become part of Western cultural heritage.

The racism directed at Romani populations is intrinsically a part of that heritage and therefore is not recognized for what it is. Just as no one would question the fear of trolls or goblins or argue for their rights, the fear of Gypsies likewise goes unchallenged. And although trolls and goblins are never encountered and the six million or so Roma throughout Central and Eastern Europe are highly visible, it is still the storybook and film Gypsy image-not the real population-that people think of.

This re-identification of Gypsies as "images" in the cultural fabric is best illustrated by an interaction between Diane Tong, a scholar visiting Romani populations in the Thessaloniki area of Greece and a local Greek Orthodox priest. After having rallied against racial intolerance in the United States, the priest brushed aside Tong's remark that Greece was similarly bigoted toward its Romani minority by saying that prejudice toward Roma in Greece didn't count; it was a different thing entirely, because "they were only Gypsies." This kind of shocking moral insensitivity on the part of a representative of a church may surprise us, but it is nothing new.

The Orthodox, Catholic, and Protestant churches legislated against Roma for centuries; the priest was merely reiterating an attitude rooted in tradition. Once ideas become institutionalized, they are seldom challenged, and misinformation can easily become the conventional wisdom. This is particularly true in the case of Roma, about whom the most bizarre things have been written and presented as fact. These range from wild statements-such as claims that Gypsies originated on the moon (or in Atlantis); that they have an intrinsic horror of water and washing; or that they have no concept of obligation or danger or ownership-to such self-serving ones as maintaining that Gypsies don't feel pain; that they enjoyed slavery; or that they have no interest in organization, education, or leadership.

Jozsef Vekerdi, the most frequently cited Hungarian "expert", has notoriously relied on this conventional wisdom in his work. The beginning of his 1988 article on "the Gypsy problem" in his country is highly illustrative:

> The Gypsies' ancestors began leaving northwest India probably about the seventh century AD. They are characterized as robbers, murderers, hangmen and entertainers. These professions were prescribed for them

by the rules of the Hindu caste system. Thus they belonged to the so-called "wandering criminal tribes" of India and were obliged to lead a parasitic way of life. Among the numerous outcast groups, they occupied the lowest rung on the social scale.

But the Romani origins assumed in it are quite wrong, and the time of the exodus out of India is off by four centuries. His acceptance of a false history is reflected in the scorn that characterizes his writings, and one must wonder whether his scholarly approach would have been more charitable had he known the true history of the Romani people. Racism is everywhere, but when it is expressed in the academic domain, to which policy-makers turn for their information, it acquires tacit institutional acceptance.

Despite the usually evident physical differences and the less obvious but hardly hidden factors of language and culture that distinguish the Romani minority from the surrounding population, administrations have generally classified Roma in terms of social behavior rather than by ethnic or racial distinctiveness. That is again the result of attitudes becoming ingrained before notions of "race" began to take shape in the 19th century. The glaring exception to that method of classification was the Nazi era, when racial considerations provided the rationale for genocidal obliteration.

In most cases, however, Roma care very much about anti-Gypsyism while having to hide their identity. For a very long time, Gypsy identity has been in the hands of the non-Gypsy specialist, especially politicians and academics, whose ideas about who and what we are have given sustenance to the Gypsy image. Non-Romani folklorists and anthropologists select those aspects of their subjects that they find appealing, while ignoring others for a number of reasons. Some might simply be more attractive or exotic.

The extent to which that selectiveness can place the expert in the position of bystander is well illustrated in Susan Lepselter's 1996 article in *Roma* magazine. Analyzing the topics covered during a ten-year period embracing the Holocaust in *The Journal of the Gypsy Lore Society*, the leading publication devoted to Romani studies, she found that the contributions dealt with, inter alia, "Welsh and New York Gypsy life, Hungarian Gypsy fiddlers, linguistic work on the Spanish Gypsy dialect, and Polish Romani vocabulary." She went on to ask "Why would professional Gypsiologists [maintain] an essentially apolitical journal at such a crucial moment in the lives of their subjects? Scholars of Romani culture did not, or could not, vigorously protest the fate of those they studied and befriended. They did not engage in political critique which might have led to action."

Claus Schreiner's introduction to the 1990 U.S. edition of his *Flamenco: Gypsy Dance and Music from Andalusia* shows that the kind of thinking where the real Gypsy experience takes second place to the expert's pet interest is alive and well among Gypsiologists: "Lately a new wave of anti-Gypsyism has reportedly again raised its head in Andalusia. If so, it might prove beneficial for Gypsy-Andalusian flamenco for pressure creates counter-pressure which could well lead to a revitalization of flamenco from within."

Non-Gypsy scholars have always striven to control and define Romani identity. When Gypsy behavior has asserted itself in ways contrary to the specialists' expectations, it has been seen as a shortcoming on the part of the Gypsy. Thus, Alexander Paspati, a 19th century Gypsiologist, claimed that "works published in Europe, several of them even by authors who wrote down what the Gypsies dictated to them, are often inaccurate because of the stupid ignorance of the Gypsies." A century later,

Doris Duncan, writing about the difficulties of analyzing the Romani verbal system, attributed this to the fact that the "major problem is that no Gypsy really knows what a verb is." Government officials haven't shied away from using that line of thinking.

As The San Antonio Express reported in March 1984, a Czechoslovak government spokesman defended his government's program of taking Romani children from their families and placing them in foster homes by saying that it was "the Gypsies' fault for refusing to let their children be civilized." Because of a history of exclusion of Roma from education and because of cultural restrictions on greater integration of Roma in the mainstream, the Gypsy image has taken on a life of its own and real Romani populations have been administrated and studied through the filter of that image.

There is another, more disturbing political aspect to the created identity, which is reflected in the increase in the presentation of the Gypsy as an illiterate, inarticulate buffoon in post-communist Europe. Such characters-played by non-Gypsies-appear in variety shows on television in Bulgaria, Romania, Slovakia, and elsewhere. Like the turn-of-the-century black and white minstrels in America, they help maintain a status quo in which Roma are merely figures of fun and are therefore non-threatening.

Only in the past few decades have the Roma been in a position to resist the manipulation of identity. When the London-based publisher of Shel Silverstein's 1984 book of children's verse, *Where the Sidewalk Ends*, was asked to remove a poem called "The Gypsies are Coming," with its accompanying illustration of a hag-like Gypsy woman with hooked nose, earrings, and scarf carrying a sackful of stolen children over her shoulder, the only concession was that subsequent editions changed the word "Gypsies" to "Googies." The illustration remained. When a British comic publishing company, John Brown Ltd., was asked to remove its 1990 cartoon strip entitled *The Thieving Gypsy Bastards* it replaced it with the sarcastic *The Nice Honest Gypsies*, keeping the offensive cartoon characters. The producers of the films *Thinner* and *The Hunchback of Notre Dame* didn't respond to a single request for fairness and accuracy from Romani organizations, at least six of which wrote to them while the films were still in production.

In order for things to change, the Gypsy image must be deconstructed and replaced by a more accurate one-in the bureaucratic structures as well as in the textbooks. Education, both of Roma and of gadje, is clearly the key to avoiding another catastrophe involving the people, and the means of attaining some measure of understanding, if not respect, for Roma and Romani history and culture. But identifying the solution goes only a short way to resolving it. Before educational programs can be put in place, the facts of Romani history must be understood and the notion of identity made acceptable to both Romani and non-Romani populations. Given the great number of differing interpretations of those very basic considerations, reaching a consensus will not be easily achieved.

Lepselter concluded from her analysis of mid-20th-century gypsiology that the Gypsies are both "the 'heart' of Europe and radically 'other' to it." The idea that Roma are really local people who have intentionally darkened their skin and who speak a deliberately concocted secret jargon dates from at least as far back as the Renaissance. In his book *The Gypsies*, published in 1973, Werner Cohn maintained that "Gypsies are thoroughly European a majority of their ancestors probably came from old European stock." Judith Okely and Wim Willems are currently the most vocal champions of that view among those who study Roma. Both of them maintain that Gypsies are "a motley rabble of diverse origin," an indigenous Western population whose identity was "invented" over time by writers and policy-makers. But neither Willems nor Okely denies an ethnic identity (or series of identities) for Gypsies; the argument is simply that Romani origins are ultimately mixed and mainly European, and that the "Rom" is a product of 19th-century European Orientalism and ideas of human-group classification.

Although the Indian origin of the Romani people is beyond dispute not only on the basis of linguistic but also of cultural and serological evidence, the issue remains largely the concern of academics. While early Romani populations on their arrival in Europe were able to say that they had come from India, that fact has become lost over time and is still generally unknown to the vast majority of Roma, many of whom have internalized instead the notion of an origin in Egypt.

Furthermore, those who minimize the Indian connection are not linguists or historians, although they frequently feel entirely qualified to make linguistic and historiographical pronouncements. (That has been a major criticism of Isabel Fonseca's recently published *Bury Me Standing: The Gypsies and Their Journey*). The most elementary linguistic evidence, such as the fact that the Romani word for "cross" (*trushul*) originally meant "Shiva's trident," is left unaddressed. It is hard to reconcile such facts with the "indigenous origin" argument that Romani language and culture were passed like a relay runner's baton from population to population along trade routes, rather than being brought with one migrating people.

Besides being scientifically defensible, the pro-Indian-origin position was corroborated in practice by Indira Gandhi's open acknowledgment of Roma as an Indian population outside of India. Moreover, the Indian government was instrumental in helping the people achieve representation in the United Nations and in creating the First World Romani Congress, and it is currently supporting the claims for the return of gold and other possessions taken from Romani Holocaust victims and currently on deposit in Swiss banks.

Quest for Compromise

For the majority of Roma, the identity issue is overridden by the more pragmatic concerns of work, shelter, safety, and providing for the family. For the average Rom, whether we are European or Asian, or neither, or both is not a matter of much consequence. For the leaders, however, it must be. The future of the Romani population is in the hands of those Romani intellectuals who interact with the representatives of national governments and human rights and educational agencies.

There are three approaches to formalizing a consensus on Romani identity: either that we are European, or that we are Asian, or that we are both. The case for being considered European rests upon the widespread dispersion throughout Europe, as a truly transnational people. But as the Romani scholars Andrzej Mirga and Nicolae Gheorghe have pointed out, we are a global-not just a European-population. Are the Roma in Peru also "true Europeans?"

One's identity has to be evaluated in terms not only of what one perceives oneself to be, but also by whether members of the population one identifies with share that perception. In other words, one might identify with a group that doesn't want to open its doors. In the late 1970s, Guyana-an English-speaking South American country with an almost entirely African and Asian population-mounted a national campaign to re-identify itself as a Latin American nation. The rest of Latin America, however, did not see Guyana as being a part of their cultural and linguistic world, and the attempt withered and died.

The arguments for stressing the "Indian connection" seem clear. In these times, when Europe is divided into nation-states, being identified with an actual homeland brings legitimacy and a measure of security. But are Roma, in fact, Indians? From the very beginning, the population has been a composite one, and acknowledging that fact constitutes a third approach. Evidence points to Dravidian, Scythian, and even East African (Siddhi) input into the early mix of militia and camp followers. Once in Europe, the migration-by this time a conglomerate ethnic population whose diverse speech had crystallized into one language-encountered other mobile populations and in some cases joined and intermarried with them.

Sometimes the Romani cultural and linguistic presence was sufficient for the newly encountered populations to be absorbed and become Roma in subsequent generations; sometimes the Romani contribution was not sufficient to maintain itself, and other, non-Romani populations such as the *Jenisch* emerged. During the centuries of slavery in Moldavia and Wallachia and under conditions of oppression elsewhere in Europe, Romani women bore unwanted babies by non-Roma fathers. Cohn has estimated the mean percentage of European "blood" in the European Romani genetic makeup to be 60 percent.

That very capacity to absorb and acculturate disparate populations is particularly characteristic of the Roma. The truly remarkable thing is that it has been possible, despite this kind of incorporation of outsiders and despite the lack of a national territory, to maintain a linguistic and cultural cohesiveness that stretches back for a thousand years. As weak as it may be, it remains strong enough to identify all Romani groups as being exactly that-Romani groups.

Many of the problems that Roma are having with

non-Roma are rooted in the vague and muddled notions of who and what Roma are, and what the Romani experience in Europe has been, and what Roma have contributed to European culture. One step toward ensuring a safe and productive future for Romani populations in Europe is to develop educational programs for the schools, both Gypsy and non-Gypsy, where Romani history and culture can be taught and the findings of current historical and linguistic scholarship made better known. Legitimization will lead to respect, and in that way the foundation will be laid for a clearer understanding of Romani identity.

Gypsies of Europe, one may envision a dark-skinned group of people, traveling in a band of wagons and playing music - seemingly unaffected by their surroundings. If one has traveled in Eastern Europe he may think of the barefoot children walking the streets and singing in the Metro stations for money. One may also remember the typical warning by others to "Beware of the Gypsies, they will try to steal from you!"

In fact, the Rroma (Gypsies) are a diverse group of people, differing in occupation, standard-of-living, historical experience of their home country, education and levels of "integration." Contrary to the typical stereotype, it has been estimated that only 5% of the entire Rroma population in Europe lead an itinerant mode of life. Though there are subtleties of different dialects, the Rroma share a common language based on old Sanskrit.

In the Rromani language, self-identification involves the word "Rrom." When encountering other Rroma, "Are you Rrom?" is asked, not "Are you Gypsy?" The designation as "Gypsy" is related to the old belief that the Rroma came from Egypt, though studies of the Rromani language in the late 18th century revealed their Indian origin.

In non English speaking countries, the Rroma are

usually referred to as Zigeuner, Zingari, Tsiganes and other variants stemming from the Greek word "Atsinganoi," which was actually a religious sect in the Byzantine Empire, unrelated to the Rroma yet attributed to this "foreign" population. For Rroma organizations and other human rights groups, the ethnic designation as Rrom is a matter of self-determination, self-identification. A comparison may be made with the Inuit of North America who were formerly referred to as "Eskimos" - an externally applied name. The principle of self-identification involves public acknowledgment of the self-designated name and the implementation of its use.

The Romanian Government "Memorandum"

Recently, the Romanian Ministry of Foreign Affairs circulated an internal Memorandum: "The problems on naming one of the ethnic groups in Romania." The Memorandum advises all public officers (civil-service workers) to address those belonging to this ethnic group as "Tigani" (pronounced Tsigan).

The Memorandum ascertains that the "ethnic Tigani" and other organizations, especially in the last few years, have attempted to use and impose the "new terms" Rom, Roma and Romani. The motivation behind the Memorandum refers to the use of Gypsy or Tigani in official documents of the Council of Europe and other international bodies and, "especially," the possible identification of the Romanians, in general, with members of this ethnic group.

The government's decision was taken without consulting members of the Rroma minority, though officially such means exist through the framework and mandate of the Council for National Minorities and the Rroma representative in the parliament.

The Rroma associations in Romania and other experts maintain that the word "Tigani" has a pejorative connotation. The link is made with the centuries of slavery, where the association of the ethnic designation "Tigani"- a socially inferior status, has remained in the social-cultural memory, later justified through racial and racist argumentation in the mid-twentieth century. It has been estimated that 5 - 600,000 of the European Rroma died in the Holocaust - a percentage of their total population comparable with the statistics of the Jewish population. .

In general, the policies (few in number) addressing the Rroma in Romania have been policies of assimilation, reflecting an intolerance toward Rromani cultures and often defining all of the social characteristics, especially those of a marginalized way of life, as something inherent in the "Rroma nature." Today, the majority of Romanian society perceive the Rroma ("Tigani") as a whole to be untrustworthy, lazy, uneducated and "rich" from illegal businesses, conniving or thievery.

As Alina Mungiu explains in her book Romania after 1989, the common attitude toward the Rroma, especially in relation to "Romania's reputation" in the eyes of the world, is one of contempt and a sense of injustice. This was demonstrated in the incident when a France Presse journalist, not knowing the pejorative connotation of "Tsigan," made a comparison between the virtuosity of the Romanian soccer team during the World Cup and the music of the Lautara - "Tsigan" (a Rromani sub-group with traditions in music). The reaction was one of shock and disgust that the "Occident sees us as Tigani". As one Romanian journalist reported, "Gypsies are gypsies, even those born in Romania, and Romanians are Romanians."

Recommendations of the Rroma Movement

Members of Rroma associations have recommended the use of double "r", which corresponds more specifically to the pronunciation in most Rromani dialects. Likewise, this spelling may help to avoid confusion between the ethnic designation and other patronymic stems such as Romania, Rome, Romand (a region in Italy), Romanism (Roman Catholicism), etc.

It is recommended that the use of all exonyms referring to the Rromani people (Gypsies, Tsiganes) and their cognates - be permanently eradicated. The process should be accomplished in stages, allowing enough time for the non-Rromani public to become accustomed to the stem "Rrom". Of course, changing everyday speech habits will take time, but references made in the media and other international documents can begin immediately with "Rroma (Gypsies)" and after a couple of years the reference to "Gypsies" can be dropped.

Since the historical events of 1989, civic associations have been able to communicate and cooperate with various international organs and bodies of the United Nations and the Council of Europe. The participation and consultation of Rroma groups and persons in Eastern Europe, is reflected in the change of language referring to this ethnic group used in the official documents.

In documents owing to works accumulated before 1990, the "Gypsies" designation is usually applied or may be used in the title with the text referring to the "Roma/ Gypsies". (Council of Europe Recommendation 1203 and Resolution 249). Others use consistently, throughout the document, "Roma (Gypsies)" (United Nations Resolution 1992/65 and many OSCE documents). Even in 1979, the United Nations Sub-Commission for the Prevention of Discrimination and Protection of Minorities Recommendation, used the terms "Gypsies (Roma)".

In 1994, the Office for Democratic Institutions and Human Rights (ODIHR) of the Office for Security and Cooperation in Europe (OSCE) created the Contact point for Roma and Sinti (The Sinti are a group of Rroma whose vocabulary and grammer have been heavily influenced by

German). Part of the mandate of the Contact Point is to act as a clearinghouse for information on Roma and Sinti issues, including information on the implementation of commitments pertaining to Roma and Sinti.

It seems clear that the reference made in the Romanian government Memorandum of the use of "Gypsies" in international documents, as a pretext for the official designation as "Tigani" in Romania, is an interpretation ignoring the fact that "Roma" is, more often than not, included in the name as well. In May, Bucharest hosted the International Seminar on Tolerance organized by the Council of Europe, OSCE/ODIHR, the Government of Romania, in cooperation with UNESCO.

The Romanian government statements maintained its position on the official designation "Tigani," even though members of international bodies stressed their concern with regard to discrimination and manifestations of intolerance toward the "Roma" populations in Romania. In response to the recommendations put forth by Rroma associations, the Council of Europe recently approved the use of "Rroma (Gypsies)" in its official documents . While this is good news for those working for the Rroma right to self-identification, there is still the obstacle of the Romanian government, paying lip service to human rights commitments, while maintaining contradictory attitudes and behaviors.

Roma in Central and Eastern Europe (CEE), it is important at the outset to stress and acknowledge that too often the plight of the Romani population has been used as a Human Rights 'big stick' with which the West can beat the East. Although the situation of the Roma in Central and Eastern Europe is almost unanimously acknowledged to be horrendous by many Non-Governmental Organisations (NGOs) (e.g., Amnesty International, Helsinki Watch, Project on Ethnic Relations), it is equally true that the established bourgeois liberal democracies of the West have similarly treated Roma living in their own countries with just as much contempt, hatred, fear and loathing as their Eastern neighbours during the last five hundred years.

Indeed, latest developments show that the doors of the European Union (EU) may not even open to the countries of CEE unless they can 'prove' their human rights slate, especially with regard to the 'Gypsy question', is relatively clean and untarnished. This EU focus on human rights, theoretically, can only be good news for the Roma.

The creation of a 'Romanestan' state has been discussed at various international meetings since 1971 but has never really got beyond the theoretical. So, the lack of a 'home' territory is a factor of some relevance, but this article will seek to deal with the main issues of discrimination and politics. According to one of most reliable and commonly referred to sources, there are between seven and eight and a half million Roma in Europe. Of this figure, about five million live in the Central and Eastern part of Europe. The ongoing transition in this area to a capitalist economic structure has meant that the 'burden' of the Roma 'problem' has been a growing concern to politicians and economists in Central and Eastern Europe, as well as to the International Monetary Fund and World Bank. However, a great deal of apathy has also been apparent when we examine the efforts made at both a local and national level to collect meaningful figures on Roma populations in their regions and countries.

International NGOs have attempted to collate sensible data on population numbers. Researchers at various European Universities have attempted likewise. The motivations and intentions behind this recent re-found enthusiasm for knowing exactly how many Roma live in Europe is noteworthy. Marek Kohn's recent work on the return of the 'race gallery' shows us the wider context of state and scientific sanctioned racism in Europe and also illustrates the positivistic and essentialist needs of a racially motivated 'science' for gathering quantitative data and thereby 'proving' the 'genetic problem' of a population who just 'breed too much' and are 'out of control'. To find a solution, as the Nazis knew with regard to the Roma in Germany, Poland and elsewhere during the 1930s and 40s, numbers first need to be known.

Kohn, as well as Powell's fascinating work in the former Czechoslovakia, highlights both the common acceptability of anti-Gypsy racism and the reasons for it. Kohn cites perceived higher birth rates among the Slovakian Roma community than the 'whites' (i.e. non-Romani), their unwillingness and/or inability to 'socially adapt', their poor physical and mental health and the general perception that the Roma are a social problem and 'are simply a great burden on this society'. The work of criminologist Chris Powell has illustrated that the common belief that 'all Gypsies are criminals' has a lot to do with this vitriolic fear and loathing that the Roma have to deal with on a daily basis. Often, as Powell comments, this belief is simply wrong and so-called 'Gypsy crime' is nothing more than petty pilfering to survive in a country where widespread discrimination in all areas of social and public life means high unemployment, poor accommodation and social exclusion.

In Europe, Roma have been victims of society's animosity. Banishment and pogroms, as well as mistreatment and discrimination, have always been part of everyday life for the 'Gypsies'. It is clear that the Roma are one of the most persecuted ethnic minority groups in Europe today. Their nomadism, economic opportunism, and supposed 'otherness' saw dominant sedentary cultures over a period of many years attempt to exclude, contain or assimilate them. Their very existence was disruptive and seen as a threat.

Racist stereotypes and myths developed to justify the persecution, concentrating on accusations of idleness, theft, witchcraft, child abduction and parasitism to name but a few. Ian Hancock, a Romanichal Linguistics Professor at Texas University has also noted how deeply ingrained anti-Gypsyism is in European tradition, evident in folk tales, beliefs and proverbs:

'The Gypsies are coming , the old people say.
To buy little children and take them away...'

In the 1990s this persecution has taken new ground in the Central and Eastern parts of Europe. With the collapse of 'socialist fraternity' came the release of far-right and ultra-nationalist sentiments, especially towards 'dark-skinned "Gypsy-looking" persons'. As we have seen recently, those Roma who attempt to escape the hatred and fear are not guaranteed any kind of sanctuary in the West: 'we do not want Gypsy refugees here' they are told by Home Office Ministers via tabloid press headlines. European Roma communities have had to endure many such hardships in different parts of the world. As Margaret Brearley writes these have included:

> '... forced evictions from homes; expulsions from villages and towns (often with the support of local Mayors); physical assault and murder by skinheads, policemen, neighbours; exclusion from public places; widespread legal discrimination; unduly harsh prison sentences and extortionate fines for petty offences; and endemic racial abuse.'.

One of the many other tragedies that could be added to Brearley's list is state-supported sterilisation programmes. Many Roma women have gone into hospital for minor operations only to return home sterilised. The *gadzho* fear of Roma as 'breeding machines' has led to such extreme actions: 'if we don't deal with them now, they will deal with us in time' as Vladimir Meciar put it in 1993. It is, however, the racist assaults and violence towards the Roma that has attracted the greatest attention from the media. Levels of attacks are increasing but are at least now being recorded and monitored if not always followed up by the appropriate authorities. For example, the Czech non-governmental organisation HOST has recorded some 1250 racially motivated attacks towards the Roma between 1991 and 1997.

It is very important to appreciate that this is not just the work of extremist neo-fascists. Opinion polls have consistently illustrated the strength, potency and acceptability of anti-Gypsy sentiments in Central and Eastern parts of Europe. One poll, conducted by Freedom House and the American Jewish Committee covering Hungary, Czechoslovakia and Poland, produced a reverse-order ranking which listed preferences for the ethnic or racial identity of one's neighbours; it read: Gypsies 78%, Arabs 66%, Blacks 53%, Asians 50%, Russians 37% and Jews 27%. Three years later the Czech paper Prognosis reported a poll that indicated 77% of Czechs had a 'negative view' of the Roma and 30% thought they should either be deported or isolated in ghettos.

What is perhaps even more worrying than the actual attacks is the way in which governments and the European Union have responded to such events. Rather than attempt to deal with the root causes and manifestations of anti-Gypsyism, organisations like the Council of Europe have deflected the issues and have instead turned their attentions to other matters. European Union has been almost obsessed with promoting culturally inappropriate *gadzho* education methods for Gypsy children rather than focussing on the rather more immediate problems they face of racist, state sanctioned violence and discrimination in housing, employment and health care.

One of the main reasons as to why official and NGO statistics are so inaccurate is because they rely on Roma self-identification. The acceptability of anti-Roma racism and discrimination means that most Roma families are understandably reluctant to reveal their ethnicity to officialdom for fear of reprisals. In many Central and Eastern European countries the freedom to proclaim one's identity only came post-1989: for example, in the Czech Republic and Slovakia it was the 1991 census that first had 'Romany' as an ethnic category.

A report written by Mark Braham for the United Nations High Commissioner for Refugees in 1993 mentions one Romani woman who refused to write her own or her children's ethnicity on the census form fearing they might be subject to harassment, attack or their house being burned out, such as the incident at Hadareni in Romania in 1993 where Roma homes were torched and three people killed. Indeed, an Amnesty International report two years earlier listed a nine page 'catalogue of injustice' which warned of rising ethnic tensions and nationalism in Romania with the Roma being principle targets.

Another 'fear factor' that causes Roma to shield their ethnicity from outsiders is the continuing legacy of *'O Baro Porrajmos'*. Grandparents today recall the numerous censuses which were conducted during World War Two in order to identify and locate Roma groups for Nazi concentration camps such as Auschwitz, Dachau, Mauthausen and Ravensbrück. Again, estimates vary enormously regarding how many Roma were murdered between 1933 and 1945. Most reliable estimates suggest half a million, though some figures have gone from the ridiculous (zero - 'it never happened' according to the revisionists) to the exaggerated (anything from 3-4 million upwards). It can be seen that in relation to the *Porrajmos* the political and economic significance of numbers are also important and contested. The number of both victims and survivors has a crucial bearing on any future compensation award that might eventually be paid out by the German government. At the time of writing progress is being made but no end is yet in sight.

What is very clear to Roma in Europe is the fact that the *gadzhe* search for the 'final solution' to the 'Roma problem' is determined and ongoing. In Britain, English *Romanichals*, such as Peter Mercer and Charlie Smith of the Gypsy Council, talk about the Criminal Justice and Public Order Act, 1994 in this light: to criminalise nomadism in the UK is to literally 'ethnically cleanse' Gypsies.

In the political vacuum that was created post-1989 in Central and Eastern Europe a plethora of Romani political and cultural groups were formed. By 1993, in Hungary alone, there were nearly one thousand local and national Rom organisations. Only three years later, according to some reports, this number had dropped to below 250 and not one of these Roma groups had a representative in the Parliament. It seems clear that the numbers of such groups have reduced somewhat and any degree of power has been elusive.

The variety of political groupings in Central and Eastern Europe is encouraging though. In Bulgaria the leading party is the Democratic Union of Roma ; in Hungary there are a variety of different parties covering the ideological spectrum – *Phralipe*, the Hungarian Gypsy Party and the Democratic Alliance of Hungarian Gypsies ; In Romania the Democratic Union of Romanian Roma, Romani Criss and the Ethnic Federation of Roma are three of the largest parties. In the Czech Republic following the 'velvet revolution' of 1989 various Rom organisations were formed, such as the Foundation for Hope and Understanding and the Romany Democratic Congress, though unfortunately the RDC has had little success in elections due to factionalism, lack of funding and apathy.

With apparently little political means to express their interests and concerns, Roma in Central and Eastern Europe will sometimes identify themselves as members of another minority that does have more power and resources. One example of this process is in Slovakia where sometimes Roma will identify themselves as Hungarian due to the relatively good standing of the Hungarian minority. This process of 'manipulating' identity illustrates the skills at adaptation, on their own terms, that Roma have when their backs are against the wall. Indeed, their adaptability has been called upon often in European history.

On one level the future does seem a little brighter for Romani politics in Europe, despite what Zoltan Barany has recently suggested. Rom activists and intellectuals are beginning to work together to create a network of groups and organisations which can tap into the corridors of power in the European Union in an effort to improve the social, economic and political situation of Roma in Europe. The work of the International Romani Union (IRU) stands out in this regard, though at least one Romani commentator has accused it of being a 'paper tiger', undemocratic and not playing 'any significant role in the Romani community'.

Real political progress and victories have been slow but at least Gypsies are now recognised as an ethnic minority in countries such as Bulgaria, Hungary and Slovakia. Indeed, even Barany, despite his pessimism, does acknowledge the political success of the Roma in Hungary and Macedonia, pointing to the way the state in both these countries has sought to encourage Roma mobilisation efforts. However, we must acknowledge that the power base of Romani politics in many Central and Eastern European countries is still localised and rather fragmented at a national level. The wider European platform would appear to offer the most hope for Romani campaigning, especially if the nations of Central and Eastern Europe are eventually admitted to the European Union.

5

Education, Living Conditions of Romas and Sinits

In many countries, Roma have been decreed illegal residents on their own property, banished beyond municipal boundaries, and left outside the community of common concern. These are not isolated incidents, but widespread practices—sometimes systematic and on occasion systemic. To redress the long and hard experience of Roma requires, therefore, considerable attention, careful analysis, development of specific policies and commitment of adequate resources.

Even against the backcloth of a decade blighted by extreme forms of racist intolerance, the phenomenon of prejudice against Roma is singular. Romani communities are the subject of hostile perceptions across an extraordinary range of countries. In some, politicians and citizens feel few scruples about expressing derogatory stereotypes of Roma. In this climate, Roma have been prime targets of skinhead violence and, at times, what must properly be called pogroms.

Therefore, the most immediate concern for many Roma is their lack of personal security. The collective violence visited upon Kosovo's Roma in the aftermath of war has been singular in some respects, but scarcely unique in others: like Romani communities who have in the past endured organized group violence directed against them in Romania, Italy and Spain in retaliation for the apparent delinquencies of individuals, entire Romani communities in Kosovo have recently been made to bear the blame for those presumed to have collaborated in or supported crimes committed by or attributed to ethnic Serbs. In other places where anti-Roma violence has flared, the victims have often faced significant obstacles in securing justice; many have been denied effective protection of the law. These are among the factors leading increasing numbers of Roma to leave their countries.

Although racist violence has claimed its largest toll in the countries of Central and Eastern Europe, where the majority of European Roma live, Romani communities experience widespread discrimination, including violence, in Western Europe as well. While several governments have in recent years made significant efforts to reverse these patterns, few have done enough to combat anti-Roma racism and intolerance. There may be no easy solution to many of the problems confronting Roma, but it is equally plain that present approaches are inadequate. Specifically, greater attention must be given to the elaboration and implementation of effective policies to combat discrimination and racial violence.

It is incumbent on government officials to provide leadership in condemning acts of racial violence and, indeed, all forms of discrimination against Roma. In particular, when racial violence occurs, political leaders must condemn the crimes lest their silence be interpreted as tolerance. When it comes to racism, what is said -words alone - can make a difference. When officials have publicly condemned acts of racist violence, they have made a significant contribution to the alleviation of racial tensions and toward preventing similar crimes.

In several countries, Roma are protected by the rule of law. As a first and indispensable step, governments must ensure that their laws prohibit discrimination against Roma and provide adequate remedies when discrimination occurs. Prejudice and intolerance are commonly fed by negative stereotypes. These must be countered through public education about Romani culture and history. In countries where Roma have been part of national history, their history and culture must be part of every child's education. Against the stereotype many local citizens had previously held of Roma as passive recipients of social benefits, the community saw the reality of highly-motivated, industrious Roma constructing homes for non-Roma as well as Romani families.

Another important measure in combating anti-Roma discrimination is to ensure that law-enforcement officials receive adequate training. Police, prosecutors and judges need to be more aware of what constitutes racial discrimination and racially-motivated crimes. Part of the solution could be to introduce conflict-management mechanisms for police and between police and Roma communities.

Education

Exclusion of Roma extends to every sphere of social life, perhaps nowhere with more far-reaching and harmful effect than in respect of schooling. In certain countries of Central and Eastern Europe, this has occurred through systematic routing of Romani children to "special schools" for the mentally disabled. Aside from the obvious disadvantage this entails in terms of the sub-standard quality of education made available to Romani children - depriving them of the equal opportunity to learn and to develop as capable and self-reliant citizens - the effect is also automatically to disqualify Romani children from admission to certain secondary and tertiary educational and professional institutions.

Exclusion from educational opportunities holds significant negative implications and gives rise to other problems. A large percentage of Romani children avoid classes and eventually drop out altogether, partly because they feel unwelcome in many public schools. Lacking basic qualifications, many Roma fare poorly in increasingly competitive job markets. Others, whose academic accomplishments satisfy basic job qualifications, face nearly impenetrable barriers of discrimination.

Their frustrations lead other Roma to wonder whether there is anything to be gained by sending their children to schools where they are all but certain to face rejection -especially given that many ultimately fail to find decent jobs even if they succeed in school. The decision of some Roma parents to keep their children out of school -even if this may be the result of discrimination, impoverishment or poor health -leads to problems later in life. It is essential that Roma children get a good start in life.

Special emphasis should therefore be put on pre-school and kindergarten education for Roma children to increase their proficiency in the language of instruction and, more generally, to prepare them for school. Like any other group, Roma have the right to establish their own schools with a view to maintaining and developing their identities.

Roma children should not be relegated to Roma classes within mixed schools. Alienation in, or even from, school strengthens the image of the Roma as perennial outsiders. These problems must be overcome not only as a matter of respecting rights and ensuring equal opportunities, but for clear purposes of public interest

Beyond exclusion from education, Roma face profound challenges in virtually every sphere of social life:

rates of unemployment, poverty, illiteracy and infant mortality are staggeringly high among Roma. In a classic downward spiral, each of these problems exacerbates the others in a self-perpetuating cycle. Equality of opportunity does not exist in the absence of minimum guarantees of an adequate standard of living. Among the most obvious and pressing problem is that of securing adequate and appropriate housing. This demands immediate attention. Resettlement projects, ghettoization and the exclusion of Roma families from municipalities have become common occurrences in many countries. There needs to be greater support for projects aimed at integrative housing. Because of the substantial resources that are required, governments should show greater readiness to assume the risk of guaranteeing loans that may be available from international organizations and financial institutions for housing projects. Targeted international, national or local support could kick-start community development.

Involving Roma in the planning, renovation, building and maintenance of houses that they live in can help advance their integration in society and avoid patterns of dependency associated with some public housing programs. Governments must, at the very least, ensure that housing projects do not foster segregation. In view of the extreme insecurity that many Roma now experience in respect to housing - whether nomadic or sedentary groups -governments should also endeavor to regularize the legal status of Roma who now live in circumstances of unsettled legality. This is particularly important in the context of nomadic and semi-nomadic Roma who often encounter difficulties in relation to encampments and halting sites.

Non-existent or inadequate access to health care is also of immediate concern. Numerous chronic tendencies bear upon Romani communities. Typical among these are a high incidence of disease, malnutrition and infant mortality. These tendencies are largely the result of endemic poverty giving rise, for example, to very high rates of tuberculosis among Roma in some countries. Such diseases underline not only the serious situation experienced by Roma, but also the clearly inadequate reach of public health.

In this relation, special attention needs to be paid to sanitation, clean water and medical care. With regard to the situation of Romani women, improvement is necessary not only in terms of immediate health concerns, such as a high incidence of frequent and sometimes unwanted pregnancy, but also more generally with respect to gender issues. Improvement in the health of Roma demands equal access to public health care with a view to achieving the highest attainable standards of health.

Perhaps no principle is more essential to the success and legitimacy of initiatives to alleviate the concerns of Romani communities than that Roma themselves should be centrally involved in developing, implementing and evaluating policies and programs. The basic democratic principle that individuals should have a say in how they are governed requires nothing less, and pragmatic considerations counsel the same approach.

The importance of minority participation in public affairs is specifically provided in paragraph 35 of the Copenhagen Document which requires participating States to "respect the right of persons belonging to national minorities to effective participation in public affairs, including participation in the affairs relating to the protection and promotion of the identity of such minorities."

Unfortunately, countless programs for Roma have been destined to fail because they were developed without Roma participation, and, correspondingly, with scant awareness of the specific culture and needs of the intended beneficiaries. Equally important, programs for Roma designed without Roma are scarcely likely to earn the confidence and commitment of Roma. At the same time, the active engagement of Roma in developing and implementing projects helps ensure that they do not inadvertently create or perpetuate a classic syndrome of dependency and passivity on the part of the intended beneficiaries.

Encouragingly, recent years have seen an increase in the dynamism of the Romani movement. Constructive and effective communication must feature mutual respect on the basis of which mutual trust may be built. More specifically, efforts should be made to engage Roma more actively in public service, and to improve the representation of Roma in elected and appointed office at all levels of government; only then will they feel that they have a stake in the system. In addition, mechanisms that are set up to allow for Roma participation must be genuine in their intentions and meaningful in their endeavors; without this they will represent nothing more than window dressing or tokenism.

The effectiveness of consultative mechanisms can be measured by a number of criteria: the scope for early involvement of Roma in Roma-related policy formation; the extent to which the process is broadly representative; transparency; and the involvement of Roma in implementation and evaluation of Roma-related programs. These benchmarks hold true for more than political consultative bodies. In order to enjoy legitimacy and success, any initiative relating to the Roma should involve Roma in the development, implementation and evaluation phases.

It is now generally agreed that Roma originated in the northwest region of the Indian subcontinent - a conclusion derived principally from linguistic science.

Despite wide variations among Romani dialects, linguists have been able to trace a common origin in Sanskrit.But if Roma share a common lineage, their migrations produced numerous distinct communities and dialects as particular groups established roots in various countries and regions.

The major migrations from India that initiated the Roma diaspora are believed to have occurred in several waves, dating between the ninth and fourteenth centuries,and successive waves of migration brought Romani communities to a range of countries over time. Among the earliest records of what may have been a Romani community are a tenth century historical account of the appearance of "Zott" in Persia several centuries earlier.

The first major migrations to Europe are dated primarily to the fourteenth and fifteenth century, and it is in Europe - principally in Central and Eastern Europe - that a majority of the world's Roma live today.These migrations produced a dispersed mosaic of peoples, united by common origins, culture and to some extent language,but also distinguished by their diverse historical experiences and the resulting impact on each group's culture.

For present purposes, the significance of this history is that approaches to Roma policy must be rooted in recognition of and respect for the plurality of Romani groups. As two scholars of Romani history and culture have observed, "Gypsies have lived (and still live) in many countries with different historical circumstances and socio-cultural environments. Hence, the search for a common and universal approach to solve the 'Gypsy problem' in all its dimensions and aspects is predestined to failure."

The second aspect of Romani history that should be borne in mind is that, despite popular associations of Roma with nomadism, Roma have been stable residents of many of the countries addressed in this study for hundreds of years. The Romani communities in Romania and Bulgaria, for example, are traced to groups believed to have settled in the territories now comprising these States between the twelfth and fourteenth centuries.

Contemporary challenges confronting Roma cannot be understood without a basic appreciation of their historical experience of persecution and rejection. Although Roma history includes episodes of comparatively benign treatment, reflected, for example, in writs of safe-conduct from fifteenth-century monarchs,the dominant European response to Roma has been one of social and legal rejection. As Jean-Pierre Liégeois has written,

> The State, officialdom, and local populations have always seen Gypsies and Travellers as a threat of disorder, be it political or psychological. Gypsies are seen not so much as strangers who are difficult to categorise, but as embodiments of the strange and different which must be driven out to be overcome. The difference of the Traveller and of the Gypsy is perceived as dissidence, and in tandem with this gut reaction, or in its wake, further attitudes and policies have developed, all of them, whatever their forms and methods, expressions of that rejection.

The instinctive reaction described by Liégeois found expression in early public chronicles of Roma that helped establish a stereotype of Romani communities as essentially sinister. In Bologna, it was remarked in 1422 "that there is no worse breed than these savages"; five years later, they were described in Paris as "sorcerers who look at people's hands."In what may be the earliest reference to Roma in Constantinople, a Georgian text composed in the early eleventh century records the presence of "a Samarian people, descendants of Simon the Magician, who were called Adsincani, and notorious for soothsaying and sorcery."

It was a short step from the social construction of Roma in these terms to the enactment of decrees effectively outlawing Roma. Liégeois recounts a few illustrative examples:

> The first response of the authorities towards nomad groups was generally one of rejection, banishing them from the territory of the State. This trend very quickly became unanimous. . . . In Germany, . . . the Reichstag, meeting in . . . 1496, 1497, and 1498, declared the Gypsies to be traitors to the Christian lands, spies in the pay of the Turks, and carriers of the plague. They were accused of brigandry, sorcery, and the abduction of children. They had to disappear. In 1500, Emperor Maxmillian I . . . repeated the demand that measures be taken. Gypsies were no longer tolerated on German territory, and could be killed with impunity. . . . In 1661, in Saxony, Elector George II published a decree imposing the death penalty on any Gypsy caught in his territory; over the following years they were hunted down by cavalry. . . . In 1721 Emperor Charles VI ordered their extermination: men were to be executed, women and children to have an ear cut off. . . . In the Czech lands in the 17 century, Gypsies were hanged all along the border as an illustration of the punishment awaiting any who dared cross.
>
> In the Netherlands, . . . painted signposts depicting hanged Gypsies were posted at crossroads as a warning of what awaited those who had slipped through the net that far. Other signs . . . informed the general public that it was

> forbidden to assist Gypsies in any way whatsoever. . . . In 1525, Charles V published an edict ordering Gypsies] to quit the country within two days. . . . Later, in the 17 and early 18 centuries, Heidenjachten -" heathen hunts" - took place; dreadful anti-Gypsy drives with the joint participation of infantry, cavalry, and the police. Anybody could murder Gypsies with absolute impunity. . . . "Gypsy hunts" took place in many countries during this period.
> [In Sweden, a] royal ordinance of 1637 . . . demands the banishment of all Gypsies; any remaining could be executed without trial. . . .
> In Norway, [ordinances in force from 1687 to 1845 provided that] "Gypsies and Travellers . . . must be arrested, and their goods confiscated, their chiefs executed and the remainder deported. Once deported, re-entry carried the death penalty. . . . After 1845, nomadism per se was made illegal, as were Travellers' traditional trades.

After providing numerous other examples, Liégeois concludes: "The bottom line was that Gypsies' very existence was forbidden: the common aim of all the legislation was the suppression of the people it was directed at. . . . Although the target group is always named, . . . [it is not] always clear exactly what they are being accused of, apart from living an independent life, being nomadic and different, and, mostly as a direct result of these, inspiring fear."

In more recent years, official policies toward Roma have included enslavement, containment, extermination, and forced assimilation. In the Romanian principalities, Roma were enslaved until the mid-nineteenth century.In eighteenth-century Hungary, Gypsies were subjected to measures aimed at eradicating their identity. To this end, the Habsburg ruler Maria Theresa decreed in 1761, inter alia, that Gypsies were to settle; to ensure this they could no longer own horses and wagons and would need special permission to leave their villages; that the word "Gypsy" should henceforth be replaced with "Új magyar" ("New Hungarian") or other constructions, such as "New Settler"; that Gypsies were forbidden to set themselves apart in dress, speech or occupation; in an effort to eradicate the Gypsy "race," that marriage between Gypsies was forbidden; and, finally, that Gypsy children over the age of five were to be taken away and raised by non-Gypsy families.

In this century, Roma have been treated as de facto aliens and inherent outlaws in several countries. The extermination of Roma and Sinti by Nazi Germany was preceded by the establishment of a central register in Munich in 1899 to collate reports of Gypsy appearances and actions taken against them.The man in charge of the register produced a book to aid police in Bavaria and neighboring Länder in eradicating what he called die Zigeunerplage ("the Gypsy plague"). Other countries, including Sweden, followed suit, establishing their own national registers.In France, a law enacted in 1912, repealed only in the late 1960s, required itinerants to carry a carnet anthropométrique, an identity document. Many communes posted signs at their borders warning "interdit aux nomades" ("prohibited to nomads").

During World War II, Roma and Sinti, along with Jews, were the only ethnic groups slated for wholesale extermination.An estimated quarter to half a million of Europe's Roma and Sinti were exterminated in the Holocaust, known in Romani as the "Porajmos" - "the Devouring." After the war, a majority of Europe's Romani communities lived under Communist regimes. Variations not only among countries but also across time within countries make it impossible to describe the post-war experience of European Roma in general terms, but certain recurring patterns should be noted in light of their enduring impact on the contemporary Romani experience.

Most important, although Roma had during earlier periods received state support for the development of their cultural identity in some Communist countries, during later periods they were subjected to policies of forced assimilation in many. In 1958, for example, Czech authorities decreed that Roma were not an ethnic group but people "maintaining a markedly different demographic structure," and enacted a law to enforce school attendance and settlement of nomadic people by registering them in one place and refusing them employment anywhere else.A subsequent policy sought to integrate Roma through their "dispersal and transfer" from settlements in Slovakia to the Czech lands. The plan was "to spread them as thinly as possible throughout the Republic."

Similarly, although earlier Communist policies in Bulgaria had provided support for Romani cultural activities, a decree of 1958 prohibited Roma from travelling. In the ensuing 30-year policy of assimilation, Romani children were forbidden to speak Romani at school, and authorities banned Roma newspapers and associations. From the 1970s, the term "Gypsy" was abolished and Roma, along with Turks, were required to take on Slavic names.

Only in the very last part of the twentieth century has a concerted effort been made within Europe to address the individual and cumulative effects of this history. While good will coupled with some effective initiatives can be observed on the part of certain authorities in some States, the overall picture remains one of the extreme alienation of a Europe-wide under-class. The challenges are many and great.

Discrimination And Racial Violence

Discrimination is a defining feature of the Romani experience. Anti-Roma bias has a profound impact on access to employment opportunities, education, housing and health care. As summarized by one specialized NGO, "Hostility against Roma is a generalised attitude, and there is particular concern over the way prejudiced attitudes and stereotypes affect public officers, journalists, and other persons working in social institutions. The racist nature of this violence and discrimination is increasingly acknowledged."

Beyond the exclusion and loss suffered by Roma as a result of discrimination in employment, education, access to public services, housing and health care, Roma are also targeted as objects of physical violence, sometimes resulting in injury and even death. Such racially-motivated hatred and violence arises not only from other citizens, but also from agents of the State including police. Aside from the fact that such experiences obviously feed alienation among Roma and reinforce their deeply held suspicions about Gadjé society and authority, racially-motivated violence is first of all a violation of human rights respecting physical integrity, including the rights to security of person and life.

In accordance with Article 3 of the 1948 Universal Declaration of Human Rights (hereafter, Universal Declaration) "Everyone has the right to life, liberty and the security of person".These rights are to be both respected and ensured by the State: in respecting these rights, agents of the State must not in the exercise of their lawful authority violate the rights to security of person and life, while the State must act to ensure these rights through legislation and exercise of lawful authority protecting against harmful acts on the part of private persons (so-called horizontal effects).

Discrimination against Roma just as clearly violates the broadly-defined prohibition of discrimination set forth in various human rights instruments. Article 1(1) of the Race Convention broadly defines "racial discrimination" as:

> any distinction, exclusion, restriction or preference based on race, colour, descent, or national or ethnic origin which has the purpose or effect of nullifying or impairing the recognition, enjoyment or exercise, on an equal footing, of human rights and fundamental freedoms in the political, economic, social, cultural or any other field of public life.

Thus "racial discrimination" is defined to include negative discrimination based not only on "race" or color, but also on "national or ethnic origin." In light of this broad definition, it is not surprising that the Committee on the Elimination of Racial Discrimination (CERD), the body that monitors States Parties' compliance with the Race Convention, has repeatedly treated discrimination against Roma as a breach of the Convention.

Not all distinctions on such grounds as "race" or association with a national minority violate the aforementioned prohibitions. The European Court of Human Rights has held that a distinction on one of the grounds enumerated in Article 14 of the European Convention for the Protection of Human Rights and Fundamental Freedoms (hereafter, European Convention on Human Rights or European Convention), might be permissible if it pursues a legitimate aim and utilizes proportionate means to achieve that aim.In similar fashion, the Human Rights Committee, the body that monitors compliance with the ICCPR, has expressed its view that "the enjoyment of rights and freedoms on an equal footing . . . does not mean identical treatment in every instance."

Distinctions based upon reasonable and objective

criteria that are undertaken in pursuit of a legitimate aim do not breach the Covenant's prohibition of discrimination.The Committee has indicated that "positive measures" undertaken by States "to protect the identity of a minority" may constitute such a legitimate differentiation (and may even be necessary), provided they "are aimed at correcting conditions which prevent or impair the enjoyment" of the minority rights guaranteed by Article 27 of the Covenant.

Employment

Although some Roma enjoy substantial economic success, rates of unemployment among Roma tend to be extremely high. For example, it is estimated that 70 percent of Hungary's Gypsies are unemployed; in some villages, 90-100 percent of the Gypsy population is unemployed.In countries that have substantial Romani communities and whose national unemployment rates are high, Roma tend to constitute a disproportionate share of the unemployed. In the Slovak Republic, for example, the rate of unemployment has reached 16.7 percent nationally-the highest level since 1990. A major portion of the unemployed are Roma, among whom unemployment rates approach close to 100 percent in some areas.

In the former Yugoslav Republic of Macedonia (fYROM), where national unemployment rates are an estimated 36 percent, the rate among Roma is 76.4 percent.Unemployment rates of Roma are also high in countries where national unemployment rates are comparatively low. In the Czech Republic, for example, government estimates in 1999 indicate that 70 percent of Roma are unemployed, compared to approximately ten percent for the population as a whole.While both Romani men and women experience high unemployment in many States, the figures tend to be even higher for Romani women.

These disparities are not solely the function of discrimination, but its impact is substantial. In some countries in Central and Eastern Europe, advertisements for job openings sometimes specify that Roma should not apply. Indeed, one government official in Romania stated that the Attorney General had taken the position that such advertisements were "much too common to be prosecuted.

In many countries, including the Czech Republic and Bulgaria, Roma frequently find that, when they apply in person for a job that has been advertised, they are told that the position has been filled even though they had been told otherwise when they made telephone inquiries. In some countries, Romani job applicants allegedly have been tracked by government employment offices. In a recent interview, the general director of the Slovak National Labour Office reportedly admitted that Slovak labor offices marked unemployed Roma with the letter "R" in their registers, and referred to the practice as a means of "identifying a risky group."

Such systematic discrimination compounds the effects of other factors that contribute to high levels of Romani unemployment. As has often been noted, Roma were particularly hard hit by the transition of formerly communist countries to market economies in the early 1990s. As state industries and agricultural collectives were closed or privatized, Roma tended to be the first to lose their jobs. Today, they are ill-prepared to succeed in a competitive labor market: in many Central and Eastern European countries, assimilation of Roma had meant their incorporation into the lowest strata of society; although employed, many worked in low-skill jobs.

In larger perspective, the phenomenon of industrialization has presented Roma with an unprecedented challenge, radically diminishing their prospects for surviving through traditional trades that sustained Roma for centuries. Low levels of educational achievement among Roma further diminish their prospects for employment. Moreover, as low levels of educational achievement persist among the Roma while required skill levels increase, especially in connection with the ever-expanding influence of information technologies, Roma increasingly find themselves simply unqualified for employment opportunities; in this way, systematic discrimination and exclusion in education result in effective exclusion from employment later in life.

In Western Europe too, the disappearance of traditional trades, the difficulties faced by people with an itinerant lifestyle, and the transition to a service economy requiring education and qualifications have all contributed to a high unemployment rate. It is to be noted that certain States have taken measures in recent years to prevent or overcome discrimination suffered by Roma in employment. For example, Bulgaria amended its Penal Code to prohibit as a criminal offence racially-motivated discrimination in employment. Similarly, Finland amended its Criminal Code in 1995 to render discrimination in employment a criminal offence.

More recently, on 29 May 1999, a Romani family was reportedly barred from using a public swimming pool in Brno when they were unable to produce health certificates. According to an eyewitness, the guard who demanded this documentation did not request similar certificates of non-Roma who were in line to use the pool. When members of this family protested that they had not previously been required to produce health certificates, the guard reportedly replied that new rules had been adopted pursuant to which Roma would be allowed to use the pool only after producing documents certifying their good health.

In a recent positive development, on 26 October 1999 the Regional Court of the Czech city of Ostrava approved the settlement of a lawsuit initiated by a Romani activist in 1998 after he had been refused service in a local hotel. The lawsuit claimed infringement of the claimant's human dignity and racial discrimination, in violation of Article 11 of the Czech Civil Code. According to the terms of the settlement, the hotel will pay compensation to the claimant and to a civic association which is supporting construction of an integrated Romani and non-Romani housing project.

The Court's approval of this settlement constitutes an important step forward in challenging racial discrimination in access to public accommodations in the Czech Republic.There have also been recent reports of discrimination against Travellers in Ireland. The Irish Olympic boxer Francie Barrett reportedly was refused admission to a nightclub in Galway because he is a Traveller. In 1998, two hotels in Dublin reportedly canceled a reservation for a dinner for participants in an international conference on discrimination when they learned that Gypsies and Travellers were involved.

Racial Violence

The past decade has seen numerous incidents of anti-Roma violence. In several countries in Central and Eastern Europe, Roma have been targets of skinhead violence and other racially-motivated attacks. In some States, including Spain, Italy, and Romania, Romani communities have been attacked. Most recently, the Roma community in Kosovo has been the target of racially-motivated violence. These pogroms sometimes bear the mark of collective retribution against the supposed offense of an individual Rom; often it is impossible to identify any precipitating event.

In several countries, victims encounter significant obstacles in their efforts to secure legal redress for these attacks. A notable example is Romania, where Romani communities were victims of a considerable number of serious incidents, in the course of which some Roma were killed while the homes of many others were burned, in the period between 1990 and 1996. There have been prosecutions in respect of only a few of these. In those cases, only some of the people believed to have been involved in the attacks were ever charged; fewer still have been convicted.

One case in which there have been convictions involves a 23 September 1993 pogrom in Hadareni, in which three Roma were murdered, fourteen houses were burned down, and five other homes destroyed by a mob of ethnic Romanians and Hungarians. An appeals court reduced the sentences of two of those convicted from seven to six years. According to Romanian NGOs, the government now asserts that the statute of limitations prevents further prosecutions in most of the cases from the early 1990s.

There have also been frequent instances of abuse of Roma at the hands of police. As with crimes of private violence, alleged instances of police abuse frequently go unpunished and sometimes are not even seriously investigated. Shortcomings in this regard led the European Court of Human Rights in 1998 to find the Government of Bulgaria in breach of the European Convention. In recent years some governments have undertaken initiatives to address these patterns. But violence against Roma remains a grave problem in several participating States.

Widespread civilian violence against Roma has been documented in recent years. Although the largest number of skinhead attacks against Roma have been recorded in the Czech Republic, Bulgaria and the Slovak Republic, instances of such violence have also been registered in Albania, Austria, Bosnia, Croatia, Hungary, Poland, Romania, Russia, Ukraine and Yugoslavia.

Collective retribution against entire Romani communities for the presumed conduct of individuals has also been common in Kosovo in recent months - in this case for the alleged collaboration of some Roma in Serb atrocities.This phenomenon has not been limited to Romani victims; the province's dwindling Serb population has also been subjected to collective reprisals for recent Serb atrocities. However obvious, the point bears reiterating: it is incumbent on the international community to do all that is feasible to protect these vulnerable communities from further attack.

Although Kosovo's Roma are not alone in their vulnerability to violent attacks, some aspects of their plight are singular. As a Kosovo field officer for the United Nations High Commissioner for Refugees (UNHCR) observed, "They are completely marginalized as a part of the Kosovar community, and that makes it very difficult to find a solution." Scarcely embraced by Yugoslav Serbs, Roma in Kosovo are said to be reviled by the province's ethnic Albanians. Thus, the UNHCR officer observed, "In a way, they may be in a more desperate situation right now than the Serbs. Nobody wants them."

Police Violence

In addition to attacks by skinheads and other private actors, there have been numerous instances in which Roma have suffered physical assaults by police. According to the ERRC, "Roma in most countries of the [Central and Eastern European] region encounter police violence in almost any . . . everyday life situation. . . Information about police ill-treatment of Roma or of use of excessive force . . . against Roma comes from almost all countries of Central and Eastern Europe, and occasionally from Western Europe as well."Between 1992 and 1998, fourteen Romani men in Bulgaria reportedly died after last being seen alive in the custody of police or as a result of unlawful use of firearms by Bulgarian police.A considerably larger number have endured physical abuse in police custody.

In several countries, entire Romani communities have been subjected to police raids, often at dawn, frequently characterized by unnecessary or excessive violence. These developments have been summarized as follows:

> In a number of countries, law enforcement authorities target Roma communities for special raids - armed assaults in the middle of the night or early hours of the morning during which houses are searched, contents ransacked, inhabitants harassed or subjected to excessive force, and young men are rounded up for arrest and questioning, in many cases in the absence of search and arrest warrants and other legal safeguards . . . In many cases, police officials readily admit that such raids target Roma communities because Roma, as a group, are said to be prone to criminality.

Racially-motivated violence against Roma and other manifestations of discrimination do not occur in a vacuum. Negative stereotyping of Roma is a notable feature of public life in countries where Roma experience frequent acts of discrimination and racially-motivated violence. In several countries, politicians have played a prominent role in perpetuating negative images of Roma. Although some of the more notorious statements of this kind have been made by opposition figures and local officials, negative stereotypes of Roma have at times been evoked in statements of government officials.

A well-known instance is a statement made by Vladimir Meciar when still Prime Minister of the Slovak Republic. Referring to Romani communities' relatively high birth rate, he publicly evoked the specter "that this [population] ratio will be changing to the benefit of Romanies. There is a recurring tenor to many anti-Roma statements: the behavior of Roma and their inherent characteristics, it is implied, account for their social exclusion and even for violence against them. In Romania, as in the Czech and Slovak Republics, racist statements have been made by the leader of an extremist opposition party. On 16 August 1998, Corneliu Vadim Tudor, leader of the Great Romania Party and Senator in Romania's Parliament, reportedly announced a ten-point "program to run the country" which included "isolating the Roma criminals in special colonies" in order to "stop the transformation of Romania into a Gypsy camp."

In the United Kingdom, reports relating to Gypsies frequently emphasize the negative views of Gypsies held by others in a fashion likely to reinforce those perceptions. After monitoring national and local press in the United Kingdom over a one year period, one analyst concluded:

> The press . . . routinely represent Travellers in such a way as to actively increase dislike of them and their way of life. The local press, in particular, more often than not cover Traveller-related issues in a manner which seems deliberately designed to inflame local tensions and damage relations between the settled and Traveller communities.

As this analyst noted, "other research has found 'that the announcement of a large number of small [Gypsy caravan] sites had been used by some local newspapers to produce the image of a major gypsy 'invasion', even though the gypsies concerned were already regularly resident in the area'."

The specter of a "Gypsy invasion" pervaded British press coverage of several recent waves of Romani asylum seekers from the Czech Republic and Slovak Republic. As noted earlier, Roma in both countries have been key targets of skinhead and other racially motivated violence in recent years and face pervasive discrimination in virtually every sphere of public life. Yet many press reports describing the arrival of these asylum-seekers portrayed them as bogus claimants seeking to exploit British welfare programs, while playing upon public fears of Roma by invoking imagery of a "Gypsy invasion."

While economic motives may, in some cases, have prompted the decision to apply for asylum in the United Kingdom, the British press failed to acknowledge the serious causes, including discrimination and racial violence, which lead many Roma to leave their countries of origin. Typical of these accounts was a front-page story headlined "Gypsies invade Dover, hoping for a handout."The article barely alluded to the fact that the Roma who had recently arrived were seeking political asylum, and implied that their real motivation was to take advantage of British welfare opportunities.

While failing to include perspectives relating to the conditions of Roma in the Czech Republic and Slovakia, the article prominently featured the purported views of the British authorities, who emphasized the "burden" the new arrivals presented and who suggested that the Roma were not "genuine refugees," but instead were abusing "the integrity of the [asylum] system." The British government subsequently made it clear that Roma who entered the country, legally, as asylum seekers would have their cases examined in the same way as all other asylum seekers, i.e. on merit.

There is a manifest need for governments to make concerted efforts to combat discrimination and racial violence against Roma. While efforts are needed on many fronts, the most sophisticated programs will fall short unless backed by the unwavering commitment of political will, manifested both in moral leadership and material resources. In the context of pervasive racial stereotyping of Roma, one measure of leadership in this regard is government officials' willingness to acknowledge that anti-Roma racism is a problem in their societies.

A non-Romani attorney in the Czech Republic made the case plainly: "Let's say openly that we have a problem that must be solved."This simple acknowledgment is the beginning of the search for solutions. The Hungarian Government approved a package of "medium term measures to improve the living standards and social position of the Roma population", in which it resolved to support a variety of anti-discrimination programs, including monitoring and evaluation of the effectiveness of existing anti-discrimination legislation, anti-discrimination and conflict prevention training for law-enforcement officials, and the activities of legal aid organizations dedicated to preventing and eliminating negative discrimination.

In September 1999, the Slovak Government approved a comprehensive strategy for Roma which states that "[the Roma] minority was really disadvantaged or even discriminated against for [a] long time", and that the protection of Romani individuals is "still insufficient" and stipulates concrete governmental measures for the improvement of this situation. In contrast to these forthright acknowledgments of discrimination and the new undertaking to redress its effects, political leaders in some countries are hesitant even to recognize that there is racism against Roma. This reluctance has sometimes been explained in political terms: Roma are so unpopular, it is said, that it would be costly politically to take up their cause. But past experience has surely taught us that we can meet the challenge of combating racism only when political leaders provide moral leadership - when they shape rather than follow public opinion.

In 1996, some Roma in Kremnica were targets of skinhead attacks. According to residents, some skinheads from Kremnica had complained about local Roma to friends of theirs in another town, air nad Hronom, who responded by coming to Kremnica and attacking local Roma. The Mayor responded by denouncing the skinhead attacks and ensuring that Roma received police protection. At the same time, he played an effective mediating role between the Roma and non-Romani communities.

The Government of the Czech Republic has, in recent months, endeavored to provide such leadership in the face of local authorities' efforts to build a "wall" between a Romani community and non-Roma inhabitants of the town of Ústí nad Labem. While the efforts of several officials provided a commendable example of leadership, this episode also highlighted the need for effective legal remedies against institutionalized racism at all levels.

In the Spring of 1998, municipal authorities in the northern Czech town of Ústí nad Labem decided to construct a wall that would separate four blocks of flats inhabited mainly by Roma families on Maticní Street from primarily non-Roma residents. The plan drew international condemnation at what appeared to be an attempt to create a Roma ghetto in the heart of Europe, and was opposed by the national government elected in 1998. For a time, local authorities indicated that they might not proceed with construction of the wall.

In May 1999, the Czech Government passed a resolution recommending that the Ústí District authority forestall implementation of the municipal resolution, and simultaneously referred the issue to the Czech Parliament. The Government maintained that a parliamentary body had authority to order the local government to rescind its decision, but the Chairman of the Parliament's Petition Committee reportedly expressed doubt about whether Parliament should review such matters, which, he said in a radio interview, are best decided at the local level; in his opinion, if such decisions are to be reviewed by other bodies, they should be reviewed by a court. Meanwhile, on 13 October 1999, local authorities went ahead with their plans, and construction of the wall was completed, under the protection of local policemen.

Shortly thereafter, the Chamber of Deputies of the Czech Parliament voted to annul the municipal council's original decision to build the wall.Local authorities, who initially insisted they would stand by their action, eventually capitulated to domestic and international pressure and had the wall removed in late November - but only after the government had provided them with funding to purchase the three homes of the non-Roma families who had originally complained about their Roma neighbors. At the same time, the Government provided the local council with additional funds to develop programs to benefit Roma.

In Hungary, racial violence was criminalized in 1996, although Hungarian law still lacks other basic legal protections against discrimination. Likewise, in 1996 Spain amended its Penal Code to make incitement to racial or anti-semitic hatred and violence criminal offenses and to add racism or anti-semitic intent to the list of aggravating circumstances for criminal offenses.

In its Resolution No. 279 of 7 April 1999, the Czech Government contemplated presenting draft legislation "restricting racial (or other) discrimination" to the Parliament, though the resolution stopped short of making a commitment to do so.The Framework Program for Equal Integration of Roma in Bulgarian Society recently endorsed by the Bulgarian government similarly includes a commitment to enact legislation that would protect citizens against discrimination. The Romanian Government's Department for the Protection of National Minorities has elaborated the draft of a Law Against All Forms of

Discrimination,which it plans to submit to the Government and the Parliament, pending signature from the relevant Government ministries. Norway has similarly committed itself to strengthening the statutory protection against racial discrimination. Such legislation should, at a minimum, prohibit discrimination in all fields of public life, including access to public accommodations, citizenship, education, employment, health services, housing, the military, and public and social services and establish effective remedies for violations.

In addition to providing civil remedies that victims of discrimination can invoke, the law should establish procedures pursuant to which State authorities can act to nullify discriminatory practices by government officials and organs at all levels. For reasons indicated earlier, it is also important that anti-discrimination laws provide clear definitions of the proscribed conduct. It is also recommended that States enact legislation mandating sentencing enhancements for offenses that are racially-motivated.

Governments should promulgate and enforce internal disciplinary standards to ensure that public officials who discriminate, including police, are sanctioned appropriately. In several countries where racial violence is common, laws proscribing racially-motivated violence that are theoretically available are rarely enforced.While this is doubtless due in part to discrimination within the legal system, in some States the problem of under-enforcement appears also to be attributable to confusion on the part of police, prosecutors and judges about what constitutes a racially-motivated crime or even racial discrimination.

Court rulings in a recent prosecution in the Slovak Republic suggest that some courts might not even find this type of evidence sufficient to qualify a crime against Roma as racially-motivated. The prosecution arose out of an incident on 11 June 1996 in which three non-Romani men accosted a Romani university student, Ivan Mako, at a bus station near the center of Banská Bystrica. The assailants spat upon Mr. Mako, called him a "dirty Gypsy," punched him and threw cobblestones at him. When Mr. Mako began to defend himself with a knife, the assailants beat him so badly that he had to be hospitalized.

On 29 October 1998, one of the assailants was sentenced for the crime of damage to health, but the court declined to characterize the crime as racially-motivated. The court found that the only reason for the attack was the assailants' hatred for Roma, but nonetheless ruled that such hatred was not "because of race" since by the court's reasoning Roma belong to the same "race" as Slovaks. Following the prosecutor's appeal, the case was returned to the district court for a new trial. On 1 July 1999, the district court of Banská Bystrica upheld the decision that the attack could not have been racially-motivated.For reasons suggested in sub-section A, this ruling applies a definition of "race" that affords substantially less protection than that set forth in the Race Convention.

While clear legislative definitions would go a long way toward addressing this type of problem, training of personnel involved in the judicial system is also clearly desirable in several countries. In the view of one Romani leader in the Czech Republic, one of the most significant factors underlying authorities' failure to punish skinhead violence adequately is ignorance of the law. In his words, the "police aren't sure it's right to enforce these laws."

In areas where Romani communities have experienced persistent abuse by police, the phenomenon is both symptomatic of, and further cause for, generally conflictive relations between the two. In these settings, efforts to curb police abuse of Roma could productively include the establishment of mechanisms for conflict-management.Such mechanisms can also go a long way toward enabling police to provide Romani communities greater protection against mob violence, which by its nature reflects conflictive relations between Roma and non-Romani communities.

Such mechanisms have been developed in Romania, with apparently positive results in at least some regions. The Romanian initiatives were triggered by a surge in mob violence against Romani communities between 1990 and early 1996 and the failure of police to provide protection. In most of these cases, the Romanian police "were seen as contributing, through direct or indirect means, to the severity of these incidents and the consequences for Roma citizens."

With the assistance of the Project on Ethnic Relations and the U.S. Department of Justice Administration, University of Louisville, the Romanian General Inspectorate of Police developed a program to improve relations between Roma and police and to enhance the capacity of the police to respond effectively in situations of tension between Roma and non-Romani communities. The first step taken by national police authorities was to organize meetings between police representatives and Roma leaders so that they could "identify the problems that [the Roma] have and . . . build together a social peace and stronger community."A hallmark of the program was to develop regular meetings between police and representatives of Roma, as well as non-Romani communities, at both the local and national levels.

As described by officials involved in these initiatives, conflict mediation is a central feature of the Government's program. One official explained that "most problems" between Roma and non-Roma "are the result of a lack of communication."Ideally, police intervene at the earliest sign of tensions that have the potential to (or already do) involve criminal behavior, and attempt to mediate among the various parties, sometimes bringing in other relevant institutions and actors.

Roma leaders are not uniformly enthusiastic about the Government's initiatives. Some regard as ominous the fact that the umbrella for the Government's program, which began as a "Mob Violence Prevention Programme" within the General Inspectorate of Police of the Ministry of Interior, was later renamed the "Institute for Research and Prevention of Criminality." In their view, this signified that a program initially conceived to enhance police protection of Roma was now more concerned with "Roma criminality."

Still, the very fact that the General Inspectorate of Police has established a framework for communicating with Roma leaders makes it easier for the latter to raise and address these and other concerns. In 1997, Roma associations negotiated a protocol with the Inspectorate to address concerns about the manner in which police dealt with Romani communities; the protocol entered into effect in 1998. Some Roma leaders involved in this initiative and others familiar with it believe that there have indeed been improvements in relations between Romanian police and Romani communities. They cite in particular the situation in the city of Sibiu, where representatives of police and of both Roma and non-Romani communities meet regularly and seek to negotiate joint methods of problem solving.

Another measure that would, if implemented properly, help alleviate conflicts between police and Romani communities and reduce instances of police violence against Roma is the recruitment of more Roma into police forces.To this end, a pilot program was instituted by the Ministry of Interior of the Czech Republic in the Summer of 1998 to prepare Roma for the police academy. According to a Rom familiar with this program, there had been only twelve Romani police in the Czech Republic before this program; ten completed the course.

The Bulgarian Government has also signaled its interest in increasing the number of Roma in its police forces: in September 1999, the Bulgarian Ministry of Defense reportedly signed an order for the appointment of 15 Roma in the Military Police structure. In a number of countries, specialized government and/or parliamentary bodies dealing specifically with issues of discrimination have made a valuable contribution toward combating racism and other forms of discrimination. A well-known example is the United Kingdom's Commission for Racial Equality (CRE), which was established pursuant to the 1976 Race Relations Act. The CRE has several roles, ranging from advising the government generally about the functioning of the Race Relations Act to investigating potential violations and instituting enforcement proceedings against persistent violators before designated courts.

Another model that has proven effective in a number of countries is that of an ombudsman. In some countries, including Sweden and Hungary, several ombudsmen have been appointed to address distinct issues, such as discrimination against minorities. Ombudsmen may also be appointed at regional or local levels. While the functions of ombudsmen vary from country to country, it is common for these institutions to receive complaints from individuals who believe that government bodies have denied their rights in areas that are within the competence of the ombudsmen. It is also common for ombudsmen to have a mandate to recommend legislative changes.

Several countries that have significant Romani communities, including Hungary, Romania and Spain, have ombudsmen whose competence includes issues of discrimination against Roma. Perceptions of the efficacy of these ombudsmen of course vary from one country to another. While it is difficult to generalize, ombudsmen who play a highly visible role in identifying problems confronting Roma and promoting reforms to address those problems appear to enjoy significant legitimacy.

In these circumstances, even critics who fault the institution of the ombudsman for lacking more vigorous enforcement powers appreciate the fact that their communities have an advocate in government - and this, in itself, can help narrow the chasm of mistrust between Romani communities and national authorities. The legitimacy of ombudsmen's offices within Romani communities is also likely to be enhanced when the ombudsman's staff include Roma.

A number of resources are available to governments that may wish to establish or strengthen such mechanisms. Examples of ombudsmen and other national mechanisms to combat discrimination have been compiled by ODIHR and ECRI.ECRI has also promulgated general principles that can productively guide governments in the establishment of such bodies. In determining the most appropriate model, two considerations are generally relevant. First, as in all areas of policy that have a significant effect on Romani communities, input from Roma should be assured in the process of shaping policy. Second, while this may be accomplished in a variety of ways, it is essential that an independent government agency be given both the responsibility and authority to enforce non-discrimination laws. While citizens must also have effective civil remedies for illegal discrimination, their private right of action is not a substitute for the government's paramount responsibility to enforce the law.

Advocates for Roma frequently note that their clients are especially vulnerable to discriminatory practices because many lack basic knowledge about their legal rights and legal institutions. In the words of one Czech attorney, "It's a world they don't understand."It is thus advisable that governments adopt measures aimed at facilitating access to justice for Roma. These may include establishing, funding and implementing effectively an entitlement to legal assistance for indigent persons, including but not limited to Roma, who have been charged with crimes and/or those bringing civil legal action in order to vindicate legal rights.

Statistical data on the ethnic composition of populations is an important tool for establishing patterns of discrimination, for facilitating efforts to enforce legal prohibitions of discrimination and for assessing the efficacy of anti-discrimination and other policies aimed at improving the conditions of Roma. Such information is routinely requested from States by such bodies as the Committee on the Elimination of Racial Discrimination, the body that monitors States Parties' compliance with the Race Convention, and ECRI.

However, more research is needed to address the legitimate concerns of minorities and others regarding the scope for misuse of such data. As recommended earlier in this report, a seminar or conference exploring the various dimensions of this issue in depth - perhaps in the context of how it has been addressed in various countries - could provide valuable insights and guidance to governments struggling to develop effective models for resolving these dilemmas. It is crucial that Roma play a central role in such discussions, and in the development of data collection policies.

In view of the crucial role of the media in fostering and perpetuating racial stereotypes, programs aimed at ensuring more responsible media treatment of stories relating to Roma, consistent with international standards of freedom of expression, merit support. Initiatives of this kind have reportedly had a positive effect in a number of countries, including the Czech Republic, Hungary,and Spain.These programs should aim at discouraging racial stereotyping in media coverage on the one hand, and in promoting greater public understanding of Romani culture and access to the media by Roma on the other hand.

In countries with substantial Romani communities, it is commonplace for Romani children to attend schools that are largely comprised of Roma or to be relegated to Roma classes within mixed schools. In its most pernicious form, segregation is achieved by routing Romani children into "special schools" -schools for the mentally disabled - or into classes for mentally disabled children within regular schools.

In some countries, many Romani parents face a Herculean challenge trying to convince directors of public schools to accept their children. To succeed in this effort is no assurance that their children will be integrated into their schools. Across a wide range of countries, the stories are remarkably similar: directed to sit in the back rows, Romani children are effectively excluded from the classroom experience. Beyond overt manifestations of bias, the educational experiences of Romani children reinforce broader patterns of exclusion: comparatively few find their own history and culture reflected in course materials. It is thus small wonder that many Romani children experience the classroom as an alien world - or, more aptly, a world in which they are the perennial outsiders.

Although not the sole factor, these experiences contribute to astonishingly low levels of school attendance by Romani children and high levels of illiteracy among Roma. In many countreis, only a fraction of Romani youth attend school beyond the primary level, and a tiny percentage receive education at university or post-graduate levels. These patterns compound the challenges Roma encounter in the realm of employment: poorly educated, many are ill-prepared to compete in an increasingly competitive job market.

International Standards

The patterns addressed in this section implicate several international standards.First, to the extent that Romani children are prevented from even enrolling in ordinary primary schools, they are denied the right to education as guaranteed in Article 26 (1) of the Universal Declaration, Article 13 (1) of the 1966 International Covenant on Economic, Social and Cultural Rights ("ICESCR"), Article 28 (1) (a) of the 1989 Convention on the Rights of the Child (hereafter, Children's Convention),and Article 2 of the First Protocol to the European Convention on Human Rights (1952).

Second, the pervasive and varied forms of discrimination encountered by Romani children in the realm of education violate the fundamental right of non-discrimination in the enjoyment of protected rights. Within the CSCE/OSCE context, paragraph 63 of the 1989 Concluding Document of the Vienna Meeting of the CSCE (hereafter, Vienna Document) affirmed that CSCE participating States would "ensure access by all to the various types and levels of education without discrimination as to race, colour, sex, language, religion, political or other opinion, national or social origin, property, birth or other status." The general right of non-discrimination and equality in respect of national minorities was reaffirmed in paragraph 31 of the Copenhagen Document, and the Report of the Geneva Meeting made clear that this obligation requires participating States to "take the necessary measures to prevent discrimination against individuals, particularly in respect of . . . education, on the ground of belonging or not belonging to a national minority."

Third, patterns of segregation noted in this section violate Article 3 of the Race Convention, which provides: "States Parties particularly condemn racial segregation and apartheid and undertake to prevent, prohibit and eradicate all practices of this nature in territories under their jurisdiction."

Fourth, the degrading treatment many Romani children encounter in public schools, particularly those who are inappropriately transferred to "special schools" for the mentally disabled, violate several international standards, including the following:

— Paragraph 40.4 of the Copenhagen Document, pursuant to which CSCE participating States undertook to "endeavor to ensure that the objectives of education include special attention to the problem of racial prejudice and hatred and to the development of respect for different civilizations and cultures";

— Article 13(1) of the ICESCR, which provides in part: "The States Parties to the present Covenant . . . agree that education shall be directed to the full development of the human personality and the sense of its dignity, and shall strengthen the respect for human rights and fundamental freedoms. They further agree that education shall enable all persons to participate effectively in a free society, promote understanding, tolerance and friendship among all nations and all racial, ethnic or religious groups . . . "

— Article 5(1)(a) of the UNESCO Convention against Discrimination in Education, which provides: "Education shall be directed to the full development of the human personality and to the strengthening of respect for human rights and fundamental freedoms; it shall promote understanding, tolerance and friendship among all national, racial or religious groups . . . "

— Article 29(1) of the Children's Convention which provides in pertinent part: "States Parties agree that the education of the child shall be directed to:

(a) the development of the child's personality, talents and mental and physical abilities to their fullest potential;
(b) the development of respect for human rights and fundamental freedoms, and for the principles enshrined in the Charter of the United Nations;
(c) the development of respect for the child's parents, his or her own cultural identity, language and values, for the national values of the country in which he or she may originate, and for civilizations different from his or her own;
(d) the preparation of the child for responsible life in a free society, in the spirit of understanding, peace, tolerance, equality of sexes, and friendship among all peoples, ethnic, national and religious groups and persons of indigenous origins . . . ."

— Article 6(1) of the Framework Convention, which provides: "The Parties shall encourage a spirit of tolerance and intercultural dialogue and take effective measures to promote mutual respect and understanding and co-operation among all persons living on their territory, irrespective of those persons' ethnic, cultural, linguistic or religious identity, in particular in the fields of education, culture and the media . . . ."

The educational curriculum for the whole population includes the teaching of tolerance and respect for human rights. In interpreting relevant international standards, independent experts have agreed in The Hague Recommendations Regarding the Education Rights of National Minorities as follows:

> In view of the importance and value that international instruments attach to intercultural education and the highlighting of minority histories, cultures and traditions, State educational authorities should ensure that the general compulsory curriculum includes the teaching of the histories, cultures and traditions of their respective national minorities.

Several patterns addressed in this section also implicate international norms relating to educational rights of minorities. Of particular relevance in this regard are paragraph 68 of the Vienna Document and paragraph 34 of the Copenhagen Document. The former provides that CSCE participating States "will ensure that persons belonging to national minorities or regional cultures on their territories can give and receive instruction on their own culture, including instruction through parental transmission of language, religion and cultural identity to their children." The latter provides in pertinent part:

> The participating States will endeavor to ensure that persons belonging to national minorities, notwithstanding the need to learn the official language or languages of the State concerned, have adequate opportunities for instruction of their mother tongue or in their mother tongue . . . In the context of the teaching of history and culture in educational establishments, they will also take account of the history and culture of national minorities.

It is often asserted that the relevance of instruction in the mother tongue, as referred to in this provision,is less pronounced for Roma than for other minorities. The basis for this claim is that, while many minorities place a high value on opportunities for education in the mother tongue, for Roma the paramount concern is that their children have adequate opportunities to learn the national language well enough to be educated in mainstream schools. While this is indeed a pressing issue, the generalization that opportunities to study Romani languages are not a priority for Roma is overdrawn.

While views on the importance of such programs vary among Roma, growing numbers place great value on preserving - and, in countries where use of Romani languages was long forbidden - reviving their own language.

Illiteracy, School Attendance and Performance

Romani children attend primary school at levels significantly below the national average; at the secondary and university levels, the disparity typically is drastic. For example, although a majority of Gitano children attend primary school in Spain, only an estimated one percent attend university. One regional study in Italy found that 1,814 Gypsy children were enrolled in primary schools, but only 193 were in "junior" school, the first few years of secondary.

In Hungary, more than 70 percent of Gypsy children attend primary school, but only 33 percent go on to secondary school and most of these attend trade schools. Less than one percent of Hungary's Gypsy population has a degree in higher education.Romani leaders in the fYROM estimate that as many as ten percent of school-aged Romani children never enroll in the first grade, half of those who do drop out by the fifth grade, and only 35-40 percent finish eighth grade. On average, only one Romani child per year finishes tertiary education.The impact of these patterns is readily evident in rates of illiteracy. As a 1996 report of the European Commission concluded, when it comes to illiteracy and scholastic failure, "no other population shows figures approaching those of the Gypsy and Traveller communities."

On the positive side of the ledger, various initiatives aimed at improving the educational prospects of Roma have registered substantial gains. In countries where programs to address these problems have been implemented for substantial periods, there have been marked improvements in the attendance and achievements of Romani students.

But even in countries where government programs have substantially elevated levels of school attendance by Romani children, the gains have often been shallow. Increased levels of enrollment in primary school often have not led to corresponding improvements in levels of attendance or in matriculation in secondary school. This is notably the case, for example, in Spain and Hungary, where concerted government efforts have led to markedly increased rates of enrollment of Romani children in primary schools, but have had much less of an impact on levels of absenteeism and matriculation in secondary schools and universities.

These patterns result from a complex set of factors, reflecting broader patterns of interaction between Romani and non-Roma cultures. In a substantial number of countries, a key factor underlying many Romani children's poor scholastic performance - and propensity to drop out of school early - is that they begin primary school with poor knowledge of the language of instruction. From the viewpoint of many government officials and teachers, low levels of Romani school attendance and performance are due above all to parental attitudes:

Formal education, they say, is not valued in Romani culture.Like many stereotypes, this one has some basis in truth and obscures the far more complex reality, including the central importance of racial discrimination combined with the fear that Roma values and identity will be lost.

Romani culture, broadly defined, is surely relevant to the patterns noted above: although education within the family structure is deeply rooted in traditional Romani cultures, participation in formal public education is not. Such education is not always regarded as a basic social cultural value by Romani communities, in contrast to non-Roma populations, and parents are not confident of the benefits to be derived, particularly where their own experience of schooling has been negative, as is often the case.

Furthermore, school as an institution entails a great deal that is at odds with traditional Roma socialization processes, alienating parents and pupils alike: "Strict timetables, immobility, group discipline and obedience to a single authority figure all conflict with Gypsy emphasis on immediacy, flexibility and shared authority. Moreover, and strangely for the gypsy child, school treats him as an individual rather than as a member of his family: brothers and sisters are separated by age, and parents have no say in the classroom".

Although attitudes toward education vary widely, many parents fear that their children will lose their Romani identity in a non-Roma environment. Writing of Vlax Roma in the United States, Professor Ian Hancock explains their concerns in this regard, noting that formal schooling "requires that Roma enter the non-Romani world, which is seen as polluting and counter-cultural. Not only is the environment unclean - particularly with regard to the toilet and cafeteria facilities, but equally unacceptable would be the seating of boys and girls in the classrooms, and the topics addressed in the curricula. . . . Schools are seen not only as environments that do nothing to teach a child to be a better Gypsy, but which seem determined instead to homogenize and de-ethnicize that child."

These concerns derive special intensity from Romani historical experience of assimilationist practices, in which mainstream education played a central role:

> Early modern policies, such as those of modernising Habsburg rulers Maria Theresa and Joseph II in the eighteenth century, attempted to change Roma into "Christians", "new citizens" and "new farmers" by removing them from Romani families, placing them with non-Romani ones, and sending them to schools to have their difference educated out of them. These strategies were echoed in CEE countries after World War II as governments used schools to enforce policies of assimilation - Roma were forcibly settled, expected to conform closely to rigid standards of sameness, and display a demonstrative loyalty to the ethnic majority. Romani children were to learn such norms by having their Romaniness removed in school, and their culture itself was viewed as a package made up of social disadvantage and deviance which a tide of systematic schooling would cleanse.

The wholesale failure of most schools to reflect Romani history and culture in their curricula reinforces these apprehensions. But these concerns do not negate the profound desire of many Romani parents to ensure that their children are educated. Even Roma who share the concerns noted by Professor Hancock are often deeply committed to enhancing the educational prospects of Romani youth.

One of the notable features of the contemporary era of Roma activism is the emergence of a new generation of Romani leaders who are committed on the one hand to reviving Romani culture, and on the other hand to helping their communities adapt to the challenges of a post-industrial age - a period where there is radically diminished opportunity to survive by the traditional trades that have heretofore sustained Romani across centuries. For these Roma, public schools - historically the embodiment of State policies of forced assimilation - are now the repository of both their aspirations and apprehensions.

Romani parents repeatedly stressed the overriding priority they attach to improving their children's access to education and scholastic achievement. In their experience, the principal explanation for poor attendance and performance levels of Romani youth lies not in "Roma values," but in their children's experience of racism in public schools.

Indeed, it is difficult to exaggerate the extent to which discrimination defines the daily experience of many Romani children. This is not to say that a hostile school environment is invariably the experience of Romani children; many have thrived under the tutelage of highly committed teachers.But for many Romani children, it can be a challenge even to enroll in a regular public school. In a number of countries, gains in this area are frequently offset by the reaction of non-Romani parents - removing their children from schools that, in their view, have too many Romani children.

It has often been noted that Romani girls are withdrawn after the first five or six years of primary school, either because they are to be married, their parents fear romantic involvement with non-Romani boys, they are expected to work at home, or for other reasons; adult educational programs for Roma similarly fail to attract many female participants. Attempts to improve the educational opportunities for Romani women, in line with Article 10 of the 1979 Convention on the Elimination of All Forms of Discrimination against Women (hereafter, Women's Convention), should be approached both with sensitivity to the cultural context and willingness to show creativity in developing alternative programs; involving

Romani women in the development of educational programs for Romani girls and women will go a long way towards ensuring this outcome.

At a recent international conference of Romani women,participants called for "specific measures of the Ministry of Education to address Romani women." They specifically recommended the employment of Romani women as "schooling mediators," to work both within schools and within Romani communities; where traditions lead to the discontinuation of formal schooling, mediators would be well-placed to design and implement programs of vocational training or alternative education.

The extreme poverty of many Roma often serves as further impediment to their children's attendance at school. Some Romani parents are reluctant to send their poorly clad children to school, fearing they will face derision. Many simply cannot afford to send their children to school. In a number of countries with cash-strapped economies, even public education is costly: parents have to pay for textbooks, school supplies and meals - expenses that impoverished families simply cannot bear.

In addition to these obvious financial obstacles, the Romani child's social and family background may negatively affect their educational performance. For instance, poor housing conditions of the family have been found to have a negative impact on children's performance; cramped, noisy living conditions are not conducive to study. Parental health problems and unemployment often make for a troubled family life.A World Bank study in Hungary found that some 70-75 percent of children interviewed in the course of their research did not have a stable family background as parents had divorced or one or both parents had died.

Although many Romani parents would like their children to stay in school long enough to obtain basic literacy skills, believing these are essential to their children's long-term prospects, some wonder whether further education will advance their children's interests. This calculation cannot be dismissed as irrational: in many countries with substantial numbers of Roma, Romani youth who graduate from secondary school face bleak employment prospects. And while the economic benefits of advanced education are highly speculative, the costs are immediate: barely able to make ends meet, many Romani parents may need older children to assist in the family trade or, in the case of daughters, to help care for younger children while the parents work.

In the words of one Bulgarian Rom, for poor Romani families, "education isn't as important as survival."Finally, the impoverishment of many Romani families has had a devastating effect on their health - and this, too, affects school attendance and performance.

In these and other respects, Romani children face a raft of challenges. The sub-sections that follow address several of the most troubling challenges, and describe various initiatives that have been undertaken to meet them.

Racially-Segregated Schools and Classes

It is not hard to fathom why racially-segregated education played a key role in triggering some of the major human rights movements of our time. From South Africa to the American South, schools divided by race epitomized the inhumane premise of institutionalized racism. It is thus a matter of the deepest concern that segregated schooling of Romani children is common in several countries.

The way in which patterns of segregation emerged varies from country to country. In some, the phenomenon of "Roma schools" is at least partly a function of segregated living patterns. For example, many Romani children attend Roma schools in Bulgaria in large part because they live in predominantly Roma neighborhoods. While some Roma neighborhoods are the product of comparatively recent housing programs, many are derived from the Ottoman-era mahala system of ethnically-distinct neighborhoods. In the late 1940s and early 1950s, the government built schools in Roma neighborhoods pursuant to its broader efforts to ensure equal education for all Bulgarian citizens. Since students attended schools according to the region where they lived, this effectively resulted in the creation of Roma schools.

Over time, the Roma schools began to decline vis-à-vis non-Roma schools. In the view of two leading authorities on Bulgarian Roma, Elena Marushiakova and Vesselin Popov, this was due in large measure - though not exclusively - to anti-Roma prejudice.That many Romani children began school without a strong command of the Bulgarian language also contributed to the comparative decline in those schools, as did the fact that Romani schools tended to have more students than other schools.

In the 1970s, Bulgarian education policy began to distinguish among schools, giving some - many of which had predominantly Romani student bodies - a special status. The idea underlying these schools, known as schools for "intensified labor education," was that there were children who could not succeed in higher education and who should therefore be prepared for menial jobs. Although this policy did not establish "Gypsy schools" as such, it had the effect of legalizing segregation - and further entrenching the idea that Roma schools were inferior.

Although the special status of these schools was abolished after the transition to democracy in Bulgaria, de facto segregation persists - and not simply as a by-product of segregated neighborhoods. Many regions have both schools with predominantly Roma students and schools whose students are principally ethnic Bulgarians. Even when Roma children are legally entitled to attend the latter, some school directors reportedly discourage parents from enrolling their children, suggesting they go instead to the neighboring - predominantly Roma - school. Although the Roma schools tend to be substantially more crowded than others, school principals have at times told Romani parents that their schools are already filled to capacity. In some areas that have mixed schools, Romani children are placed in separate classes.

These patterns are by no means uniform; many Bulgarian schools are genuinely mixed, particularly in smaller towns and villages. Those who are fortunate enough to have unbiased teachers have thrived in this environment. As their experiences make clear, the chief barrier to Romani achievement in education is not the attitudes of Roma parents but, all too often, the biases of educators.

While de facto segregation of Romani children is often justified as an unintended by-product of non-racial factors, in many instances prejudice seems the only plausible explanation. For example, Gypsy children at the Ferenc Pethe school in Tiszavasvári in eastern Hungary were assigned to separate classes, not permitted to use the gym, and forced to graduate in a separate ceremony from non-Gypsy students in 1997. The discrimination was so clear that a Hungarian court of first instance ruled that students who filed suit had suffered discrimination based on ethnicity - the first time a Hungarian court had ruled on discrimination against Gypsies in schools. On 22 April 1999, the second instance County Court of Szabolcs-Szatmár-Bereg county in central Hungary upheld the decision of the first instance court.

Although Hungary's courts ultimately vindicated the rights of students at the Ferenc Pethe school, one aspect of Hungarian law discriminates prima facie between Gypsy and non-Gypsy children. The 1993 public education law provides for a national and ethnic minority normative allowance to support special programs which promote and develop minority identity (i.e. language classes, cultural programs, etc.). Controversially, the law stipulates that in the case of Gypsy children, this normative allowance should be utilized to fund special "catch up" programs. One Hungarian educator summarizes the operation of the law, which discriminates against both Gypsy and non-Gypsy children, this way:

> Lots of Gypsy kids need remedial classes; but so do lots of kids who merely come from disadvantaged backgrounds. I don't know on what grounds it has been decided that Gypsy children should be shut out from the same possibilities available to children of any other nationality - they have a culture, too; they have a language, too. This money is for national minorities, but some children are accorded positive discrimination on the basis of their ethnicity - cultural classes, national song and dance, language classes - while others, the Gypsies, because of their socially disadvantaged situation, are determined to be in need of remedial classes - as if possessed of some special disadvantage on the basis of their ethnicity. In all the other cases the law is positive; the same law, however, treats Gypsies as a kind of 'negative minority,' which has yet to be brought up to the level of all the others.

Hungary's Parliamentary Commissioner for National and Ethnic Minority Rights agrees that the law is discriminatory. In his 1998 report on education of minorities in Hungary, the Commissioner observed:

> According to Section 45(2) of the Act.gen.ed it is possible to create special frameworks of

> education in order to reduce the educational disadvantages of the Gypsy minority. We consider the above regulation of the Act.gen.ed as extremely disquieting in its wording, since it talks about the disadvantages of the Gypsy minority and not of certain students. Thus it practically suggests that the Gypsy minority as a minority has disadvantages in terms of education which is indubitably untrue...."

The Parliamentary Commissioner also condemned "the education of Gypsy children in separate classes without any special educational programme and without the approval of their parents." He continued:

> We have no precise information as to the number of Gypsy classes of this type functioning in Hungary but after comparing legal regulations we may declare that the organisation of separate Gypsy classes which are operated without a Gypsy catch-up programme, or on the basis of a programme which is not in accordance with the Directive for the School Education of National and Ethnic Minorities, as well as run without the knowledge and agreement of the parents is against the law, since it constitutes the negative discrimination of Gypsy students. . . . Where separation is not justified either for reasons of minority rights or for educational reasons, the organisation of students into integrated (mixed) classes is advisable.

If the injustice of racial segregation is manifest, experience has taught that there are no easy paths toward reversing its legacy. What is clear, however, is that governments must summon the will to meet that challenge through an unstinting commitment of political leadership as well as material resources. By equal measure, they must find the solution with, and not for, Roma.

Exclusion from Enrollment

As already touched upon in the preceding subsection, Romani parents often encounter resistance when they try to enroll their children in mixed or predominantly non-Roma schools. Several women in the Bulgarian town of Plovdiv described the barriers Romani mothers have encountered when trying to enroll their children in predominantly non-Roma schools. They claim that the headmaster of one school in the Stolipinovo neighborhood accepts only four or five Romani children out of every hundred students.

According tc these mothers, the headmaster explains that the school does not have any more places when, according to them, spaces are still available. This response is a matter of deep concern to the mothers; they believe that Romani children learn more when they are educated with non-Roma children, in part because this forces them to learn to speak Bulgarian which, in turn, enables them to acquire other knowledge. Further, in the view of a young Rom who began his education in a Roma school and then transferred to a mixed school, "teachers in Roma schools teach in an elementary way; they don't demand that much from the children."

In the Romanian city of Timišoara, parents encountered so many barriers in this regard that they prevailed upon a Romani educator to organize an alternative educational program in her home. Located near the western border of Romania, Timišoara has large numbers of Romani families who migrated abroad in the early 1990s, principally to Western European countries, and who were forced to return home by the countries to which they had emigrated. In a number of instances, parents encountered resistance when, upon their return, they attempted to enroll their children in public school.

Having lost several years of schooling during their years abroad,these children would have been older than most of their classmates if they had been allowed to register. Although this should not have prevented their enrollment, many were, their parents recalled, denied the right to register on the grounds that they were "too old."According to one mother, the teacher and principal of her son's school at first said her son could not register because he had missed the first two weeks of class, and finally relented when she argued that her son would be much older than his classmates if he had to wait another year to begin school. Another mother reported that the principal of a local school rejected her seven-year-old Romani child without explanation, saying only "you must go to the other school." A number of children lost a year of schooling because of paperwork: their parents, citizens of Romania, were required to track down birth certificates of the children, who had been born abroad.

These experiences took place against the backcloth of widespread discrimination against Romani children in Timišoara's public schools. It has been a common experience for them to be directed to sit in the back row of classrooms, where they are ignored by teachers.Accounts of physical assaults of Romani children by non-Romani classmates are not infrequent, and some report having been kicked or hit by teachers. When their parents have raised these problems with the school principal, they have encountered responses along the lines of "if your son was beaten, it must have been his fault." After such experiences, some Romani children have been unwilling to return to school.

In the beginning of the school year 1999, the Romani educator found that children were being redirected to her home school program by a teacher from the nearby public school, despite the fact that she has been unsuccessful in repeated requests to local authorities for the use of classroom space.

Special Schools

Perhaps no legally-sanctioned practice affecting Roma is more pernicious than the phenomenon of channeling Romani children to "special schools" - schools for the mentally disabled.

This section focuses on the illustrative case of the Czech Republic, but the practice of routing Romani children to classes for mentally disabled children within regular schools is also prevalent in the Slovak Republic and Hungary.Although the practice is less prevalent in Bulgaria and Romania, in both of these countries Romani children appear to be disproportionately referred to such schools or classes.

A recent policy resolution by the Czech Government estimates that "approximately three-fourths of Romany children attend special schools for children with light mental defects, and that more than 50 percent (estimations are again close to three-fourths) of all pupils attending special schools are Romany children."

Sending Romani children to schools for the mentally disabled has effected a particularly degrading form of segregation - one that brands Romani children as mentally defective and consigns them to a life in which their brightest prospect is menial work. As one former special education teacher put it, graduating from such a school at best provided Romani children the opportunity to assist a carpenter; they could not even theoretically qualify as professional carpenters.

Until recently, Czech law generally prohibited children who completed such schools at the primary level from matriculating in mainstream secondary schools.They were legally eligible to apply only to a technical training center or a practical school, which prepares students "for the performance of simple tasks."In October 1999, the Czech Chamber of Deputies - on the recommendation of the cabinet - approved an amendment to the School Act, by which graduates of special schools are granted equal access to secondary schools if they pass the entrance examinations.

Many educational authorities in the Czech Republic concede that the overwhelming majority of Romani students who are sent to special schools are not mentally disabled. Why, then, do they end up there? A key part of the answer lies in the role of psychological evaluations. Under Czech law, any of the following can recommend placing a child in a special school: "the pupil's legal guardian, the school already attended by the pupil, an educational psychologists' center, a health establishment, an organ for family and child care, an education center or a diagnostic institute of social care for mentally-handicapped youth."Both by law and in practice, psychologists play a key role in the process of referring children to schools for the mentally disabled. As the ERRC has chronicled, the evaluation process is highly discretionary - allowing large scope for the influence of racial biases.

Equally important, tests used to measure the intellectual ability of students are culturally-specific; they include questions whose frame of reference is that of the dominant society. Thus, Romani children may and often do get questions "wrong" because they simply lack familiarity with such concepts as "insurance companies" or "cutlery."

> This phenomenon is not unique to the Czech Republic. Educational specialists in Hungary, where Romani children are frequently referred to special schools, describe testing processes there in which children are asked to answer questions that invoke concepts that are basic in Hungarian culture - and unknown in Romani culture.

Similar problems in understanding stem from linguistic differences between Romani children and their teachers. In the Czech Republic, for example, educators sometimes refer Romani children to special schools because they appear unable to comprehend their teachers' questions. But the impediment is not a mental impairment; rather, it is a linguistic barrier. As noted, many Roma children speak a Romani dialect at home, or their parents speak a significantly different version of the national language than that spoken at school. Even when a Romani child's family ostensibly speaks the language in which public school is taught, vast cultural differences can make for profound gaps in communication. The ERRC describes this phenomenon:

> Communication depends heavily on non-linguistic signals. Romani children, coming from Romani environments, often meet with non-Romani culture for the first time on their first day of school. Here they are confronted with the extremely alien figure of the (in almost all cases) non-Romani teacher. They do not understand this person and their almost completely alien system of signals and sounds. As a result, even in cases in which the home language of the Romani child at issue is Czech, there is a strong probability that the Romani child will not understand what is being said to her.

Many teachers realize that Romani children perform poorly in school because of their deficient knowledge of the Czech language rather than because of a mental impairment. But, as one Czech educator explained, teachers "had no time to teach them more, so it was easier to send them somewhere else." In his words, while there may well be problems that lead school authorities and psychologists to route Romani children to special schools, "there is a different problem than their inability to be educated."

In addition to their deficient knowledge of the language of instruction, these problems often include difficulties adapting to a new environment. Behavioral patterns that others take for granted may be alien to a Romani child. One Czech teacher who has taught many Romani children offered an example: "Mostly they have no toys [at home], so they have no feeling of owning something. They have to learn certain new things of European culture."However, many teachers find it easier to refer the child to a special school than to take the time to educate her.

By law, the consent of a child's legal guardian is required before she can be enrolled in a special school in the Czech Republic.In practice, according to the ERRC, Romani parents are often pressured to consent or are misled about the consequences of their consent. Sometimes, the ERRC has found, the requirement of parental consent has been disregarded.Even when consent is freely given, it may signify above all resignation to a disturbing reality: knowing that their children will be isolated, neglected, and in all likelihood left behind in the regular schools, parents may readily follow the opinion of a psychologist that their children will receive more attention and support in a special school. Further, many Romani parents prefer to keep their children together. Thus, once they have placed their oldest child in a special school, parents may be more inclined to agree to send their younger children there as well.

The most compelling - though deeply flawed - argument made for referring Romani children to special schools is that, however inappropriate, this alternative may be the best option available in an imperfect system. Defenders of the practice argue that, if kept in regular schools, many Romani children will rapidly fall behind because of their comparatively weak language skills. In special schools, it is asserted, they will learn at their own pace and receive greater attention from their teachers.

In several countries, financial incentives operate to draw or keep students in special schools. In Hungary, schools receive a state financial quota for each student enrolled in special education in addition to the regular quota schools receive for each child.Directors of special schools may therefore have a disincentive to recommend that their students be transferred to a regular school. In both Bulgaria and Romania, all costs associated with special education are covered by the State, providing an inducement for poor Romani parents to assent to their children's transfer to such schools.

While the question of how best to end the practice of channeling Romani children to special schools is complex, one step in the right direction can be readily taken in the short-term: States should eliminate financial incentives for schools and parents to transfer children to special schools. This is not to say that States should not provide supplemental financial support to assist children who need special educational programs. Rather, such support should be made available in a manner that does not skew placement decisions in favor of "special schools" for financial reasons.

In those States where Romani youth are disproportionately referred to schools for the mentally disabled, governments should commit themselves to abolishing this practice as a matter of the highest priority. Notably, the Czech Government has taken a first step in this direction: it has formally committed itself to ending abuse of the special schools.

But if the urgency of ending this practice is manifest, the question of how best to do so is more complex. Most Romani children who were inappropriately sent to special schools would fare poorly if they were immediately transferred to regular schools, as the level of educational performance at special schools is significantly lower than that at regular schools.

In the view of some Romani activists in the Czech Republic, there should be a period of transition during which special schools that are, in the ERRC's terminology, "Romani ghettos" would be transformed into transitional Romani schools. During a period of several years, students at these schools would be prepared to make the transition back to normal schools. The obvious risk, however, is that these schools would continue to be special schools by another name.

What is needed, of course, is a program in which Romani students who have been inappropriately referred to special schools receive the support necessary to prepare them either to transfer to a regular school or to take an examination that would enable them to obtain a diploma equivalent to that of a regular school.But thoughtfully-designed phase-out programs are not enough: it is also necessary to address those aspects of mainstream education that prevent Roma from enjoying the same prospects for academic achievement that other children enjoy.

In this regard, States in which Romani children are inappropriately referred to special schools must be prepared to pursue far greater flexibility and innovation in their educational strategies than has heretofore been common.It is not a solution to say that Romani children must adapt to the prevailing classroom environment; schools, too, must adapt.

It is encouraging to read in the Czech Government Policy Concept that a radical change in the present system of education for the Roma is envisaged. The Concept states:

> The Government will create conditions for a change of educational system in order to ensure that Romany children will be as successful as the

> others. In order to achieve this goal we shall use methods of pulling down language barriers, preparatory classes, Romany language as supplementary teaching language, Romany assistants at schools, and, in particular, [an] individual approach to students. The system in which a large majority of Romany children pass through special schools and thus . . . . are assigned to the last qualified work for their whole lives will be replaced by a system of flexible, permeable, equalizing classes at elementary schools with [a] smaller number of pupils than in normal classes.

It is to be hoped that this new approach will soon be put into practice. Above all, as argued already, racial biases must be eliminated from schools. But also, educators must become literate in the skills of multi-cultural teaching - an area in which significant strides have been made in recent decades.

An elementary school in Ostrava, the Premysl Pitter School, provides one model of how schools can more effectively respond to the distinct culture of its students while ensuring that they receive an education commensurate with their potential for academic achievement. The school, which is run by the Catholic organization Caritas, was founded in 1994 by several educators who had previously taught at special schools in Ostrava.In their experience, many of the Romani students in special schools "shouldn't be there." These teachers were also concerned about the fact that, when these students graduate from a special school, "their possibilities are very limited."And so they established the Premysl Pitter School to provide quality education to students who might have difficulty in most schools but who would thrive given the proper pedagogical support. Although not restricted to

Romani children, the Premysl Pitter School has a student body that is 95 percent Romani.

Teachers at Premysl Pitter seek to make the classroom a less alien place for Romani children. To this end, the school employs seven Roma assistants to work with the teachers.Because this enables Romani children to see someone from their community in a position analogous to that of a teacher, "they receive [what is taught] better." The Roma assistants also bridge the communication gap between Romani children and their teachers - an especially important function during the first year or two of schooling, before Romani children have been able to develop a strong command of the Czech language.

The school also incorporates aspects of Romani culture, such as music and dance, in its programs. Another important aspect of its approach is that it welcomes Romani parents, some of whom come to the school every day while others come for special programs. This enables parents to develop a sense of confidence in the school environment.

The Premysl Pitter School employs a social worker, who helps maintain social contact between the school and students' families which, in turn, further enhances parental confidence in the school. Equally important, the social worker is able to help families address problems that, if not resolved, could have a deleterious effect on the child's education. The social worker has, for example, assisted families in addressing problems with their flats and with social benefits, as well as medical problems.

Finally, the Premysl Pitter School makes a concerted effort to overcome the language barrier that, in the view of the school's teachers, is the key problem confronting Romani students. In addition to the assistance provided by the Romani assistants, the school has a "zero class" - a pre-kindergarten class aimed at preparing children for kindergarten. This year, it has obtained permission from the government to offer an additional hour of Czech language instruction until the fourth year. It is too soon to be able to measure whether these aspects of the school's program will enhance the long-term prospects of its students. What seems clear, though, is that its students - and their families - are more enthusiastic about school than many other Romani children in the region.

Improving Romani Education

Issues relating to illiteracy and education of Roma have received substantial attention for many years within the European Commission, the Council of Europe, and many other countries. In recent years, there have been a rich variety of innovative projects aimed at addressing the problems noted above. A substantial number of pilot projects have been instituted with funding from the European Commission and various innovative projects have been supported by the Open Society Institute. of these initiatives is beyond the scope of this report, we note several dominant trends in this subsection.

Multi-Cultural Curricula and Training

One point that has repeatedly been emphasized by Romani students and parents, as well as by many educators, is that Romani children's experience of exclusion in public schools is based not only on overt acts of discrimination, but also on the commonplace absence of their history and culture from the basic curriculum. Beginning school is said to be a profoundly unsettling experience for many Romani children, who feel as though they have been torn from a familiar and supportive environment and thrust into an alien and alienating world. That their own cultural experience is absent from the history, music, art and other forms of culture that are taught exacerbates their sense that they have entered a foreign universe - one in which they have no place.

This is a key reason why many support the introduction of material on Romani history and culture into the general curriculum. Not surprisingly, such material has figured prominently in educational programs initiated by Roma themselves. Further, the development of such material has been a key priority of educational initiatives supported by the European Commission and the Council of Europe.

In the view of many Romani activists and non-Roma educators, the introduction of such material into school curricula is also an essential step toward combating racial prejudices against Roma. It is common wisdom that ignorance of minority groups is the taproot of racist stereotypes, and, indeed, the exclusion of Romani culture and history from the curricula of most public schools has allowed negative stereotypes to fill the resulting vacuum.

While a number of countries have introduced or are working to introduce such material into school curricula,in many the efforts have been sporadic and incomplete. In Greece, for example, the teacher of one predominantly-Roma primary school reported that she had previously used, with effective results, a primer on the Greek language that was written from a Romani perspective.

There is also widespread consensus on the crucial need to provide teachers with training about Romani culture and history. An example of such an initiative is the opening of a Romany Culture Department at the Nitra University of Pedagogy in the Slovak Republic. The Department, which has an outpost in Spišká Nová Ves, has a special emphasis on training primary school teachers in areas that have a large proportion of Romani students. Such programs serve two important ends: some are designed principally to enable educators to teach their students about Romani culture and history.

Especially notable contributions in this regard have been made by the Council of Europe, which has prepared and updated a publication with this in mind.Others have as their principal aim better equipping teachers to respond effectively to their Romani students. As noted, many teachers have either ignored their Romani students or transferred them to schools for mentally handicapped children because they lack multi-cultural teaching skills; these programs aim to address this failure. A key premise underlying some programs is that many teachers, biased themselves, are likely to communicate their own prejudices to other non-Romani students.

Romani Schools

Deeply concerned by public schools' failure to meet Romani children's educational needs, some Romani leaders have supported the establishment of Roma schools. In contrast to the segregated "Roma schools" established by public authorities, this model envisages schools created and administered by Roma themselves, ideally with State support. The leading example of such a school - and a model that has inspired Romani activists in other countries - is the Gandhi Gimnázium in Pécs, Hungary, which began operating in February 1994. The school is administered by the Gandhi Foundation, which was founded in 1992 by more than 30 individuals, some affiliated with NGOs, with the support of the Open Society Institute, and which became a public foundation in 1995.

Its founders conceived of the Gandhi Gimnázium as a vehicle for fostering the development of a Gypsy intelligentsia through high-quality education aimed principally at Gypsy students.The school's "most important aim is to educate a significant number of Romany professionals who are devoted to their people and who will be capable of reorganizing the disintegrated Gypsy communities." Its leaders "also consider it important to change the prevailing opinion that Gypsy children are less teachable and less capable of reaching educational success."To these ends, the gimnázium seeks to prepare students to attend university. But while providing education of the highest academic standards, the Gandhi Gimnázium also offers a program that fosters pride in students' ethnic identity. Although the language of instruction is Hungarian, the curriculum includes courses in the Lovári and Beás languages, and features various courses in Romani history and culture.

The very establishment of the Gandhi Gimnázium is, in the eyes of its supporters, a powerful symbol of Gypsy achievement. As one of its founders explained, during the Communist period, "if a Gypsy finished vocational school, it was really something." To go to a gimnázium - a far more academically demanding form of secondary school and one which, unlike trade schools, can lead to university - was beyond Hungarian Gypsies' imagination.

But while the Gandhi Gimnázium has inspired many Hungarian Gypsies and Romani leaders outside Hungary, its path has been anything but easy. Some of the difficulties the school has encountered fall into the realm of inevitable growing pains. More than half of the school's first class, which is due to graduate in 2000, has dropped out.Still, measured against national rates, for even half the class to graduate represents significant progress. The dropout rate has declined from year to year - suggesting that the school administration has effectively adapted its methodology to the special needs of its students.

Further, initially some parents were reluctant to allow their children to leave home - often in a small village - to attend boarding school in Pécs. The Gandhi pedagogical program takes these concerns into consideration. School administrators establish early contact with parents, visiting the homes and schools of prospective students to explain the school's objectives and methodology and to answer their questions. This contact is maintained through regular parent-teacher meetings at the school after the student has enrolled. The school also provides material and logistical support for students to return home for a long weekend every second week.

In recent years, as the reputation and standing of the school has grown, parents' fears of sending their children into an unknown and untested environment have diminished. For many Gypsy parents, the Gandhi school represents their only possibility for sending their children to secondary school. Perhaps the most significant challenges have been financial. To this day, the Gimnázium has obtained less than half the funding its administrators seek and has been unable to finish constructing its physical facilities. Preoccupied with fund-raising, its administrators can spend far less time on issues of pedagogy than they would like.

The Gandhi Gimnázium is, to be sure, a comparatively expensive school like the Premysl Pitter School in Ostrava, the Czech Republic, it employs a social worker to assist students' families across a broad range of concerns and covers all of its students' educational costs, including transportation to the school. In the view of its administrators, however, this is not the only cause of their financial challenges: some question whether Gypsy youth need a state-of-the-art gimnázium like the Gandhi school.

Others have questioned the very premise of the Gandhi Gimnázium, apparently suggesting that it is a form of segregation. There are, in fact, a range of views among Roma leaders, educators and parents about the most desirable means of addressing various educational problems described in this section. This is, of course, hardly surprising given the complexity of these issues and the diversity of experiences among Roma. But there should be no questioning the basic principle that Roma, like other national minorities, are entitled to establish their own educational institutions.

It is too early to know whether the Gandhi Gimnázium will ultimately prove an effective alternative to the more problematic models of education typically available to Romani youth. Surely, though, it deserves the opportunity to try to realize the estimable objectives of its founders. As its late principal, János Bogdán, believed, the school may already have registered significant successes: "By its very existence, [the Gandhi Gimnázium] has stimulated local schools in the region to change, because more attention has been focused on them by our search for talented Gypsy students. Moreover, it has created a competitive atmosphere in which Gypsy students have some possibility held out to them - a focus for their ambitions."Other observers have noted that the school generates positive secondary effects as well.

In addition to providing education directly to Gypsy students, the school also "educates" the broader population: people living in Pécs who may have been hostile to having the school placed in their neighborhood can observe that Romani children are capable of achievement, and that having a Roma school in the city can also be a source of pride. Recently, Pécs was honored with a UNESCO award for multiculturalism. While the Gandhi School is something of a path-setter in the field of education of Roma children in Hungary, a number of other private institutions have been established in Hungary over the past decade, aimed at improving secondary education opportunities for Roma children.They do not all cater exclusively for Roma students, but were established in settlements where the proportion of the Roma population is known to be high. These programs are essentially grass-roots initiatives which have evolved in response to the existence of locally experienced demands and needs not being met by the public education system. A feature of many of these institutions is that they provide special educational activities in addition to traditional teaching.

Many of these initiatives cater for pupils across the age spectrum from early teens to mid-twenties, in an attempt to meet the needs of Romani children who never entered or who dropped out of secondary education. As a result, the age of children is on average more advanced in these schools than in other secondary schools educating non-Roma pupils. The Kalyi Jag School, for instance, provides a two-year education for 14-25 year-olds who finished primary school but are not involved in public education or are unqualified. The aim is to prepare pupils to continue studying in secondary schools that lead to the final secondary examination. The aim of the "Roma Chance" Alternative Vocational Foundation School, Secondary School and Students' Hostel is to give professional qualification to disadvantaged Roma and non-Roma pupils alike.

Some institutions work with a small family-like staff; in others, the ratio of teachers to pupils is quite high. In addition, the use of Roma pedagogical assistants as well as technical staff members, social workers and psychologists have been found useful and in some cases indispensable. The benefits of employing qualified teachers sensitive to the needs of Roma pupils, and the need for qualified Roma teachers has been highlighted by these institutions. Moreover, efforts to develop good communications with parents are also found to be helpful in ensuring that children, once enrolled, continue with their education.

Romani Teachers' Assistants and Mediators

In a substantial number of countries, schools have hired Roma assistants.This approach has often been undertaken at the initiative of Romani NGOs, and in some cases has received government support. One of the key ideas underlying this approach is that Roma assistants can help bridge communication gaps - both linguistic and cultural - between Romani students and parents on the one hand, and teachers on the other.

Further, their involvement in the teaching process can alleviate the alienation of Romani students, who rarely find Roma in positions of authority at the schools they attend. Ideally, of course, there should be more Romani teachers as well as teachers' assistants. But the problems relating to educational achievement addressed in this section make for a marked deficit in the pool of Roma teachers. Until greater headway is made in this area, Romani teachers' assistants can play an invaluable role.

A related model, which is sometimes combined with that of teachers' assistants, is that of Roma mediators - Roma who serve as a liaison between schools and Roma communities. This approach is based in part on the premise that the divide between schools and Romani communities cannot be bridged solely in the classroom; it is also necessary for schools to interact with Romani communities.

The headmaster of a Bulgarian school whose student body is 90 percent Romani explained the role that such mediators play at his school. "It is normal," he explained, "for a Bulgarian teacher who doesn't know much about Roma culture and values to be in conflict with Roma parents." He offered two "typical" examples. First, Bulgarian teachers often interact with Romani parents in what he termed an authoritarian manner - which, he said, tends to enlarge the distance between Romani communities and the school. He gave the specific example of a teacher suggesting to Romani parents that they should not have so many children, "which communicates that they do not value the Roma value system." Second, teachers often celebrate Bulgarian holidays while disregarding important Romani holidays.

In Finland, the teaching of the Romani language started in primary schools in 1989. Since 1995 legislation has provided the possibility for teaching the Romani language also in secondary schools.According to Finland's Advisory Board on Romani Affairs, the position of Romani children has improved in those schools which have availed themselves of this opportunity, largely because of the presence of Romani teachers in the school. As the Board notes in a recent report: "the teacher of the Romani language often also acts as an intermediary between children's homes and the school, making at the same time the attitude of children and their parents towards learning at school more positive."

As with any initiative that is sound in principle, however, the use of Roma mediators can be ineffectual if not implemented properly. The experiences of some Gitano mediators in Spain may exemplify the risks in this regard. Ten years ago the Spanish government initiated its program of hiring Gitanos to serve as liaisons between public schools and Gitano families. The principal aim of these liaisons has been to help increase levels of school attendance by Gitano children. One of the most important laboratories for this program is the region of Andalucia, where almost half of Spain's Gitanos live. To the government's credit, regional authorities recognized that educational initiatives would not succeed without the active involvement of the Gitano community itself. It thus engaged the Federation of Roma Associations in Andalucia (FARA) to identify Gitanos who could serve as liaisons with Gitano families.

At one level, the program has been a notable success: when it began, some 90 percent of the region's Gitanos did not attend school at all. Now, the level of non-registration has dropped to seventeen percent in some areas of Andalucia.But the program has been less successful in reducing the drop-out rate of Gitanos: the government's efforts have succeeded in getting Gitano children to school, but not in keeping them there for very long.

Many Gitano activists have enthusiastically supported the mediator program in principle. Committed to advancing the educational prospects of Romani youth, some highly-educated Gitanos enlisted as mediators. But some became disenchanted and resigned in frustration. In the view of two former mediators, the principal problem with the program as implemented was that authorities placed overriding importance on the sheer numbers of Gitanos enrolled in school. Although these former mediators wholeheartedly embraced the challenge of trying to convince Gitano parents of the value of education, they say they felt pressure to apply coercion to this end: government authorities threatened to terminate parents' social welfare benefits if they did not send their children to school, and it fell to the Gitano mediators to communicate this.

In the view of the two former mediators, the coercive approach ultimately backfired: while it increased Gitano enrollment in schools in the short-term, it reinforced many parents' sense that school was something imposed from outside.That the mediators' role was effectively confined to "controlling for how many days kids were missing from school" undermined the value of their involvement.

But these two former mediators fault the government less for using unproductive strategies to increase Gitano enrollment than for failing to follow through with effective programs in the classroom. Like many other educators and advocates, these two believe that substantial efforts should be made to include the Gitano experience in school curricula and program activities. Beyond their specific concerns relating to program design, these two educators regret that their supervisors did not seem to value their insights concerning the effectiveness of the methods they were employing.

It is difficult to know how representative these mediators' experience is: while their role was largely confined to that of attendance police, other Gitanos who have collaborated with government authorities have helped develop more substantive initiatives.But their experience highlights the importance of ensuring that Romani participation in Roma programs is meaningful. To the extent that it failed to draw upon the insights of these two mediators, the government lost the opportunity to benefit from a valuable resource.

While the use of Roma mediators and teachers' assistants is increasingly common, a current initiative by the Romanian government represents a new variation on this model. On 1 March 1999, the Ministry of Education adopted a decision to appoint a Roma Inspector in each of Romania's forty-one counties. While it remains to be seen how this policy will be implemented, the basic approach is salutary. In particular, it is noteworthy that Roma are to be involved at the level of governance where the impact of educational policy is most keenly felt.

Pre-School and Kindergarten Classes

A recurring factor contributing to the difficulties Romani children encounter in school is that many begin with a poor command of the language of instruction. In some countries, such as the Czech Republic and Slovakia, many Romani children speak a Romani dialect at home and thus begin school with a substantial disadvantage. Even when they speak the national language at home, many Romani children speak a different version than that of the majority. Further, profound cultural differences -

reflected in such basic matters as spatial conceptions - produce major barriers to comprehension.

The resulting problems are compounded by the fact that most Romani children who attend elementary school do not begin until the mandatory age of attendance. Although many countries provide kindergarten classes, it is still relatively uncommon for Romani children to enroll. Thus, they often begin the first grade that much further behind their classmates who attended kindergarten. In this area, the diagnosis of the problem suggests its own solution: enrollment of Romani children in preschool programs that improve their proficiency in the language of instruction and, more generally, acculturate them to the classroom.

Many recent initiatives in the area of Romani education have, in fact, included the development of such classes. A substantial number of these programs have been developed with support from sources other than the government, including the Open Society Institute, the PHARE Program of the European Commission and various Dutch foundations, such as the Netherlands Organisation for International Development Co-operation (NOVIB). Because the programs examined are only a few years old, it is not yet possible to assess their success. Nonetheless, several programs seem to have been designed and implemented in a fashion that augurs well for their success.

Extra-Curricular Support Programs

In recent years, a raft of innovative programs have been initiated with the aim of providing extra-curricular support to Romani students. Notably, many of the most impressive programs of this kind have been developed by Romani individuals and NGOs - a testament both to the keen motivation of many Romani leaders and parents to enhance their communities' educational prospects and to the value of Romani participation in programs for Roma.

Higher Education

As noted earlier, the percentage of Roma who matriculáte in university is minuscule. Even so, the achievements of those who have graduated from university is a testament to the potential efficacy of efforts to increase Romani participation in higher education. Among the younger generation of Roma leaders, some attended university with the assistance of government programs aimed at enabling Roma to obtain advanced degrees. These range from the use of quotas to the provision of scholarships.

An example of the former approach is a Romanian policy pursuant to which the government has set aside places for Roma students at public universities since 1993. The program started with ten reserved spaces for Romani students at a university for social work in Bucharest; in 1999, the program had expanded to potentially cover some 150-200 Romani students. The system does not necessarily ensure that every reserved place will be filled; applicants must still pass a qualifying exam. But it does make it more likely that Romani students will attend university.

Another approach has been that of providing special training and/or scholarships to enable Romani students to qualify for and attend university. According to the Hungarian Government, 1,115 Roma secondary school students received scholarships in 1998 and, in past years, the State-funded Public Foundation supported 200-300 Roma students attending institutions of higher education.A different model is the American University in Bulgaria, sponsored by the Open Society Foundation, Sofia, which for several years funded approximately 30 Romani students to attend a one-year program at the university. Participants in the program studied English, computer skills, and other subjects thought helpful in preparing them for university.

Here, as in other areas, there are a range of views about the most effective approach toward increasing the numbers of Romani students at university level. But there is wide agreement on the importance of this goal. Beyond qualifying Roma graduates for professional employment, their graduation from university is seen by many activists as critical to the emergence and effective leadership of a Romani elite. In addition, many believe that, as role models, Romani university graduates can help inculcate among younger Roma positive attitudes toward academic accomplishment as well as self-confidence in their own potential for achievement.

Living Conditions

For those Roma who maintain a traditional nomadic or semi-nomadic lifestyle, the availability of legal and suitable parking sites is a paramount need and, indeed, a precondition to the maintenance of their group identity. Many Western European countries where the incidence of nomadism is comparatively high have regulations encouraging or requiring relevant authorities to maintain camping sites.For example, France's 1990 Besson Act requires every municipality with more than 5,000 inhabitants to maintain sites where nomadic groups can either stop or stay.

But this law and others, including legislation in The Netherlands and Northern Ireland, also make it illegal to park on unauthorized sites.(The latter law criminalizes unauthorized parking of caravans only when done by "any person being a traveller.") Typically, even in countries that encourage or advise local authorities to maintain parking sites, the number and size of available sites is insufficient in light of the need. The effect is to place nomadic Roma in the position of breaking the law - in some countries, committing a crime - if they park in an unauthorized location, even though authorized sites may not be available.Often, too, sanitation and other basic facilities provided on public sites are inadequate.

Beyond basic housing concerns, the lack of legal parking sites typically entails an interlocking set of social and civil problems. Gypsies who cannot find lawful halting sites are, for example, hard-pressed to keep their children in school. In France and other countries, moreover, difficulties establishing lawful residence - even semi-permanent residence - may effectively disenfranchise nomadic groups and disqualify them for social benefits.

Gypsies and Travellers in the United Kingdom

The lack of adequate halting sites is a relatively recent problem in the United Kingdom. In the words of Mr. Justice (now Lord Justice) Sedley:

> For centuries the commons of England provided lawful stopping places for people whose way of life was or had become nomadic. Enough common land had survived the centuries of enclosure to make this way of life sustainable, but by section 23 of the Caravan Sites and Control of Development Act 1960 local authorities were given power to close the commons to travellers. This they proceeded to do with great energy, but made no use of the concomitant powers given to them by section 24 of the same Act to open caravan sites to compensate for the closure of the commons.

Responding to the resulting scarcity of caravan sites, Parliament passed the Caravan Sites Act 1968 with the principal aim of transforming into a duty the discretionary power of local authorities to create such sites. Section 6(1) required local authorities "to exercise their powers . . . so far as may be necessary to provide adequate accommodation for gipsies residing in or resorting to their area", and the Secretary of State could direct local authorities to provide caravan sites where it appeared to him necessary.Parliament's aim in enacting this law was, in the words of a British judge, "that there should be sufficient sites to accommodate the whole of the gipsy community within the law . . . ."

In exchange for ensuring that all Gypsies could find lawful caravan si'es, the law made it a crime for Gypsies - but no one else - to station caravans in unauthorized areas pursuant to a system of "designation."The distinction between Gypsies and others has since been eliminated from U.K. law. At the time, if the Secretary of State was satisfied under the 1968 law that a local authority had made adequate provision for the accommodation of Gypsies - or that it was not necessary or expedient to do so - he could "designate" the relevant district or county.Some achieved this status without providing any caravan sites; most did so despite their failure to provide sufficient sites. Upon designation it became a criminal offense for a Gypsy to station a caravan within the designated area with the intention of living in it for any period of time, on the highway, on any other unoccupied land or on any occupied land without the consent of the occupier.

Local authorities proved highly reluctant to establish caravan sites, and the Secretary of State rarely used his authority to direct them to do so.A study undertaken by Sir John Cripps at the Government's behest, completed in July 1976, found that

> provision exists for only one-quarter of the estimated total number of gypsy families with no sites of their own. Three-quarters of them are still without the possibility of finding a legal abode . . . Only when they are travelling on the road can they remain within the law: when they stop for the night they have no alternative but to break the law.

Nevertheless, the 1968 Act achieved substantial - if still inadequate - results. Perhaps spurred by legal actions seeking to compel action under the 1968 law, local authorities established more than 300 new caravan sites over the 24-year period when the Caravan Sites Act 1968 was in effect.

In 1994 the British Government nonetheless successfully pressed for repeal of the Caravan Sites Act 1968, explaining:

> That system has been in operation for 24 years, and the fact is that levels of unauthorised camping - in terms of numbers of gypsy caravans on unauthorised sites . . . - have hardly changed since then . . . The Government had to decide to do something. . . .
>
> The conclusion we reached . . . was that local authority site provision was not likely ever to meet that apparently growing demand for sites . . . . [I]t is the Government's view that public provision has now reached a satisfactory level and that further provision should be made by the gypsies themselves through the planning system.

The provisions of the Caravan Sites Act 1968 summarized above were repealed by Section 80(1) of the Criminal Justice and Public Order Act 1994 ("CJPOA"). Local authorities are no longer statutorily required to provide adequate sites for Gypsies, although councils still have statutory pcwer to establish caravan sites.

While eliminating local authorities' duty to provide adequate caravan sites, the CJPOA 1994 enlarged the circumstances in which unauthorized parking may be determined illegal. Section 77(1) of the CJPOA 1994 gives local authorities the power to direct unauthorized campers to move;for these purposes, unauthorized campers are persons who appear to be "for the time being residing in a vehicle or vehicles" on any land forming part of the highway, any other unoccupied land, or any occupied land without the consent of the occupier. Failure to comply with such a direction as soon as practicable or re-entry upon the land within three months is an offence.

Under current law, Gypsies have three options for lawful camping: parking on public caravan sites - which the Government acknowledges to be insufficient; parking on occupied land with the consent of the occupier; and parking on property owned by the campers themselves. The British Government has issued guidance to local authorities aimed at encouraging the last approach.In practice, however, and notwithstanding official recognition of their special situation and needs, many Gypsies have encountered formidable obstacles to obtaining the requisite permission to park their caravans on their own property.

Under United Kingdom law, one is not entitled to park a caravan on property merely by virtue of owning it; planning permission is required for carrying out any development of land.For these purposes, a change in land use for the stationing of caravans can constitute a development.An application for planning permission must be made to the local planning authority, which is required to make its determination in accordance with the local development plan unless material considerations indicate otherwise.If a development is carried out without the required planning permission, the local authority can issue an "enforcement notice" if it considers it expedient to do so having regard to the provisions of the development plan and to any other material considerations.

This scheme allows wide play for the exercise of discretion - and that discretion has repeatedly been exercised to the detriment of Gypsies. A 1986 report published by the Department of the Environment described the prospects of applying for planning permission for a

Gypsy site as "a daunting one laced with many opportunities for failure."In 1991, the last year in which the success of application rates was evaluated, it was ascertained that 90 percent of applications by Gypsies for planning permission were denied.

In contrast, 80 percent of all planning applications were granted during the same period.It is to be noted that, as a category, Gypsy planning applications are relatively unique insofar as they typically request permission to park caravans in areas or sites which are subject to restriction by local planning authorities. As such, virtually all Gypsy planning applications are highly contentious.Nonetheless, the fact remains that there is inadequate provision or availability of authorized halting sites (private or public), which the high rate of denial of planning permission only exacerbates. Moreover, there are indications that the situation has deteriorated since 1994. One recent study of Gypsies and the planning system concludes:

> ...since 1994 the pace of authorised (public and private) provision has decreased to approximately 250 caravans per year from 320. The current rate of yearly increase in authorised provision accounts only for the reduction of the same number of caravans on unauthorised sites. Evidently, since Circular 1/94 has been introduced, the pace of private site provision has not increased sufficiently to counterbalance decreases in public site provision . . .

In the face of these difficulties, the itinerant life style which has typified the Gypsies is under threat. As Justice Henry observed when he cited the need for the policy embodied in Britain's Caravan Sites Act 1968 (now abandoned) of making adequate provision for caravan sites: "If there are not sufficient sites where gypsies may lawfully stop, then they will be without the law whenever and wherever they stop. This will result either in them being harried from place to place, or in them being allowed to remain where they should not lawfully be."

The UN Committee on Economic, Social and Cultural Rights in interpreting Article 11(1) of the ICESCR regarding the right to housing has emphasized in particular that "instances of forced eviction are prima facie incompatible with the requirements of the Covenant and can only be justified in the most exceptional circumstances, and in accordance with the relevant principles of international law."

While not all involuntary evictions violate the ICESCR, they generally are incompatible with the right to adequate housing when individuals are removed against their will from the homes they occupy "without the provision of, and access to, appropriate forms of legal or other protection."The Committee has also admonished that evictions "should not result in individuals being rendered homeless or vulnerable to the violation of other human rights. Where those affected are unable to provide for themselves, the State Party must take all appropriate measures, to the maximum of its available resources, to ensure that adequate alternative housing, resettlement or access to productive land, as the case may be, is available."

As noted, a major consequence of the various housing quandaries recounted above is that many Roma live in conditions that are not legally sanctioned. Their lack of settled legal status can have profoundly deleterious implications for virtually every aspect of life, ranging from children's ability to attend school to adults' ability to vote. In some countries and under certain conditions, illegal occupancy can expose Roma to criminal sanctions. In many European countries, entire communities have been vulnerable to eviction. In these circumstances, pervasive discrimination against Roma has often served to block any community from accepting the displaced Roma.

Health

Inadequate attention and resources have been devoted to the pressing health concerns of Romani communities. The resulting dearth of information about specific patterns of health-related problems among Roma in turn contributes to scant allocation of vital public resources to address these problems.

Health patterns among Roma are also negatively influenced by high levels of poverty, low levels of education, and limited access to health care and services. Discriminatory and prejudicial attitudes are one of the key factors in the marginalization and sometimes exclusion of many Roma from public health campaigns and programs; lack of practical access to health care generates specific concerns for Romani women.

Statistics from many countries show that the incidence of certain types of environment-related illnesses is typically several times higher for Roma than for the general population.Communicable diseases such as tuberculosis (TB), hepatitis, poliomyelitis, and measles are all reported to be prevalent amongst Roma communities in various States.The last reported cases of poliomyelitis in Bulgaria, the fYROM and Romania, for example, all occurred in Romani communities. Romani children, in particular, are also susceptible to dermatological problems such as scabies and impetigo which are more easily communicated in unsanitary conditions.

While the number of cases of TB is generally on the increase, both in Western Europe and Central and Eastern Europe, it is the most socially and economically disadvantaged groups, such as Roma, who are most at risk, not only in terms of infection rate, but also in terms of recovery. In 1990 in Bulgaria the morbidity rates for TB among Romani children was 60 per 1000 compared with 22 per 1000 for the national average, and in former

Czechoslovakia the rate was more than double the national average.

Sedentary, crowded living conditions also contribute to the high incidence, in many Romani communities, of smoking, alcohol and drug addiction.The burden of dealing with the health consequences of these problems is borne disproportionately by Romani women, both as mothers and as the primary health-care providers within the family.

Frequently, the perception within non-Roma society is that Roma are more exposed to infections than other groups and that, consequently, they are responsible for spreading epidemics.This perception must be countered by efforts to ensure that discriminatory attitudes in society which hold Roma responsible for spreading disease and view the illnesses that afflict Roma as being exclusively their responsibility are combated. Health problems related to the social condition of Roma, such as the prevalence of communicable diseases, must be regarded as a matter of public health.

Causal factors

a) Inadequate living conditions

The infrastructure available to Romani communities is often disastrous. Romani settlements in rural areas are frequently either isolated or located on the outskirts of a town or village, with limited access to public amenities such as water supply, sewage systems, electric power or gas supply, and access roads. Roma living in urban areas are often relegated to particular districts or neighborhoods, usually characterized by slum-like conditions, poor or non-existent public services, and severe overcrowding.

In a recent policy pronouncement, the Slovak Government noted that "Romany settlements have substandard municipal hygiene, [and a] polluted and devastated environment. Potable water supply is missing."Those communities that lack running water inevitably suffer from water-borne diseases and poor hygiene. Assessing the situation of one Romani settlement in northeastern Croatia, one international official recently noted:

> [In the Gypsy settlement] close to 200 individuals live in a state of poverty. They only have one well of unclean water and no telephone line. The settlement is about 500 meters from the village. In case of emergency, they have to walk on a long and difficult dirt road to get help.

Moreover, Romani neighborhoods are often located close to rubbish dumps or contaminated industrial sites, which creates environmental health problems. A 1999 World Bank study on the health status of Roma in Hungary refers to one Roma settlement in Ózd where many Roma survive by collecting and selling metal refuse from an industrial waste site; a number of Roma have lost their lives when dump pits suddenly collapse.Recent publications in the United Kingdom and Ireland highlight the concerns of Gypsies and Travellers with regard to the condition and location of Traveller's sites (both official and unofficial), and specifically inadequate provision of services, including fresh water.

b) Unemployment

The high rate of unemployment among Roma noted earlier in this report, in addition to contributing to an ever-greater degree of social exclusion, marginalization and poverty, also has a dramatic and direct impact on health conditions. The relationship between poverty and health is well established;the effects of poverty are pervasive, but are perhaps nowhere more immediately apparent than with respect to diet. One comparative study conducted by UNICEF in 1992 found that under-nutrition was of major concern for Roma in Italy, the former Yugoslavia, France and the former Czechoslovakia, and that the poor diet of

Roma children leads to chronic health problems in later life.

Moreover, the type of employment in which Roma are often engaged can itself entail health risks. In the 1960s and 70s, large numbers of Roma in Central and Eastern European countries faced occupational health hazards as semi-skilled or unskilled laborers in heavy industry. Today, Roma throughout Europe are faced with an increasingly tight labor market, and often accept "black-market jobs" as seasonal or day-laborers, thus foregoing health and/or social insurance. Others are legally employed in areas, such as city sewer maintenance, street-cleaning, or municipal refuse collection, which require - but do not always receive - special public health measures. Médecins du Monde, an NGO working in Greece, systematically vaccinates Roma against rabies because of the hazards of their work in these areas;the existence of this program suggests that the situation is not being addressed by the public health system.

Roma who become ill under such uncertain working conditions are trapped in a vicious circle: lacking insurance and/or working papers or registration, it is difficult to gain access to and pay for health care after an accident or an illness; with ill-health, it is difficult to look for and secure employment.

c) Education

Lack of education or vocational qualifications is one factor affecting the employability of many Roma. Education is therefore recognized as key in improving access to employment and improving the living conditions for Roma. Some studies suggest an even more direct relationship between education and health; a World Bank report on the health status of Roma in Hungary concluded that individuals with a higher education degree are likely to live up to twenty years longer than persons who are illiterate.Reportedly, programs ostensibly focused on raising general levels of education have proven effective in improving health conditions as well. In this context, the Council of Europe's Recommendation of the Committee of Ministers to Member States on the Education of Roma/ Gypsy Children in Europe explicitly recognizes the need for comprehensive educational initiatives which acknowledge the link between education and economic, social and cultural factors.),

Considering the high level of isolation and marginalization of many Romani communities, targeted health education programs could play a particularly important role in improving their health conditions. There is a demonstrable need for public health initiatives to inform Roma communities about available health services and how to utilize them, as well as about specific issues such as immunization. Preventive immunization is not actively sought by many Romani communities, and vaccination coverage among Romani children in many countries has been low.

One recent study conducted in Romania found that Romani parents refuse vaccination for their children due to a mistrust of injections, and fear that the vaccine will spread the illness;another, in Hungary, found that illiteracy was a determining factor, as parents were not able to read relevant public health notices. Clearly, more effective distribution of health-related information is warranted. On the other hand, immunization policies which have concentrated effort on reaching Romani families have posted positive results.

Other health issues, such as the spread of and protection against the HIV virus and other diseases transmitted sexually or through intravenous drug use - known to be on the increase amongst Roma in some States - would also benefit from preventive educational efforts.

Recent research undertaken in Bulgaria, for example, revealed an increase in the spread of Hepatitis B and C infection amongst Roma intravenous drug users and warns of enormous health and social costs for the Roma population if preventive efforts to avert the possibility of an epidemic, followed by an epidemic wave of HIV, are not urgently implemented.

Given the large gap that must often be bridged between the perspective of public health officials and institutions and Romani communities, the training and employment of Roma as consultants in the development of health education policies, and as mediators in the implementation of these policies, is likely to have a positive impact on their effectiveness.Because the burden of childcare and meeting the basic needs of the whole family falls almost exclusively on women, they are often the principal point of contact between Romani communities and school, health and social services.Health-care training for Romani women, therefore, could play a particularly important role in facilitating communications between public health workers and Romani communities.

d) Discrimination and Exclusion

Access to health care for many Roma is also limited - and sometimes precluded by discriminatory and prejudicial attitudes.

Cultural differences can raise barriers between Romani communities and health care institutions. Roma who are not proficient in the majority language are at an automatic disadvantage in accessing health care; even where language as such is not a problem, vastly differing perceptions and expectations regarding health care on the part of Roma and health care workers often make communication difficult. Some culturally-determined behaviors, such as standing watch over a sick patient, can directly conflict with institutional culture.Such misunderstandings contribute, over time, to a cycle of mutual mistrust and antagonism—and to qualitatively worse care for Roma than for the general population.

Some innovative health programs have sought to bridge the gap by employing mediators. A Médecins sans Frontières (MSF) program in Romania provides Roma with "escorts" on their first visit to the health center, to provide reassurance and support in familiarizing themselves with the health care system, and in establishing an initial relationship with doctors and other health care workers.As noted above, Romani mediators can also play a positive role in constructing co-operative relations between Romani communities and key health institutions and practitioners.Likewise, programs to educate health care workers about the situation, background and cultural attitudes of Roma could also be beneficial.

Other Roma are excluded from public health care by virtue of the fact that they lack birth certificates, identification cards, or other official proofs of registered residence. The Romanian daily Ziua reported on 7 September 1999 that Roma without either the means to pay for health services directly or proof of state medical insurance had been banned from the Iasi County Hospital. State health services are provided for all citizens who are employed and pay social security benefits, and for those who are officially registered with the State as unemployed. Apparently, many Roma in the area are not registered with the government and therefore, in the eyes of the local Fund for Social Security and Health, were not eligible for state health care.

Some Romani communities also experience practical problems accessing health care due to their relative isolation. For example, public transportation does not serve many Romani settlements; when public transportation is available, many Roma can not afford to pay fares. Some isolated communities do not have doctors or nurses in residence, and are not regularly visited by public health care workers because of poor roads. The consequence is that many Roma seek health care only under the most urgent conditions.

States should focus sustained effort to see that no group is systematically or even inadvertently excluded from public health care services. Where special registration is required to access health care, it is the responsibility of public authorities to see that all segments of the population receive relevant information and adequate opportunity.

Women's Health Issues

The demography of Romani populations is characterized by high fertility and infant mortality rates (IMR). Romani women tend to marry and start families earlier and have more children, often at short birth intervals, compared to other sectors of the population. The young age of mothers and the number of pregnancies implicate not only the health of the mother, but the health prospects of the new generation as well.Low birth-weight, linked with early and multiple pregnancies, is common.The comparatively low nutritional status and weight of many Romani mothers also increases the risk of low birth weight, as well as having serious implications for lactating mothers and their infants.

Available country evidence indicates that there was a general improvement in infant mortality rates between 1960 and 1989 for Roma populations in Europe. Nonetheless, the IMR for the Roma population in, e.g., the former Czechoslovakia in 1991 was over twice the national average and in Hungary it is almost double the national average.The 1989 rate in Bulgaria was even more alarming: 240 per 1000 for Roma compared to a national average of 40 per 1000 , i.e. a 600 percent greater risk for Roma infants. Child mortality rates are similarly higher for Roma populations living in Western European States.

In the United Kingdom, for example, the rate was 1,500 percent higher than the national average in 1983. A key factor influencing the trend in fertility rates among Romani populations is a lack of education and information with regard to contraceptive practices. According to the studies available, knowledge of contraception varies between Romani women in different communities;in general, however, knowledge among Romani women has been found to be poor in comparison to other sectors of the population. Access to an affordable supply of contraception is another major factor in determining the contraceptive practices of Romani women.

Women's choice of contraceptive method may also be determined by factors related to traditional gender roles in Romani culture and, specifically, to spousal relationships. MSF in Romania found that many Roma women preferred the intra-uterine device as the best modern contraceptive, because it did not require the collaboration of their husbands. Indeed, one of the lessons learned from the MSF experience was the need to bring men into discussions regarding contraceptive efforts at an early stage in order to ensure their co-operation in family planning efforts.

In the absence of access to and/or knowledge of contraceptive measures, abortion is reported to be prevalent among Romani women in some countries as a form of "contraception".High numbers of abortions not only increase the risk of gynecological illness for the woman, they jeopardize the success of future pregnancies. From the aspect of the unborn child, one of the most serious factors is a negative obstetric pathological history, including artificial and spontaneous abortions.

Reproductive health education for Romani women is important not only with regard to contraception, but also in relation to hygiene and nutritional practices which impact on the health and development of the child, both before and after birth. The evaluation of a joint UNICEF/ Rromani CRISS local primary health care project in Balta Arsa, Romania, for example, revealed that Roma women tended to be unaware of the need to modify their lifestyle during pregnancy, including in terms of food, vitamin intake, physical effort and work.In this context, the high incidence of smoking among Romani women is also significant.Apart from obvious impacts on the health of the mother, smoking during pregnancy can increase the risk of infant mortality.

Romani women are less likely than others to seek prenatal and antenatal care -a trend which is influenced by those factors affecting access to health care generally, such as a lack of funds or mistrust of non-Roma medical institutions, as outlined above. In addition, women may not prioritize their own need to seek medical care and support. Studies suggest that many Romani women do not conceive of their own health as being a significant factor in making decisions.

In planning public health initiatives it should be recalled that family planning and reproductive health are sensitive issues, particularly in the light of allegations that at various periods in the past the Roma populations of some countries have been induced to accept sterilization.Romani women leaders emphasize that public health initiatives should focus on providing women and their families with information and choices (including access to contraceptive measures if desired) rather than seeking to impose a particular solution.

Political Participation

Policies and laws aimed at improving the situation of Roma will no doubt fail without the active participation of Roma in the identification and analysis of specific problems, the design and elaboration of programs and projects and, ultimately, their implementation. Like other minorities, Roma face special challenges in their efforts to participate in the fundamental promise of democracy - the right to govern themselves. In some respects, these challenges have been especially acute for Roma.

Anti-Roma discrimination has engendered a pervasive sense of alienation among Roma from the political life of their countries; some traditional Romani leaders have remained aloof from national political processes. The importance of Roma participation in these processes speaks for itself; the challenges to their meaningful participation remain considerable. Although governments generally acknowledge the importance of Roma participation, many are unaccustomed to engaging Roma as partners. For their part, many Romani leaders who are committed to participating in the development and implementation of policies have expressed the desire for programs that would enable them to hone their expertise and skills in this arena.

While principal responsibility for meeting these challenges lies with national governments and political communities, international organizations can play a helpful role. A notable example in this regard has been that of the European Commission which has encouraged some EU candidate countries to ensure that Roma participate meaningfully in the development of national Roma policies in the context of the EU accession process. International actors can also make a substantial contribution by sponsoring programs aimed at assisting Roma in acquiring the expertise and skills necessary to participate effectively in political processes.

6

Tibetan Nomads

China's economic reforms since the 1980's, known as the "household responsibility system" in rural China, have shifted communities away from collectivization and towards entrepreneurship and privatization. This reform has led to major changes for rural Chinese families involving household composition, marriage arrangements, and childbearing . Local variations in culture and economy have also influenced those transformations in specific ways . Therefore, the impact on the family system has not been uniform; rather there have been distinct consequences in different areas.

While changes in families in rural China have attracted the attention of many scholars of Chinese studies, little has been published on ethnic minorities and even less on Tibetans, who have also experienced farreaching social and economic transformations. Scholars also have differentiated families according to types. Murdock-classifies families into five types based on kinship relationshipoı

— The nuclear family, which consists of fathers and mothers with their unmarried children. This type is also known as an "elementary family" or "simple family" .

— Compound families, formed by uniting two or more nuclear families through a common husband and wife, as in polygyny or polyandry, respectively.

— Extended families, normally consisting of at least two siblings or cousins in each of at least two adjacent generations.

— Lineal families, comprising of at least one individual in the senior generation but at least two individuals in the next generations.

— Stem families, usually consisting of one or two related families, other than polygamous unions of the same generations.

Murdock defines lineal families as "small extended families", and stem families as "minimal extended families." Following Murdock, other researchers have divided families into two types, referring to lineal and stem families as "extended families", and nuclear and compound families as "independent families".

This last definition is similar to the classification provided by Dargyay in her discussion of Tibetan families. According to Dargyay, Tibetan families normally fall into two types: the nuclear family, based on the relationship of husband and wife, and the extended family, consisting of kinsmen of various generations living in a common home . In addition, polyandrous households were widespread in Tibet in the past . Some nomadic areas still have polyandry even today . This type of household, ordinarily with only one wife present in a generation, is described by Levine as generationally extended linearly and fraternally expanded laterally .

Scholars of the Chinese family studies usually identify two types of families based on the number of couples in each generation . The different types of Tibetan families as follows:

1. Nuclear Families, consisting of a couple and /or their unmarried children.
2. Extended Families, consisting of parents with two or more children along with their spouses and children.
3. Mono-parental families, consisting of either an unmarried mother or father with his /her illegitimate children.
4. Other families, including families containing brothers and sisters, families of grandparents and grandchildren, nuclear families with either a husband's or wife's unmarried siblings, polyandrous families; or singlepersons with adopted children and one-person families.

Comparative data suggest that most societies have small, nuclear family households; corporate extended families are rare . However, why do some societies have extended families while some have small, nuclear families? Is this determined by economic and social structures, as asserted by some scholars or affected by religion and traditions in specific cultural contexts? Although efforts have been made to try to formulate a general theory of family systems and changes within them, the correlation between family type and a variety of determining factors is still a controversial issue.

If we can classify family systems as "independent" (nuclear) or "extended" (stem, lineal, or fully extended), extended families are more common among agricultural and nomads societies, and that nuclear systems are more prevalent among residents of Lhasa and other small towns. It can be said that the mode of subsistence influences family type through demands for family labor. It is clear that there is some association between traditional agriculture, animal husbandry and extended family households. There are close correlations between specific types of families and particular subsistence systems. No matter what the production system is, the appearance of extended family is due to its ability to provide extra labor for various divergent activities within the family.

The family becomes increasingly nuclear to fit the requirements of urban life because the nuclear family is the unit most compatible with industrialism and urbanization. It is clear that all of China as well as Tibet are moving towards industrialization and modernization. The family systems are also approaching some variant of the conjugal system. According to Goode's theory, the conjugal family is peculiarly appropriate to the needs of industrial urban society because of its geographic and social mobility and because its members can take up specialized occupational roles in a fluid labor market. As can be observed in Lhasa city, the nuclear family predominates among the land-less and animal-less laborers and waged workers. Yes, the nuclear family predominates widely, even in rural areas of Tibet.

Furthermore, nuclear families existed even before urbanization and industrialization occurred in Tibet. Therefore, it may not be a necessary connection between urbanization or industrialization and the small, simple, nuclear family of contemporary Tibet. Even in Lhasa, maintaining the extended family kinship system constitutes the basis of the economic and financial power of privileged social groups. Goode's model drew heavily on the experience of Western Europe and North America and has failed to explain family structure among many Asian and African populations.

Clarke, who is among the few western Tibetologists studying Tibetan communities, carries out his field research among a Tibetan pastoral nomadic community in Qinghai Province. He focuses on reform and its impacts on pastoralism in Tibetan areas. Clarke argues that with the introduction of the "responsibility system" into Tibetan nomadic areas, "the joint rights of the household to pasture, together with the economic and management advantages of a division of labor that can be made because of the larger numbers in an extended family, militate against fission into nuclear families". Thus, Clarke suggests that nomads in Qinghai retain extended families primarily for economic considerations.

However, another case study in a southwestern Tibetan farming community shows that the new system of land tenure after the 1980's has actually led few young people to establish traditional co-residential marriage and families; instead these young people prefer informal unions which require no coresidence of family members and pooling of resources. Since these young people tend to stay with their natal family members, this inevitably reduces the potential for the establishment of extended families involving a married couple, although it still could be a generational-extended family containing only siblings.

In addition to the demographic and social factors that shape the developmental cycle of Tibetan families, economic reforms and transformation in land ownership also brought about changes in domestic organization. After the "responsibility system" was implemented in the early 80's, household size in Yid-Chab village dropped slightly to 5.5 persons, on average.

According to the 4th nationwide census in 1990, the average household size in Amdo County in 1982 was 4.8 persons, and rose slightly to 4.91 persons in 1990. Meanwhile, the average household size in Nagqu Prefecture increased from 4.9 members in 1982 to 5.26 in 1990. Thus, one might presume that the average household size of the nomadic population in Tibet began increasing after the new economic reform policy was carried out in the 80's. As in other Chinese rural areas, nuclear families were the prominant type in the nomadic Amdo area.

Many scholars of family studies held that economic factors should be primarily responsible for changes in family size. For instance, Pitkin indicates that families tend to extend when they assume full economic responsibility for their subsistence. Hammel cites a diverse mix of "economic" or "ecological" variables, including; labor needs in production, defensive needs, care of children and taxation as the "underlying functional reasons" for the variation in the size of the domestic group.

Regional diversity, developmental cycle of domestic groups, gender sexrole systems and kinship as a symbolic system should also be taken into consideration when studying domestic organization. Rather, changes in land tenure should be responsible for the changes in family system in Tibetan nomadic areas.

The family as a basic economic unit needed enough members so that various essential activities could be carried out. Besides, households with more members benefited economically through shared expenses, labor, security and companionship. Thus, households welcomed more members to increase the work force.

In addition to economic interests, a large family was favored because it could fulfill heavy corvee labor, for long-distance trade, and for military obligations to tribal leaders. In a data the four-to-six person household accounted for 50.1% of the total thirty-eight households, and this was also found in Serthar, a nomadic community in eastern Tibet with 62% of the total households.

However, the interesting difference was that, in the traditional society in Serthar, 50-60% of families were extended while only 26% were extended among the population . Gelek attributes the prevalence of extended families in Serthar to the demands of labor in diverse pastoral activities. Democratic reform between 1959 and 1966 did not cause significant changes in household size and structure because in the nomadic Amdo area after 1959, ownership of livestock remained the same as before-in the hands of the nomad families. The only difference was that the ownership of grassland was transferred from estate owners to the collective. This change did not lead to a reduction in household size.

On the contrary, the average size of household after the democratic reforms increased slightly. Among the twenty-three old households in Yid-chab Village, ten experienced an increase in the number of household members, seven remained the same, and the remaining six households became smaller. Meanwhile, the number of nuclear and extended families remained almost identical. Thus, it seems that the democratic reforms, which involved no devolution of grassland ownership to individual households, had no significant impact on household organization.

During the Commune period, as elsewhere in rural China, the collective owned not only grassland, but also livestock. In the North Wind Commune in Amdo County, each household member in the commune received three head of livestock for subsistence. Production and labor allocation were the responsibility of the "production teams." Therefore, the productive functions of the traditional economic unit - - individual households-were diminished. Collectivization not only weakened the household as a productive unit, but also reduced the power of the family-head over the sons because once the control over the utilization of grassland, livestock and labor that used to belong to the family-head was now taken by the collective. In this system, every family member made a living by earning points awarded by the production teams. This provided opportunities for siblings to separate from their natal family and set up their own families with the points each of them earned. Leaving one's family had no impact on ownership of grassland and livestock. Therefore, it could be expected that the declining role of the family as an independent productive unit would lead to earlier division and reduction in the number of extended families.

The average household size during this period of time was larger than in any of the other three periods: Families consisting of seven and more persons were numerous, and the number of extended families was also more than in the other two periods. Huang who found that the extended families prevailed in a farming village in southern China. Johnson , in his study of a northern rural community, claims that government policies restricting mobility and emphasizing village self-sufficiency have strengthened patrilineal extended families practice.

Two additional factors could also be responsible for this change. First, before the 1980's, China's birth-control policy had not been enforced among the minority populations, and particularly not among the pastoral nomads in such a remote, isolated frontier region.Nomads did not use birth control. Besides, infant mortality declined due to the improved health care services. The crude birth rate in Amdo is 33.1 per 1000. This is consistent to Goldstein's findings among another Tibetan nomadic community which is similar ecologically with the population . Both data show that the CBR in Tibetan nomadic areas resembles the CBRs of high growth countries such as India and Mongolia. Therefore, families may have increased in size due to a high rate of reproduction and improved child survival.

The second factor is related to the point system imposed during the commune period. At that time, each family member made a living by earning points which made it possible for children to separate from their natal families. Nevertheless, there were still a number of families that preferred to keep the family large. According to one of my informants, these families wanted to prevent the partition of a family to pool the points together to make a better life, operating on the presumption that everyone was equally paid by the commune. Thus the more labor force one family possesses, the more points it would accumulate, and potentially the richer it would become. Also, sharing might reduce living expenses of the whole family. Still, others may argue that, separation from the natal family was made possible since each could make a living with the points each earns and the partition would not diminish their own standard of living.

De-collectivization, in the early 1980's, followed by nationwide agricultural reform, was initiated in Tibetan nomadic areas. Pastureland and livestock were allocated to individual households. One feature that deserves close attention is that the livestock were allocated to individuals by head count. The grassland, however, were allocated to households as a whole, rather than individuals within each family. This allocation system actually makes dividing the household difficult to realize since members can bring the livestock with them upon separation, however, the grassland is impartable and it is very difficult for out-marrying children to bring a piece of grassland with them, although it happens in other nomadic areas.

Besides, the household contract system weakened the former collective structure and strengthened the role of households as productive units in agriculture, in sideline production and in market activity. As elsewhere in rural China, capitalist reforms led nomadic pastoralists into market activities and stimulated various sideline occupations. Direct access to the Qinghai-Tibet Highway has provided the people of Amdo with new opportunities.

It has stimulated some of them to pool labor resources to engage in pastoralism, while other carry out long-distance trade outside the local areas, or operating restaurants, tea houses and gasoline stations along the highway . The average annual income per capita among Amdo nomads, which was only RMBY 526.0 (US$92.3) in 1986, jumped to RMBY 1,490.0 (US$173.3) in 1994.

From 1986 up to 1994, the incomes from transportation, handicrafts, commerce and restaurants increased from 14.9% to 41.1% of total annual per capita incomes . Once again, each family found that it needed to pool its labor to conduct various tasks, as it did during the pre-commune period of time. Although the average size of the household decreased slightly during this last stage, the number of extended families increased while the nuclear families decreased considerably. Involvement in the market economy prompted nomad families to conduct profitable sideline production in addition to subsistence production. Assume that the involvement in the sideline work also potentially favored the spread of extended families. However, this is merely a hypothesis requiring further investigation.

In addition to the land tenure changes that have considerably influenced household patterns of this nomadic community in the TAR, the distinctive characteristics of the local economy might have favored the existence of the extended family in nomadic communities. It should be noticed that the subsistence economy, particularly the mode of production, has remained unchanged for centuries in pastoral production and still heavily relies on the strength and size of the labor force because of the generally low technological level of the area and its challenging natural environment.

Modernization has not altered the mode of production in Tibetan nomadic areas. Although certain kinds of machines, such as milk separators, have been introduced in pastoral production and have effectively reduced the intensity of labor, the size and the strength of the labor force decide the wealth of each family. Extended families and those with more laborers were much better off than those with fewer members, a weak labor force and large numbers of dependents. The potential relationship between the wealth being of a family and the labor forces.

Kinship as a symbolic system should also be given equal attention when domestic organization is being studied. The existence of extended families throughout the four decades and its steady increase in numbers should not only be explained by nomads' economic rationality, but also by the well-kept ideology of traditional life-style, both among pastoralists and agriculturalists. Traditionally, the ideal Tibetan family pattern was three generations living in one household.

According to Tibetans, large families bring good luck and prosperity. Being a research assistant in a research project conducted in the Summer of 1994 in another Tibetan nomadic community in northwest Sichuan Province,I collected data on the household structure there as well. In 1983, 76% of the seventeen households were nuclear households while 18% was extended family. In 1994, the total households in this village increased to twenty. The 60% of families were nuclear while the extended families accounted for 30% of the total households. Most significantly, the average household size increased sharply from 3.9 in 1983 to 7.1 in 1994.

The two nomadic communities are similar ecologically. Both communities experienced an increase of extended households. A large family is preferred among Tibetan nomads. If this is the case for Yid-Chab Village, one can infer that the extended family is not a new phenomenon appearing in Tibetan pastoral areas, but rather a revitalization of a traditional life style driven by traditional Tibetan ideologies.

One particular feature that distinguishes Tibetan nomadic areas from inland rural China is that mono-parental families have always existed. In nomadic areas, people may have children without being married. Some women never marry and remain in their parental tents. If they have had children with someone they are not blamed but can also gain a few animals and occasional assistance from the child's father when the time for seasonal migration comes. Both mothers and the illegitimate children were accepted by the society, shared equal rights to family property and faced no discrimination.

According to 1990 statistics, there were ten illegitimate children in Yid-Chab village and they enjoyed the same inheritance rights as legitimate children. As another example, in Washul Serthar, a Tibetan nomadic area in the northwest of Sichuan Province, there traditionally existed a tribal alliance consisting of forty-eight tribes, and the tribal leader was an illegitimate child from a mono-parental family.

Household Patterns

The factors that might have brought about changes in family patterns in the Amdo nomadic community. They are mainly social, cultural, economic and political variables. However, that individuals, who are agents of society also play a crucial role in the formation of the social system. This is evidenced by the prevalence of magpa households in the population under study. One notable and interesting feature in Tibetan kinship is the prevalence of magpa, or uxorilocal marriage, that is the change of residence of the man to his wife's tent. It is well documented that the Naxi people and Tibetans in Yunnan Province mostly practice matrilocal residence.

Interestingly, among the twenty-two extended households in Yid-chab village in 1995, there were ten uxorilocal marriages, accounting for 45% of total extended households. Ekvall argues that this "called-in-sonin-law" marriage is to keep family wealth intact, which results in an extended family. He suggests that it occurs mostly in affluent households. When a family has only one daughter, or when all but one of the daughters have married and left, a son-in-law, usually from a family of less wealth, is brought in as a surrogate son. Clarke also asserts that matrilocal residence is likely to happen if there is no son in the house of marriage for direct inheritance, or if there is lack of labor in that tent.

According to a data, there existed three types of matrilocal residence. One was the typical family with only one daughter and there are six cases like this. The second was when there was one daughter and one son in the parental homes and the son-in-law married into the family while the son stays too. There were three such marriages. The third occurred in unusual circumstances. The family had three daughters and one son. In 1989, the elder daughter brought in a magpa, with whom she had two daughters.

In 1992, the second daughter married and she also brought in a magpa to live together with her parents, her sister's family and her brother. In family C, the parents were middle aged, and the son was also old enough to work as a full laborer. Thus, the lack of labor force or sons for direct inheritance were not sufficient to explain these two magpas. When asked about the reason, the household head just simply said: My two daughters are very filial, and we just can not bear them leaving us and moving into other people's houses. Besides, the two daughters are also happy to stay with us after marriage.

Obviously, harmonious family relationships are highly valued in this magpa extended household. The head of another magpa household told that it was because the son-inlaw lived in another village which would take half a day of horse-riding. This made it inconvenient for the daughter to visit her parents frequently. Since the son-in-law has a young brother staying at his natal family, he moved into her family after marriage. From those two examples, the type of family is largely determined by individuals' responses to their social and personal circumstances, even though the motivations which drive people to choose matrilocal residence have not been fully understood.

Goldstein , in his study among another Tibetan nomadic community in western Tibet, suggests that there is no rigid rule regarding who marries and moves out. One of Goldstein's respondents said that he decided to keep his daughter with him and the prospective groom had to move into his household although he still had other two unmarried sons living with him.

Goldstein further points out that, in reality, nomads decide which of the children should stay at their natal family upon his/her marriage depending who will take the best care of them as they grow old, rather than by following a fixed "custom." Basically, in the village, matrilocal residence occurs no matter whether there are sons or there is more than one daughter staying at the natal family.

Apart from the fact that the magpa households result from decisions based on individuals' circumstances and by members of the two households- the son's family and the daughter's family, this type of family can be explained by women's domestic roles. Female labor in Tibetan nomadic areas is highly valued. Women's contribution is virtually identical among all Tibetan nomadic areas .

Women do the milking, churning, cooking, collecting dung for fuel, fetching water, taking care of tents and so forth. Women are not merely valued as childbearers, but also as important members of the labor force and they make far greater contributions toward the subsistence economy of their society than the men do. This fact is well explained by a saying popular in Amdo area: Calluses are on children' feet (herding); calluses are on women's hands (working); calluses are on men' bottoms (sitting and drinking tea).

This division of labor and the importance of women' labor is also well described from one summer time schedule of a nomadic household:

— 4:30 The elder daughter gets up, lighting the stove.

— 5:00 The mother gets up, milking their eighteen dri (female yak); then separates the baby sheep from the baby goats.

— 7:00 Two elder sons get up, go herding after breakfast; then the elder daughter makes butter while the mother cleans the shrine and does housework.

— 8:00 The father gets up and twists wool thread after breakfast.

— 12:00 The mother prepares lunch. After lunch, the mother and the elder daughter tie the baby yak and milk their dri and the female sheep. Afterwards, they return home making yogurt and cheese.

— 21:00 The son and the younger daughter bring the animalsback home. The mother and the elder daughter milk the animals while the younger daughter cooks dinner.

— 21:30 Family dinner.

Although this time schedule is not complete, it still reveals that fact that women play an important role in the subsistence economy. Losing female labor means an enormous loss for the family. In order to keep their daughters working for them, some families would rather allow the daughters to bring in their magpa than having the daughters move away. This might be another factor that favors the existence of magpa extended households.

Martial Payments

Among most ethnic groups of the world, marriage is associated with economic exchanges which customarily take the forms of bridewealth or dowry. Bridewealth is a gift of money or goods given to the bride's relatives by the groom or his kin, whereas dowry involves goods or money given by the bride's family to the bride, the groom, or the groom's family. Jack Goody has theorized that the nature of marriage payments depends on the extent of women's contributions to the domestic economy and that such contributions are more substantial under horticultural and pastoral regimes. Moreover, he explains dowry as a kind of inheritance system for women, paid out in advance of their parent's deaths.

The nomadic way of life has been followed for centuries. Among Serthar nomads, the exchange of gifts has been a very important part of the betrothal and marriage process, similar to other Tibetan pastoral areas. Bridewealth is paid to a bride or her family before the wedding ceremony takes place, and a dowry is brought by the bride with her to the new family. In the local dialect, dowry is called 'bagskal' and refers, namely, to the gifts or property given by parents to their daughter at her marriage. Bridewealth is called 'mag-skal', meaning gifts given to the girl's parents by the future husband or his family, or property the man brings when a magpa marriage is introduced. (Magpa refers to the change of residence of the man to his wife's family's tent) The word "skal" means "a share".

According to the traditions of Serthar nomads, when children marry and move out, the family calculates what its property includes and gives an equal or fair share to the marrying child. Each child takes their share of the family property into their own marriage. If a person is from a wealthier family, then the share of property that they bring to marriage will be greater on average.

Marital payments usually include tools of production and other necessities such as tents, clothes, household goods, and so forth, but cash gifts are seldom given because people don't have much cash. Livestock is given priority as a marital payment, since domestic animals are essential to work and life, and the quantity of livestock directly reflects a nomad's wealth. So, whether poor or rich, the parents try to provide animals for the children upon their marriage.

Traditionally, in the Serthar area, large amounts of gifts for marriage were prepared and provided by the groom's family, but the bride's family provides more than that of the groom's. There also is a difference between the quantity of livestock provided by the man's family and that of the woman . The bride's family, furthermore, tends to provide more grain and tea, on average, and more clothing.

Customarily, tents should be provided by the man's family, but the woman's parents are also willing to send a tent as part of the dowry if the groom is too poor to afford it. Marital payments often include sheepskin coats and wool coats. Because Serthar is located in an area where the average altitude is over 4000 m, the climate is harsh, and the difference of temperature between day and night is extremely sharp. Therefore, the nomad's basic garments, a sheepskin robe and a wool robe, are very popular marital gifts. They are worn as a garment during the day and used as a quilt at night.

Expensive ornaments, such as headdresses, necklaces, belts and other jewelry are also included in dowry. In general, these ornaments are usually kept by the woman herself during her marriage and not by her husband or his parents. Later, if the marriage fails through no fault of the woman's, or as the local people say, it is a "reasonable divorce," then the wife returns to her kin with all these ornaments, just as guns go with the man. However, if the marriage fails and the wife is to blame, then the husband will acquire all of this jewelry into his own possession.

The kinds and amounts of marital payments in the cooperative and commune era are distinctively different from those given after 1981. The first difference concerns the giving of livestock. During the cooperative and commune periods, the average number of animals per household given as dowry and bridewealth was two and four, respectively. However, these numbers increased to an average of twenty-two and eight, respectively, after the introduction of the responsibility system, which started in 1982.

The second difference concerns the types of goods given as marital payments. During the cooperative and commune periods marital payments usually included the basic necessities of life, such as livestock, grain, clothes, tea, etc. Since 1982, however, marital payments have not only included those things mentioned above, but also some goods that are considered luxury items, such as sewing machines, wool blankets and so forth. Also, before 1982, jewelry was seldom given in dowry, but since 1982, jewelry has become a common gift.

The third difference concerns the cash value of marital gifts. The value of marital payments averaged 1,766 RMB per dowry and 1,839 RMB per bridewealth, during the cooperative and commune periods. But those averages increased to 14,086 RMB per dowry and 5,378 RMB per bridewealth after 1982. That means cash payments were eight times higher for dowries and three times higher for bridewealth after 1982, according to the value of these same goods in 1994.

Why the sharp increase in marital payments between the periods prior to and after 1982? First, during the cooperative and commune periods, most animals and productive implements were owned by the commune. Nomad households were able to keep one milking cow of the yak species, or dri; per person and one horse for every two people as kashul (Kashul is the minimum number of animals required to provide basic subsistence.) When children married out, they were able to take only their share of kashul and clothes. However, larger families had more kashul/animals. By pooling their resources, these larger families might have been able to get by on less "family kashul," in order to provide more animals to their out-marrying children. This would be the only way a family could give animals as part of marital payments to their children.

Second, a work points system was practiced during the cooperative and commune periods. All the pastoral tasks such as milking, shearing, and so forth were assigned a work-point value from one to ten. Work points were awarded each day depending on the nature and amount of each person's work. These work points would eventually be converted to a monetary figure, from which the nomads could "buy" basic necessities at the end of the year, at a large distribution of goods.

Each nomad could obtain some mutton, yak meat, butter, grain, skins, and other necessities by "cashing in" work points they had earned. Thus, whenever a nlop (matrilocal), patrilocal or neolocal marriage was engaged in, the couple would bring their work points with them to the marriage. In consequence, during the period when the work point system was used, fewer goods (in kind) were given as marital payment because of the share to be received in the more intangible work points.

The amount and kinds of marital payments largely depend upon the economic background of the individual's natal family. For instance, households which are rich in livestock provide a large marital payment, while those who are poor in livestock provide lower payments. In the Serthar area, women enjoy equal rights of property with men. This is evidenced through the method employed in dividing property in the event of divorce. If there is no child, each party takes back their own property that they had brought into the marriage. But if a divorce involves a third party (e.g. if one spouse is involved in an extramarital affair), the spouse involved must pay out a certain amount of his property to the other. If no children are involved and the husband marries again, he must pay the former wife 'mossier' (a compensation fee). Paying mossier has been a unique cultural feature in the Serthar area. Property acquired after the marriage should be divided equally among all family members (both spouses and any children) in the event of a divorce. Even the family tent may be torn apart, with each family member taking his and her own share.

In the Golog Nomadic area, male and female siblings within a family enjoy equal inheritance rights, the only difference being that the female's inheritance takes the form of a dowry which she takes to another tenthold at marriage. If she divorces, she is entitled to the full dowry she brought to the marriage, as well as her equal share of the rest of the family property (as it is divided equally among the spouses and each child). For example, if the tenthold has increased its livestock holdings, she is entitled to a share of that incremental increase, for through her role as tent mistress, she has contributed to its prosperity.

In the southern nomadic area of Qinghai Lake, there is an equipartition of livestock between sons if they move away from their tent of birth after marriage. A daughter, if she leaves her natal tent at marriage, is likely to receive only clothes, jewelry and a horse. If she is permitted to bring a magpa in (to bring a husband into her natal family), she will have a right to share in the livestock of her natal household. Similarly, among the Songpan nomadic communities of the Kham area, all outmarrying children, whether sons or daughters, receive what must be considered a dowry at the time of their marriage. This dowry is less than a full share of their family's property. For example, parents prepare only clothes and jewelry for the out-marrying daughters and provide only a skin coat, a riding horse and a rifle as gifts for their son if he moves to his wife's family's tent or into his own tent. However, in the latter event he assumes the inheritance rights of his wife's total property.

Pastoral Development in Tibetan Rangelands

Modern pastoral development began in Tibetan nomadic areas in the late 1950s and 1960s. Thousands of years of traditional pastoralism were radically and abruptly changed with the formation of Chinese communist collectives and all animals and the tools of production became the property of the collectives. Large, state farms were established in many nomad areas.

Nomads, who previously were largely responsible for their own livestock, although usually under the control of a large estate or monastery, now had their animals put into collectives and the collective made decisions regarding production and the use of the rangeland. The government, through the collectives, provided inputs for fencing, veterinary services, crossbreeding with improved breeds, and the growing of artificial forage. In many areas, pastures were fenced and set aside for winter grazing or as special lambing and calving pastures. Nomads built houses around commune headquarters and constructed barns and shelters for livestock. Many rangelands were plowed up to plant grain.

In 1983, the Household Responsibility System was initiated in Tibetan nomad areas. Communes were dissolved and all animals divided equally among the nomads. Each family became responsible for its own livestock production and the marketing of livestock products. Rangeland remained the property of the state but nomads used the rangeland communally, often in groups that reflected the previous communal structure. In other areas, the traditional tribal structure, in existence prior to the 1950s, became the basis for rangeland tenure. Under the Household Responsibility System, many nomads that were more industrious or better skilled in taking care of animals were able to increase the size of their herds over time.

About ten years ago, in Tibetan nomad areas near Qinghai Lake, in Qinghai Province, pastoral development programs were initiated by the government that promoted the settling down of nomads and the division and allocation of rangeland to individual nomad households. Starting first in the traditional winter grazing lands, each nomad family was allocated a specific amount of rangeland on a long-term contract (30-50 years) in what was essentially a privatization of the grass-lands.

Pastures were also fenced to demarcate boundaries between pastures belonging to different nomads. The amount of land each nomad household was allocated was based on the supposed carrying capacity of the rangeland and the number of live-stock the family had. The construction of houses for nomads, sheds for live-stock, fencing, and development of artificial pasture was encouraged and heavily subsidized. Roads, schools, health clinics, and service centres were also established in nomad areas. Nomads were encouraged to restructure their herds to raise more breeding females and to sell stock for slaughter at a younger age. In some areas, with government concern about overgrazing, limits were placed on the numbers of animals nomads could raise.

This program was later expanded to privatize all the grazing lands used throughout the year, not just the winter pastures. This same pastoral development program of 'settling the nomads' and allocating and fencing the rangelands is now being rapidly extended throughout the Tibetan nomadic areas of western China.

Pastoral Policies

Pastoral development policies on the Tibetan Plateau, as elsewhere in much of the pastoral world, often maintain that nomads are 'backward' and that their traditional nomadic practices need to be 'improved'. Nomads' vast ecological knowledge and animal husbandry skills are often not well recognized or appreciated by scientists and development planners. As a result, nomads have largely been left out of the development process, with neither their knowledge nor their needs and desires considered. Nomads should, however, be thought of as 'experts' even though they may be illiterate.

Many old Tibetan nomads have probably already forgotten more details about rangelands and yaks than many young range ecologists and animal nutritionists will ever learn in college. Lamentably, the utility and economic viability of nomads' existing herd structures are largely unappreciated by most officials in Tibetan nomadic areas. Pastoral policies for restructuring nomads' herds usually do not acknowledge the reasons behind the existing herd structure in the first place.

Too often, policies for Tibetan nomads are conceived by people who do not know which end of a yak gets up first. Herd structures commonly found in commercial livestock operations in North America, Australia, or New Zealand are usually impractical for most Tibetan pastoral areas, yet many aspects of Western style livestock operations are often recommended for rangelands in Western China as 'modern' and 'scientific' means of livestock production.

Pastoral Misconceptions and Realities

Misconceptions abound regarding the rangelands, nomads, traditional nomadic practices, and pastoral development on the Tibetan Plateau. Sifting fallacies from facts is often confounded by the lack of good ecological information on the ecology of the range-lands and the poor understanding of nomadic pastoral production systems. In addition, information that does emerge about pastoral systems that contradicts official policies and development approaches is often ignored.

In China, the prominence of cultural attributes such as 'loss-of-face', generally makes people reluctant to admit to past mistakes, especially of officials or senior people. The political and donor-driven pressure to develop the hinter-lands of China and to alleviate poverty among nomads also often means that many of the underlying technical and scientific issues in pastoral areas are not adequately addressed before development programs are undertaken.

Popular misconceptions about the sustainability of Tibetan nomadic pastoralism include ideas such as: live-stock numbers have greatly increased in recent decades; rangeland degradation is widespread; overgrazing by livestock is the cause of rangeland degradation taking place; degraded ranges could be improved if stocked at carrying capacity; large herds maintained by nomads are uneconomic and only a status symbol of wealth; and that new institutions and organizations need to be put in place to improve range resource management.

The realities are that in many Tibetan pastoral areas, livestock numbers have not increased greatly in recent years and current attempts to limit animal numbers may be ill conceived. Even if seemingly uneconomical, nomads oftentimes will not be willing to reduce animal numbers since large herds provide insurance against losses and competitive advantage in exerting control over grazing resources in addition to social status and livestock products. The absence of viable markets and high transaction costs also often preclude nomads from selling more animals in the marketplace. Since costs for maintaining animals are low, it is usually profitable to hold animals, although critics of Tibetan pastoralism often claim that nomads keep large numbers of live-stock just as a status symbol.

In China, views are widespread that Tibetan nomads wander freely across the grasslands in a migratory manner with no permanent home and without any management of the grazing lands. Current policies for privatization of grasslands are based on the mistaken belief that traditional pastoral systems did not give nomads any responsibility for the rangeland and that, therefore, nomads tried to maximize herd sizes with no regards to carrying capacity. The fact of the matter is that Tibetan nomads do not move randomly across the landscape and hardly ever have. Rather, their movements are usually well prescribed by complex social organizations and are highly regulated. In some areas, under the traditional pastoral system, quite elaborate systems were in place to periodically reallocate grazing land among herders depending on rangeland condition and livestock numbers.

It is a widespread opinion that grazing lands on the Tibetan Plateau are overgrazed and in a degraded state.

While much of the rangeland in the agricultural valleys of Central Tibet is heavily overgrazed and in a badly deteriorated condition with desertification a spreading problem, the situation in many of the nomadic pastoral areas is not nearly so bad. Many rangelands in the pure nomadic areas of Tibet are, in fact, in good to excellent condition, despite centuries of livestock grazing.

Overgrazing is an issue in some nomadic pastoral areas and rangeland degradation is a problem in places, but sweeping generalizations about overgrazing and rangeland degradation only confuse the issue. Due to concern about overgrazing, policies for limiting livestock numbers have been enacted, but they are inappropriate when applied to pastoral areas where rangeland conditions are still good and where the nomads could actually be raising more animals. Overgrazing and rangeland degradation needs to be looked at on a local level.

There is increasing evidence that a general climatic trend of desiccation and warming may be responsible for vegetation changes taking place in the alpine meadows of many parts of the Tibetan Plateau. Livestock grazing may just accentuate natural ecological processes taking place instead of being the cause for the vegetation changes. It is also becoming increasingly apparent that existing paradigms for explaining the dynamics of rangeland ecosystems have not captured the dynamic nature of Tibetan rangelands and, therefore, traditional measures for range conditions and carrying capacities may not be effective gauges for management in these grazing lands.

Future Challenges

Despite their extent and importance, rangeland ecosystem dynamics on the Tibetan Plateau are still poorly understood and good, scientific data on ecological processes taking place throughout the rangelands are limited. Many questions concerning how rangeland vegetation functions and the effect of grazing animals on the pastoral system remain unanswered for the most part. The socioeconomic dimensions of the Tibetan pastoral production systems are also not well known. This lack of information limits the proper management and sustainable development of the rangelands.

Improved pastoral production in Tibetan nomad areas requires that ecological principles regulating range-land ecosystem functions are linked with the economic principles governing livestock production and general economic development processes. New perspectives emerging about non-equilibrial ecosystem dynamics and new concepts about plant successional processes in pastoral systems provide interesting frameworks for analysing Tibetan rangelands. Exploring the relevance of these new perspectives could have important implications for the management of Tibetan pastoral areas. Innovative, pastoral development paradigms that actively involve nomads in the development process also suggest new possibilities for and fresh approaches to working with Tibetan nomads.

Greater efforts should be directed towards developing a better understanding of current nomadic pastoral production systems. Practices vary considerably throughout the Tibetan rangelands and these differences need to be analysed. Analyses of the socioeconomic processes at work in Tibetan pastoral areas are a key challenge for researchers. It will also be important to determine which aspects of indigenous knowledge systems and traditional pastoral strategies can be used in the design of new development interventions for pastoral areas on the Tibetan Plateau.

With current pastoral development policies, Tibetan nomads are being transformed into commercial livestock ranchers. While these developments are certainly improving nomads' standard of living, the long-term susceptibility of the large subsidized investments in fences, buildings and range improvements needs to be questioned. Fencing and barns are expensive, relative to the benefits. Given the generally poor experience with settling of nomads in other pastoral areas of the world, it will be interesting to watch the process of sedendarization as it unfolds on Tibetan rangelands. Pastoral development programs for Tibetan rangelands must involve the nomads themselves in the initial design of interventions. Nomads' needs and desires must be heard and the vast body of indigenous knowledge nomads possess must be put to use when designing new projects. An important message for pastoral policy-makers and planners is the need for active participation by the nomads in all aspects of the development process and for empowered nomads to manage their own development.

7

Nomadic Education and Economic Perspectives

For nomads there is no realistic chance to benefit from the formal education system. Even if a nomadic family could arrange to send a child to school by living with member of the family, the type of education he/she could get in the formal school would not help him or her in the nomadic environment.

Providing education for nomadic people in the traditional manner confronts the teaching profession with a series of headaches. School buildings, classrooms, benches, desks, teaching equipment and timetables of subjects and activities for the term are all irrelevant for people who do not stay in one place for more than a few weeks at a time.

The nomad is certainly an awkward customer for the services and structures of the modern education system. They are seen as dispersed and somehow aimless, obstinate and an inferior sort of person. It is very difficult to provide them with classes or clinics, or take any of the advantages of social services. Nomads are always blamed for causing their own problems.

The education system was never conducive to Somalia's pastoral communities. Since the colonial era the country's education has been generally characterized by low enrollment, male-biased and urban (or settlement) orientation features. Available statistics indicate that 5-10 percent of all school children were enrolled, of which girls constituted less that 20 percent of the total enrollment.

A major problem that affects nomads' accessibility to educational facilities was the urban-orientation of Somalia's education system. Almost all educational facilities were built in towns or major villages that served settled communities only. One manifestation of this bias is the fact that in 1969, about 90 percent of primary schools were located in urban settings that were inaccessible to pastoralists. Similarly, in 1988, 59 percent of all secondary school graduates were from the capital city Mogadishu. What could be the share of the pastoral nomads? Thus, nomads are neglected absolutely and relatively when it comes to access to education.

A crucial problem is how the sector was financed. In the first place the bulk of education expenditure was covered by the budget of the Ministry of Education and Culture. During the 1975-79 period Somalia spent 12 percent of its recurrent expenditure and 7 percent of it development expenditure on education, which equalled to only 3.2 percent of the Gross Domestic Product.

During 1970s, however, defence and security needs absorbed increasing amounts of government budget, and expenditure on education drastically declined, reflecting a shift in government priorities and an apparent loss of its commitment to education. From 1986 through 1988, the Ministry of Education's share of government spending dropped to less than 2.0 percent of its recurrent expenditure and about 3.0 percent of its development expenditure. Total basic expenditure on education was about 0.6 percent of the Gross Domestic Product.

Inadequate finances led to a precarious decline in primary school enrollment, teachers left the system at an unprecedentedly high rate, resulting in the subsequent closure of many schools. This trend discouraged even the settled communities to send their children to school, where conditions were appalling, let alone pastoralists who always had their doubts. If interventions aimed to meet some educational needs of pastoral nomads are to become sustainable, they have to be coupled with other efforts in improving nomads income generating capabilities, whereby women are given special attention in strengthening the pastoral production system.

The underdevelopment of pastoral communities could be explained as a result of a number of factors, including lack of access to basic education. Yet availability of education cannot be assumed a panacea for the sector's problems. However, it is a general belief that education is a key to progress and that its purpose is the liberation of nomads from the restraints and limitations of ignorance and dependency. Therefore, if this service is provided to pastoral nomads, it is assumed it will make differences such as:

— It will enable them to participate in the planning, implementation and evaluation of projects affecting their special living conditions, as well as their future;

— While cultivating their awareness on their rights and problems it will encourage nomads to form community organizations and participate in the political realm effectively;.

— It will enable nomads to understand and utilize their environment better and increase productivity;

— It will give them the capacity to absorb and utilize sustainable technology that reduces the number of working hours for the nomads, liberating children to enroll in schools;

— It will open communication channels for nomads to understand their surroundings and develop a better relationship with urban and agricultural communities.

Pastoral Nomads

A nomad could be defined as a livestock owner who keeps the productivity and survival of his herds through extensive yet cyclic wandering in areas where there are not enough resources to remain in one place permanently. While pastoral refer to people whose main livelihood is herding. With the exception of southern agricultural land along the Shabelle and Juba rivers and the northern, Borama-Gebilay enclave, Somalia is a territory exclusive suitable and used for grazing.

This lifestyle and form of livestock production has survived through centuries, and even today pastoral nomadism is recognized as an efficient cost-effective method of utilizing marginal lands. Nomads have special ways of adapting to the arid and unreliable climatic conditions. Nomads have a strong and viable social system and community organization which (before it was manipulated and misused by the last dictatorial regime) enhanced their self-reliance and survival capacities to meet their needs, even at times of disaster such as drought.

According to I.M. Lewis, the Somali nomad, particularly the northerner, is independent and an individualist. He noted that the "informidable pride of the Somali nomad, his extraordinary sense of superiority as an individual, and his firm conviction that he is sole master of his actions and subject to no authority except that of God". Nomads are symbols of survival. They have survived long droughts, epidemic diseases, all kinds of hardships without any external assistance or from the government. They have a functioning and self-contained system based on individual abilities and strong and well-balanced social structure, based on the 'economy of affection' where the needy is supported through clan or marriage relationships.

Over the years, pastoralists have developed their own methods of treating livestock with a fair degree of success. They acquired accumulated knowledge on various herbs to treat people and to cure their animals. For centuries milk produced on the rangelands constituted the main diet of the nomads during several months of the year, depending on the size of the herd and pattern of droughts. But since the market economy came in contact with nomads their diet has substantially changed. Since then pastoral nomads have not been as remote and out of touch with other sectors of the Somali society as their geographical location may suggest.

Nomads make regular trips to markets in agricultural and urban settlements. And lately, cereals, some of them imported, e.g. rice, constitute the nomad's staple food, and not dairy products of milk and meat as commonly believed. The mode of living among nomads has permeated and influenced the very roots, thinking, behaviour and culture of present day Somalis. Nomadism as a way of life was a logical, valid and productive mode of existence. Pastoral nomads proved to be resistant to external forces. Their land, culture, lifestyle could not be overrun by modern civilization.

The world economy is changing drastically, and pastoral nomads everywhere must feel the impact. They have been at the mercy of shifting commodity prices, tariff regulation, and trading patterns over which they have little or no control. As the monetized economy expanded to engulf the pastoral nomads, they have become more and more dependent on goods from settled communities, and their sensitivity to macro change is increasing.

Pastoralism could be assumed the only practice that does not threaten the arid environment and nomads know how to exploit it. The continuous cyclic movement of men and animals allows vegetation to replenish itself and does not threaten water sources and the grazing land around them. Nomads have more or less full control over the management of pasturage. They restrict and direct their wanderings and focus on tribal holdings, depending on the availability of food supply (fodder) and the technology for exploiting it. Each clan has focal sites that they occupy for a considerable period of the year.

In Somalia, pastoral nomads constitute between 60 and 70 percent of the country's sparse population, and are entirely dependent on livestock. Their livestock production is the mainstay of the country's economy, accounting for some 40 percent of the gross domestic product (GDP), providing subsistence to about 75 percent of the population, furnishing some 80 percent of foreign exchange earnings, and employs between 55 and 60 percent of the nation's labour force.

Inspite of their significant economic contribution, 57,000 of Somalia's 500,000 nomadic and semi-nomadic families are considered "poor all the time", and 300,000 are poor during drought. The total population who are in need of permanent support before the war was estimated to be approximately two million.

Education of pastoral nomads

Children of pastoral nomads go without modern education, but not without education at all. They receive traditional education that is oriented to their ways of making a living and which contains the cultural and societal values of society. For example, herd boys learn the value of different kinds of grazing for each species of stock by watching animals and the environment and through direct teaching by male elders, while girls acquire household related activities from their mothers and sisters.

The Koranic school is by far the most pervasive, steady and permanent education facility in the country. Since the advent of the Islamic religion, the nomadic children received some sort of formal education, which has shown some success. This was the teaching of the Koran. In general, this played a very different role in the children lives from those involved in modern or formal schools, because such teaching takes place in a familiar environment and carried out by individuals from the same neighbourhood.

Among pastoral nomads, children (mostly boys) aged 5-14 years are brought together for some hours (normally early morning and or early evening) six days a week to be taught how to recite the Koran by a nomad teacher, who is supported by voluntary annual contributions and who enjoys the respect of the community. Facilities are rudimentary, barely proving shelter and the equipment is simple: wooden slates, ink, and a wooden pen. An advantage of these schools is their mobility; the Koranic teacher moves with his students and his school wherever the new camp is constructed.

The Koranic schools, however, face many problems. Teachers are not well trained. Many of them are barely literate and only teach the Koran with no supplementary courses in Islamic studies. The teaching approach is often rigidly unyielding and consists largely of note-taking, memorization and copying.

Nomads are not their own masters. They have no control over the ups and downs around them that directly or indirectly influence their future. In this country in the Horn, regional and sectorial unequal distribution of resources is the dominant scene, whereby pastoral nomads are impoverished, dominated and underprivileged. Like other services, education facilities are unequally distributed among different communities of the Somali society. Since the beginning of formal education in Somalia, schools were urban-oriented or settlement-biased (concentrated in towns and villages).

In the years following independence, education was focused on the minority urban population and the majority of children in the 'miyi' (rural rangelands) did not share the fruits of the post-independence. In 1969, for example, 90 percent of all primary schools were located in settings of permanent residence e.g. towns and villages of different population sizes. Although the delivery of basic education was urban or settlement oriented, the disparity is more explicit depending on the degree a certain region is nomadic. Regions which people derive their livelihood from livestock have had the lowest primary school enrollment.

The provision of schools for nomads, and the adoption of schooling to the special needs and circumstances of nomadic society, has made less progress in Somalia than for other basic needs. Although it is generally accepted that without proper schooling pastoral communities (settled communities) will remain poor and discriminated upon, there have been few attempts to solve this problem. Where nomad children do get schooling, it is at immense personal cost both to the child and its parents, and denotes a complete and often permanent separation of the child from the nomad community. Few benefits from such sacrifices are returned to the nomad community.

Most efforts at providing schooling for nomads have been through the extension of ordinary schools into the remote areas generally inhabited by nomads. In the first place small towns and villages are generally equipped with a day school. The pupils are normally town or village children and children of local officials and traders. A few nomadic children, almost invariably boys and generally from richer families or those with an urban connection, attend school and live with kin in the town or village. Assistance and support through the extended family or the "economy of affection" is part and parcel of nomad's means of survival. Since independence nomad family members have been moving into towns and villages, and once established, supported certain numbers of nomad school-age children through some level of education.

Even though the government may recognize the special problems that nomadic movement and distance from town creates, it does not provide affordable and accessible boarding facilities for nomadic children. The last military regime closed down nearly all boarding primary schools in the country, on the unsubstantiated assumption that such facilities were utilized by the well-off urban class. The truth was just the opposite. Boarding schools provided an opportunity for education to many children from rural areas, a chance without which many politicians, businessmen and professionals wouldn't enjoy their present status. The facilities were reasonable and furnished good quality education. The annual cost to the nomadic household was during 1960s between $40 and $50, equivalent to 7 head of goats or sheep, a number most families could afford.

Attendance by nomadic children at day schools has had limited success. Few children managed to overcome the obstacles involved, have graduated to secondary or higher education and have risen to senior positions in government administration. But this is despite, not because of the system. There are many problems. Few nomad children go to such schools, and for those that do, drop out rates are high. Girls rarely ever start school. Curricula are often irrelevant to the needs of the pastoral nomads and teaching standards are low. Following are the factors related to pastoral way of life:

(a) *Mobility and Sparse Population*: Sparse distribution of the nomad population is the foremost obstacle limiting children's attendance in school. This low population density makes it difficult to gather enough pupil population to make it cost-effective. If facilities are provided to such sparse population, costs per pupil are far higher than schools in towns and villages.

(b) *Child labour*: Because of the labour-intensive nature of the herding economies, children of pastoral nomads are significant contributors to the household income through their labour, even from an early age. Among these communities children (especially boys) are viewed as an economic asset. Such economic benefits are cultivated in the short term, the children being useful to help the family raise livestock. They look after animal herds (e.g. sheep goats, camels, etc) and undertake most household duties. Therefore, parents need to maintain their children's contribution and at the same time avoid the cost of schooling. Thus a limited number of rich families will be inclined to send their children (preferably boys) to school. Physically handicapped children considered not-fit for the nomadic way of life are sometimes given the chance to attend school in towns or villages. For some time pastoral communities have been aware of the long-term benefits of educating children, but the cost of educating remains a major obstacle.

(c) *Direct Costs*: If a pastoral nomad's children are to receive uninterrupted education and in suitable facilities, they have to be sent on scholarship to towns and villages and parents must meet all the costs in cash. As long as most pastoral nomads do not consider schooling a long-term investment, they are not willing to pay for their children's education.

Although in Somalia education was pronounced free, the cost of school uniforms, exercise books, and transportation expenses, constituted a substantial burden to add to the expenses to cover the pupil's living in town or village.

(d) *Attitude and Values*: Nomads in Somalia view both schools and schooling as alien things that do not contribute to the pastoral way of life. Pastoral nomads' independence and reluctance to change their traditional ways poses a major obstacle. They believe that such facilities will in the end alienate their children from them and the society at large. Parents with such attitudes are illiterate and have never experienced the benefits, if any, of modern education.

School Related Factors

(i) *Curriculum.* The contents of the curriculum is generally considered inappropriate for the children of pastoral nomads. It does not provide practical skills to improve the livelihood of nomads. Rather, it is believed, it focuses on academic achievements that only suit the needs of urban children. There is a lack of demonstrable practical benefits for the pastoral economy .

(ii) *Quality of schools/Teachers.* Rural primary schools which pastoral nomads may have access to are qualitatively poor in terms of facilities and teaching staff. The management and supervision of officials are not effective either. Low salaries of education personnel creates a reluctance to live away from their urban families, leading to an unequitable geographical enrollment of schools and an unwillingness of younger staff to leave urban centres. It is therefore very difficult to place quality staff in schools accessible to nomads.

Interventions to Educate Nomads

The government of Somalia realized the importance of education for overall national development but did not acknowledge, let alone obligate itself to extend this service to the bulk of the population. Innovative projects which addressed the educational needs of pastoral nomads are limited and those which took place were either short-lived or not sustainable.

Nomadic Resettlement Programme

Pertinent lessons could be learnt from the experiences of 1975 drought-stricken nomads resettled in agricultural and fishing settlements. By August 1975, at least 120,000 nomads had been moved to three agricultural resettlement areas along the Shebelle and Juba rivers and to fishing villages along the southern coast. The resettled families gradually learned to adjust their traditional values to the new surroundings. Instead of passing the days herding, men and women had set patterns of agricultural labour, aimed at making them successful communal farmers. On the coast the men were trained to become off-shore fishermen.

For some of the resettled nomads, the change was too drastic and when the good rains came in 1977 and 1978, many of the men set off again for their traditional pastures. Primary school facilities were supplied to the newly settled communities by the Ministry of Education with assistance from UNICEF, to a population with little or no previous formal education. It was also possible to cater for the adult population, and the government made tremendous efforts to ensure the delivery of basic services.

The benefits of the settled way of life were particularly appreciated by mothers and children. They had schools and day-care centres, medical help and mother and child health care centres. The resettlement areas were large and quickly took on the shape of small towns, where the new arrivals fully participated in the running of the 'new towns'.

Rural Development Campaign

The 1974-75 rural development campaign was the first and last of its kind in which more than one million persons of the rural population, including pastoral nomads, attended classes. This literacy programme targeted adult nomads. Around 25,000 students over sixteen, as well as school teachers were instructed to set off into the Somali countryside, attach themselves to the nomad groups, and become their tutor for a while. The teachers, most of whom came from relatively sophisticated urban families, were given no money, no resources, nothing except a portable blackboard and a box of chalk. They were to teach nomads how to read and write.

There was a lot of skepticism over whether the ambitions of the Rural Development. The cynics were confounded by the results. Even though the year was 1974, and the nomads were enduring the country's worst drought, a survey conducted at the end of eight months suggested that one million previously illiterate people were now able more or less to read and write in their own language. As many as 875,000 people passed the final exam.

Part of the success derived from the appropriate phrases and subjects selected for the campaign. This was a chance to introduce Somalia's people to new ideas related to livestock management, domestic welfare, health and sanitation, plus suggestions for relieving the least comfortable aspects of their precarious way of life out on the margins of desert existence.

Education Centres

It was not easy to reach pastoral nomads on a permanent basis. But through the nationwide organization of regions, districts, and villages, settled people could be easily reached, informed, oriented, taught and cared for. It took the Somali government more than two decades before it started some sort of permanent training for pastoralists. The end of 1978 saw the beginning of a new experiment under the Adult Education Programme, to set up six Nomadic Education Centres in different parts of the country, concentrating on providing the skills and knowledge which nomadic people can best utilize.

If it is difficult to teach nomads through formal approaches, it is almost impossible to teach nomads accidentally. It will not be an easy job for the few extension workers, who lack transport, drugs and, in many cases, lack knowledge, as often stated by nomads, for example, in the field of veterinary services. Since it is difficult to follow nomads, the Somali government ventured to embark on a programme based on the construction of six Nomadic Education Centres. This pilot project is based on the assumption, that some members of a nomadic family could be delegated to participate in the residential training course. The provision of food would be a kind of attraction for the nomads to come and stay for a limited time.

Generally, in political terms the Nomadic Education Programme can be seen as an attempt to apply justice and equal rights for the nomads. For years the nomads produced up to 80 percent of the nation's foreign exchange earnings, but the livestock sector received only 10 percent of the government budget.

The programme was designed to enable nomads to use technical procedures and methods of individual or joint organizations, likely to improve their standard of living without obliging them to abandon their own values. The programme was to help modernize the attitudes and values of the nomad so that he could be an active agent for progressive change in his own environment, and capable of better adjustment and better environmental control, modification and exploitation.

Although the Somali government sympathizes with the idea of settling nomads, sedentrization is not the main aim of the programme. The programme was of an experimental nature and remained in danger of a number of failures. If, for example, the nomads were not satisfied with the educational programmer, with the food or with the time or duration of the training course, they would not come, or they would leave the center in the middle of the course.

Educational training programmes aims to:

— A mixed programme combining various areas such as health, livestock, agriculture, community development, etc.

— A training course for traditional birth attendants (TBA) and community health workers (CHW), who were supplied with TBA kits and First Aid kits respectively.

— A literacy training programme to enable participants to read course materials.

Economic Perspectives

The pastoral nomads in East Africa breed camel, cattle, goats, sheep and donkeys altogether, which is called the multiple-stock herding. The balance among the various types of livestock varies according to regional ecological differences. The principal stock shifts gradually from cattle combined with small stock to camels combined with small stock, as aridity increases. Also, the relative degree of the social and cultural values vested in livestock is different from society to society. The Eastern Nilotic Maasai, Samburu, Ariaal, Turkana, Karimojong, Jie peoples, and the Eastern Cushitic Boran and Dasanetch peoples value cattle more than camels, and conversely, the East Cushitic Somali, Rendille and Gabbra peoples value camels more than cattle.

In all the pastoral societies, however, herders make for their own living within the socio-ecological framework of the openland. Living as they do symbiotically with their livestock, their rhythm of life is dominated by the needs of the animals. Anything that affects the life of flocks and herds affects humans just as acutely.

These pastoral nomads live off their livestock who provide them with the pastoral diet of milk, blood and meat. Far from treating their livestock merely as sources of meat, milk, and cash, they display an obsessive reverence for their livestock. They use them in marriage settlements to acquire wives and children, as compensation for injures and death. Livestock are used in social exchange to adjust and activate personal relationships. Also, they offer livestock to gods and spirits, and communicate with the spiritual world. With these and a multitude of other social and symbolic significance, livestock represent the ideal prestige wealth, the measure of a man's substance and success.

However, pastoral nomads' comprehensive and obsessive concern with livestock is accused as pre-modern, obstructing the development of state economy which aims to incorporate livestock into market economy. In Kenya, so many range-land specialists have criticized the maximizing strategy of indigenous herders as leading to the destruction of ecological balance through overgrazing and overstocking. These specialists presume that livestock should be bred according to the carrying capacity of rangeland. Therefore, every policy effort has been to maintain ecological balance by culling "excessive" livestock from the herd that outgrew the optimal size.

This rangeland policy was already in effect during the colonial times. The government changed taxation to be paid from livestock to money. At the same time, herders were assigned and restricted into their "tribal" zone. Furthermore, livestock were extracted from the indigenous herds on the grounds that overstocking should be avoided. The independent government has followed the colonial policy of market economy for pastoral production. The IPAL (Integrated Project in Arid Lands) project, started in 1976 in Marsabit District, was put in effect to integrate the local pastoral production into state-wide market economy. Many herders were employed by this project and itinerant auctions and shops were facilitated to advance consumerism. Moreover, the livestock auctions were frequently held in order to enforce livestock supply from the herders. Consequently, opportunities for wage labour and commodity exchange increased, and market economy of livestock was promoted by the IPAL project.

A policy to promote livestock supply to the market intended profit expansion through market exchange. But such economic transactions were principally different from indigenous livestock transactions that aimed to promote social coexistence through reciprocal interpersonal relationships. It is a serious problem how the indigenous transaction is balanced with the market economy transaction because it lies at the core of how subsistence economy and credit transaction should be.

Concept of Optimal Herd-size

Market economy policy depends on surplus livestock steadily supplied to the market under the condition that optimal herd-size is kept in balance with the carrying capacity of the rangeland. This idea is derived from ranching management in the temperate zone, where livestock is bred within an enclosure with waterhole and pasturage. In this case, a rational target is that the feeding efficiency of livestock should be in balance with animal growth to cut down feeding cost. In contrast, nomadic herding is accompanied by rearing livestock and movement of humans and livestock, and does not work with the efficiency of the man-made environment.

The concept of optimal herd-size was emphasized by Hardin in the thesis of "tragedy of commons". He had two presuppositions. First, the pasture of joint ownership is freely open to private use. Second, livestock are owned privately by individuals. The cost increase of a communal pasture for a head of livestock should impose equal burden on the individuals who share it. But each individual tries to maximize his herd-size, because each monopolizes the profit earned by increasing the herd-size. This leads to overgrazing, exceeding the limit of carrying capacity of the pasture. Hardin thus denied the communal system of the pasture.

But, Hardin has come under criticism. First, the presupposition of communal resources for individual freedom is completely unrealistic. The pursuit of private profit does not escape communal control. Second, the carrying capacity of the pasture is difficult to determine precisely, and it is a vague and unpractical concept in the tropical zone where the livestock population fluctuates violently. Moreover, it is doubtful whether livestock grow to the limit of carrying capacity in reality. Dietz, who studied the correlation between livestock population and climate change in Pokotland of western Kenya, concluded that overgrazing never occured in reality, because livestock died in periodical droughts, before ever reaching the limit of carrying capacity.

Furthermore, the concept of optimal livestock population is not realistic in the drought-ridden zone of arid East Africa. When Turkanaland was devastated by the severe drought of 1979-81, so many livestock died a natural death, and many people starved. People were forced to give up herding. Only the households with relatively many livestock managed to weather this drought. This demonstrates the adaptive meaning of maximization strategy.

It has been reported that herding has higher pastoral productivity than ranching. Cossins concluded that herding productivity in the Boranland of southern Ethiopia was higher than that of ranching in Australia with a similar climate to Boranland. The pastoral Boran produced four times as much protein and six times as much food energy as the Australian ranching in terms of productivity per hectare. Also, the Boran herding was more favourable than the Australian ranching in terms of input cost. One-kilogram of protein was produced at the monetary cost of 1.9-3.9 US$ by Australian ranching, and of 2.0 US$ by Laikipia ranching in Kenya, whereas the Boran herders produced 1 kg of protein at the cost of only 0.1-0.3 US$.

Per capita productivity is generally presumed higher for ranching than for herding. However, comparison by production per unit area of protein quantity and food energy and the amount of monetary investment, herding turned out to be more productive than ranching. Thus, different conclusions can be drawn with different measures of productivity. It is wrong to apply the general idea of the optimal herd-size, which is standardized for the temperate ranching system, to the herding system in the arid land with unstable and drought-ridden conditions.

Multiplication and Reduction of Herd-Size

The East African herd compositions by age and sex are fragmentally available. Based on 20 herds of Rendille camels, an average herd-size was 49 heads of camels, including stud-camels (3%), ox-camels (15%), cow-camels (62%), juvenile camels (10%), and calf-camels (11%). An average herd of camels of the Ariaal in the southern part of the Rendilleland had similar composition to the Rendille's. The compositions of cattle herds in four cattle-raising societies of the Turkana, the Karimojong, the Bodi, and the Lokoro revealed that the percentage of oxen increased from 1 to 23% as the average herd-size increased.

This means that more surplus oxen are kept in larger herds. Oxen are used in household consumption, social transactions and sales.

Beyond the number of heads necessary for the socio-economic life, oxen are neither culled entirely or increased, but are kept as surplus at hand. On the other hand, as herd-size increased from 20 to 181 heads, the number of the cows to a bull increased from 6 to 11 heads, and conversely the percentage of cows in a herd decreased from 43 to 34%, and that of bulls from 7 to 3%. Every herd of any size is assigned at least 1-2 heads of bull, whereas bulls are not assigned to a herd in proportion with the number of cows. A bull can copulate with as many cows for breeding. Comparing the herd-size of camels with that of cattle, the camel herd is smaller than the cattle herd. The ratio of breeding males is lower in the camel herd than in the cattle herd. The ratio of castrated animals and that of adult females is higher in the camel herd than in the cattle herd. It is because the ox-camels are reared for meat, cash and packing that more castrated males are kept at hand.

The ratio of cow-camels is higher than that of cows because cow-camels have a longer reproductive period than cows. A cow gives birth to its first calf at 3-4 years of age, and continues giving birth for approximately 10 years thereafter. The cow-camel reproduces at 4-5 years of age, and continues giving birth for approximately 20 years thereafter. Thus, adult females are more abundant in the camel herd than in the cattle herd. The annual rate of herd growth is estimated at 3.4% in the camel herd, 4-10% or 5.6-14% in the cattle herd. Dahl & Hjort simulated the increase rate of livestock variety by using many suppositions, and showed that a little change in the variables such as the year of age for the first childbirth, birth rate, and death rate would result in a great fluctuation of herd population. Such drastic changes threaten the herd population dynamics in East Africa with periodical droughts. When a herd population declines due to a drought, the death rate of juvenile and old-aged animals increases, and the birth rate also decreases. Also, the off-take rate of animals increases with household consumption and sale.

According to Itani, when the Turkana experienced the devastating drought of 1979-81, goat population decreased by 41%, sheep by 7.4 %, cattle by 70 %, and camels by 41%. The Turkana made every effort to keep the cattle they culturally esteem the most. This tendency was also pointed out in the Somali society with its importance attached to the camel . The recovery process of the herds, has been reported for the Isiolo Boran and the Maasai. The annual rate of increase was 28% a year for the cattle herd, three years after the 1975-76 drought in the Boranland.

In the Maasailand, it was at 24% for the cattle herd in 1964, three years after the 1960-61 drought, but it declined to 7% in 1968. Herd-size is subject to drastic fluctuations by the drought. Furthermore, the kind of livestock kept at the time of the drought is determined by the cultural value. The higher the cultural value for a livestock species, the more effort is made to keep them. The model of optimal herd-size should be applied to actual herds with consideration of cultural and time factors.

Economic Aspect of Livestock

Pastoral nomads live on the pastoral diet of milk, blood and meat from their livestock. Yet not all the members of a household can be supported with their livestock, depending on the number of livestock. Some herders (the Samburu) thus supplement livestock products by imported grain of maize or sorghum. Others (the Rendille) vary their diet between settlements and herding camps. They have mainly livestock products in the herding camps and eat more grain in the settlements.

Milk is the most stable food of the livestock products. It is consumed as fresh and sour milk, and consumed with tea, blood and grain. The milk yield is determined by the quality and quantity of pasture and the lactation cycle of the milking animals. Herders milk the lactating animals according to the milking schedule, allocating the milk between themselves and the calves. According to Field, the experimental camels in the Rendilleland yielded the largest quantity of milk 3-7 weeks or 1-2 months after childbirth. The milk yield of 1-2 months after childbirth counted as 1 unit decreased to three-fourth in the third month and to a half during the 4-6 months.

The Rendille leave the calf-camel to suck all its dam's milk for a month after childbirth. Then, they share the milk with the calves. A dam-camel has four nipples, and is milked respectively from two nipples twice a day in the morning and at night for the second month after childbirth. In other words, a calf-camel shares a half of the milk of its dam with the Rendille. During the 3-8 months after childbirth, the Rendille milk the dam-camel from two nipples in the morning, and from four nipples at night. After 9 months, milking is done from four nipples both in the morning and at night, and for the first time the calf-camel is kept from finishing off what milk is left.

According to the Rendille milking schedule, about 38 (three-eighth) - 56% (nine-sixteenth) of the total amount of milk lactated by a dam-camel is consumed by the people. Whereas the milk yield varies with the lactation cycle, human milk consumption is not determined by the lactation cycle. Rather, with the milking schedule, the Rendille secure about 40-60% of the total amount of lactated milk. In general, the dam-animals lactate more milk in the rainy season when good pasture is available, but less in the dry season. Under a severe drought in Turkanaland, 200 g of milk a day per dam was estimated as an average for the cattle, and 1,400 g a day per animal for the camel.

In the 1975-76 drought in the Rendilleland, 800 g of milk a day was estimated as an average for the cattle and 1,300 g for the camel. Normally in 1982, a dam-cattle supplied the Rendille with 1,200 g of milk daily, and a dam-camel, 2,000 g of milk daily. Camels can stably supply more milk than cattle. Unlike milk, meat remains a luxury and is largely reserved for special occasions. These include both times of festivity and of emergency. In fact, small stock are most frequently killed in the dry seasons when milk is scarce, and their skins are then sold or exchanged for grain and other foods and necessities. Thus the herders tend to sell livestock and its products, not when they have a surplus, but when they are hard up. Herders drink milk in the rainy season when livestock yield much milk, and eat meat, blood and grain in the dry season when milk dries up.

Both cattle and camel herders, use small stock as cash animals for elastic small money besides as food source for home consumption. Cattle and camels, however, are treated differently. Cattle herders, who keep donkeys as pack-animal, readily sell more camels for cash, although they use meat and milk of camels. Conversely camel herders strive to keep their camels, used for transportation, milk and meat. Following the laws of supply and demand underlying market economy, herders are recommended to sell their livestock at the highest price as the rational economic behaviour. Yet generally speaking, they do not sell their livestock in the rainy season when milk is abundant. Conversely, as milk decreases with the advent of the dry season, they sell their livestock.

Livestock is fat in the rainy season and lean in the dry season. When demand is the greatest and prices the highest, supplies of livestock actually declines. In other words, herders tend to sell livestock in time of depression rather than boom. Under favourable conditions, they engage in what might be called target-sales, where the objective is to acquire a certain cash sum for certain purposes. Once this is achieved, the motive for selling livestock diminishes or disappears. The herders' selling behaviour is reinforced by the mutual and reciprocal relationship with their livestock dealers, most of whom run either retail or wholesale shops. The persons left behind in their settlements have less food and cash as the dry season advances, because their livestock are taken away to the herding camps. They purchase necessities on credit for a while, and in the rainy season when their livestock are back in the settlements, they repay the debt with their livestock.

The dealers also can take advantage of such credit transactions. The cost of keeping livestock to fatten is high in the dry season even if livestock is purchased with low price from the herders. Through the above credit transaction, the dealers can place the herding cost on the herders, and also acquire fattened livestock in the rainy season. Furthermore, they can acquire livestock in the rainy season when supply of livestock actually declines, and gain more profit at the livestock market when demand is greater than supply and the price is favourable for suppliers. Thus the relationship between the herder and the dealer can be described as symbiotic.

When the purchasing policy for livestock from herders was put into effect by the itinerant auctions of cattle, the Ariaal cattle herders did not respond positively. But the Rendille camel herders supplied more cattle to the auctions. Importance is attached to small stock as cash animals and camels as animals for milk in both the societies. However, the Ariaal maintain a cattle-oriented culture under the influence of the Samburu, the neighbouring cattle herders, and attach more importance to cattle than to camels for ritual use and bridewealth payment. In contrast, the Rendille can readily sell their cattle because they attach more importance to camels than to cattle. Again, the type of livestock vested with higher social and cultural value is kept at hand.

Household and the Livestock

In the pastoral societies of East Africa, a household composed of man and wife (or wives) with her (or their) children, is the communal holding group of livestock. The agnates of the household exercise the legal management of household livestock. Sons cannot separate their own livestock from their father's without difficulty, whereas the household head is obligated to support his household members by distributing livestock as the need arises.

Upon a father's death, his legacy is inherited by the children. Whereas the eldest son is responsible for allocating the legacy livestock, societies follow either the primogeniture inheritance or the division inheritance . The former is the inheritance in which most of the legacy livestock are retained within the eldest son's household with a few livestock allocated among other children. The latter is the inheritance in which the legacy livestock are divided among the children.

The Rendille, Gabbra, and Boran peoples follow the primogeniture inheritance. For them, a father does not transfer the ownership of his livestock to his eldest son during his lifetime. Instead, the eldest son may be given some livestock by his mothers eldest brother. At his father's death, he succeeds to the patrimony and inherits most of his legacy livestock. The larger part of household camels are successively retained by the eldest sons from generation to generation, maintaining the primogeniture inheritance. This does not necessarily mean, however, that an eldest son monopolizes all of his father's camels. Upon inheritance, he is obliged to redistribute a few heads of livestock to each younger brother and sister.

The division inheritance is typically followed by the Turkana, Karimojong and Jie peoples. For them, a father transfers the ownership of his livestock among wives with children during his lifetime for subsistence use and marriage payment, and the remainig few heads of legacy livestock are inherited by negotiation among his children. Household livestock are thus dispersed from generation to generation. The bridewealth livestock, mainly consisting of large livestock, are handed over to the bride's close kin by the groom upon marriage.

Bridewealth payments can be classified roughly into two types: the fixed and negotiated payments. In the former, the groom is responsible for collecting and paying bridewealth to each conventionally designated recipient. For example, the Rendille groom has to hand eight heads of camels (four male and four female) over to the bride's brothers, mother, and mother's eldest brother. In societies with fixed payments, the amount of bridewealth livestock ranges from eight heads, through four of cattle, to three of camels, which is equal to 0.7 - 2.7 times as many as per capita holdings of large livestock.

In the negotiated payment, the amount of bridewealth livestock is negotiated and agreed upon each marriage between the close agnates of the groom and bride, and the groom is responsible for collecting bridewealth livestock and handing them over, ideally in toto, to a close agnate, usually the bride's father, who redistributes them in turn. Among societies with negotiated payments, the amount of bridewealth livestock ranges from five to eighty heads of cattle (the Turkana, whose per capita holdings is 2.8 heads), thirty to seventy (the Jie, whose per capita holding is 3.5 heads) and thirty to fifty, and is thus equal to 1.8 - 28.6 times as many as per capita holdings of cattle as a whole.

Bridewealth tends to be more abundant in societies with negotiated payments than in those with fixed payments, and conversely, per capita holdings of livestock is less in the former than in the latter. Moreover, the former follows the division inheritance, and the latter, the primogeniture. The paradoxical correlations among bridewealth types, per capita holdings of livestock and inheritance systems can be explained by both the ways bridewealth livestock is collected by the groom and redistributed by the recipient.

According to the fixed payment, the groom is responsible for collecting bridewealth, and then hands it over directly to several recipients who are conventionally designated as the bride's elementary kin, namely her brothers, mother, and mother's brothers, instead of handing it over in a lump to a specified person, such as the bride's father. This way, the number of participants in the transactions of bridewealth livestock is very few, and such interpersonal relationships are conventionally stereotyped. Moreover, it is easier for the groom to collect his bridewealth, usually by himself and infrequently aided by "his persons," because the amount of bridewealth is small.

On the other hand, in negotiated payments, the groom is responsible for collecting bridewealth, hands it over in a lump sum to a responsible recipient, who in turn redistributes it. No groom can collect the sufficient amount of bridewealth without requesting "his persons" for aid, because the amount of bridewealth needed is far and away from per capita holdings of livestock. Usually, the responsible recipient also has been already heavily in debt to "his persons'" for his own marriage aid, and thus, when his daughter gets married, he is pressed to pay back his debt and to redistribute some portion of his daughter's bridewealth.

It should be remembered that most societies with negotiated payments follow division inheritance, where household livestock are diffused over the descendants as generations proceed. It means that the corporate identity based on the communal holdings of household livestock weakens with the generations, so that each descendant is driven to strengthen his own reliable partnership with "his persons". The bridewealth livestock are collected and distributed within a wider interpersonal relationships beyond household members, and thus has functions of defining and strengthening the personal networks of the groom and the bride's father beyond individual households, besides confirming affinal relationships.

It has been said that the bridewealth payments can be expected to be high where livestock play a relatively insignificant part in the total economy, and that the negotiated payments derive from the economic motive, whereas the fixed payments derive from the social . These arguments, although usuful to some degree, neglect the fact that livestock are transferred within the framework of social structure.

The negotiated payments are different from the fixed payments in that the former has the function of defining and strengthening personal networks of both the groom and the bride's father. Such function is closely correlated with the unstable intrastructure of household. The fixed payments are more pervasive in societies where the intrastructure of household is regulated and stabilized by the primogeniture inheritance. In contrast, the negotiated payments are more pervasive in societies where the intrastructure of household is weakened by the division inheritance. Bridewealth livestock are used for surmounting such inherent weakness of intra-household solidarity by activating interpersonal relationships beyond the individual household.

Social Transactions and Transfers of Livestock

Among the pastoral societies of East Africa, livestock

are used for social transactions that bind and regulate societal interactions. When certain livestock are transferred between partners, one recognizes that the breadth of one's decision-making is different from society to society because the motives and occasions for livestock transactions and the types of livestock involved are prescribed by social conventions. The East Cushitic peoples, such as the Rendille, Gabbra and Boran peoples, have the peculiar system of livestock transfer classified as the trust system, whereas the East Nilotic peoples, such as the Turkana, Karimojong, Jie, Maasai and Samburu peoples, do not. Such difference is derived not only from the number of animals reared and the scarcity of livestock.

For example, the Rendille have four forms of transaction, namely, gift, exchange, loan and trust. Gift transaction means transferring one's personal camel to another for no direct return, whereas exchange transaction is for a direct return. Loan transaction means transferring a camel to another on condition that the transferred camel itself is returned in the future according to a prescribed convention, and trust transaction means transferring female camels in accordance with the rules of the trust system.

In any camel transaction, there is a clear distinction between the personal camel (alal) and the trust camel (maal), and this is confirmed by the persons concerned. Personal camels are valued higher than trust camels. A man who keeps his personal camel can dispose it as he pleases. All male camels are categorized as personal camels, whereas female camels can be either personal or trust camels. The trustee has no ownership of the trust camels, but holds usufruct rights to their milk, blood, and male offspring. He has to return the camel to his trustor at his request. As long as any trust camel, including the one originally entrusted and its female offspring, is alive, the eldest sons of both parties inherit the credits and debts of their fathers over generations.

The trustee can sublease either the entrusted camel itself or its female offspring to a third party of his choice. A chain of trust relations is then formed on the basis of the dyadic interpersonal relation between the trustor and his immediate trustee. Along the chain of trust relations, any trustee must mark the trust camel as instructed by the first trustor. The first trustor (the owner of original personal camel) retains the ultimate credit, so he is regarded as the owner of all the trust camels transferred through the chain of trust relations. When he irrevocably falls out with the trustees, the first trustor can forcibly withdraw all the trust camels.

The first trustee never subleases the trust camel to the close agnates of his trustor if he belongs to the same clan as the trustor; nor does he sublease it to the clansmen of his trustor if he belongs to a different clan. In the whole chain of trust relations, the close agnates and clansmen demarcate a double boundary, which functions like a semi-permeable membrane. Those trust camels which have been once placed beyond their boundary cannot be brought back in through subleasing. In other words, the solidarity among the close agnates and clansmen becomes obvious in the trust system.

As mentioned above, the trust system works through the medium of the unity of a father with his eldest son. Fundamentally it works on the basis of the favourable societal relations, and at the same time it works together with the structural frame-work of the more corporate groups of close agnates and clansmen within the patri-lineal descent group.

On some occasions and in some social relations, a man is obliged to donate his personal camels to another. Such occasions include the death of parents, circumcision, the killing of an enemy, and marriage. If an eldest son is circumcised or kills an enemy, he is entitled to at least one female camel from his mother's eldest brother, whereas on the same occasion, the other sons are entitled to at least one female camel from his father. Upon marriage, the groom has to pay eight personal camels (four male and four female) as bridewealth to the bride's elementary kin, such as her mother, brothers and mother's eldest brother. Moreover, the bride's eldest brother is expected to give one female camel out of his sister's bridewealth to his father's brother's son. Since the bride's father has no share in the bridewealth camels of his daughter, he cannot divert them to his own marriage.

The above occasions are landmarks in the developmental cycle of the household as well as in the age-set cycle. The eldest son is obliged to donate personal camels to his own and his wife's elementary kin, his father's brother's eldest son, and his sisters eldest son, and conversely he can receive personal camels from his sister's husband, his sister's daughter's husband, and his mother's eldest brother. The relationships among the effective kindred are maintained and reinforced by the reciprocal donation of personal camels, and are structured not only by the unity of a father with his eldest son, but also by the relationship of a mother's eldest brother to a sister's eldest son, and by the relationship among the eldest sons within close agnates.

Pliability of Camel Transaction

For the Rendille, the four forms of transaction above are formal classifications. In reality, one form of transaction can turn into another, depending on the relative degree of solidarity between the giver and recipient, and the circumstances of transaction. Sometimes, a calf-camel is adopted in order to ensure milk from the mother-camel. When one requests a calf-camel from another for the purpose of adoption, the latter usually gives away either one male calf as a personal camel or one female calf as a trust camel. In this case, a man was donated a female calf by his mother's eldest brother in return for the female camel which his father once handed over to the latter as a personal camel in compliance with his request for bridewealth aid.

A lactating camel is temporarily lent out to someone for the duration of lactation, and soon after lactation stops, the borrower has to return it to the lender. But, there was a case where a son-in-law lent out a lactating female with a suckling calf to his father-in-law and then turned it into a trust camel. The reason was that the loan camel with milk should be treated as trust camel once it bore a calf in the borrower's pen. That camel bore a calf while the son-in-law refrained from requesting its return. The above transactions were made through moral reciprocity.

The Rendille have a standardized exchange rate for one type of livestock to another. For example, one head of heifer-camel is equivalent to either one head of heifer or 12 heads of adolescent small stock. Also, one female calf of either camel or cattle is exchangeable for one ox-camel or ox. This exchange rate is applicable to neither transactions with livestock dealers nor those at the livestock market, where transactions are negotiated, but applicable only to transactions within the communal Rendille society. Also, one type of livestock may be exchanged with livestock combined with other goods, for example, sack of maize.

Some conventional barters may take place over time, even as long as after twenty years, within Rendille society. Usually, the giver of female camel can claim cancellation of the barter, either if his camel reproduced overly in favour of the recipient, or if the transaction had violated the conventional exchange rate. Such unexpected profit on the part of the recipient or subjective hindsight of distorted exchange is sufficient for the original owner to contest the transaction. The contestation is never treated indifferently and taken up publicly. This suggests that excessive profit through barter of livestock is checked by public opinion and that the owner of personal camel can exercise very strong discretion.

Whereas camels are esteemed more than cattle by the Rendille, there is less demand for camels, and prices offered often fall short of the herder's expectation. Therefore, he first exchanges the less demanded camel for the more demanded cattle using the conventional rate in his network, and then sells that cattle in the market. This manipulation of the local dual economy enables the he rder get through the disadvantage to market economy.

8

Distribution of Houseless (India, States, Union Territories, Districts 2001)

Houseless Population (2001)

India/State/ District	*Total/ Rural/ Urban*	*Number of House-holds*	*Persons*	*Males*	*Females*
(1)	*(2)*	*(3)*	*(4)*	*(5)*	*(6)*
INDIA	Total	447,552	1,943,476	1,136,322	807,154
	Rural	259,742	1,164,877	633,978	530,899
	Urban	187,810	778,599	502,344	276,255
JAMMU & KASHMIR	Total	2,123	12,751	7,206	5,545
	Rural	1,641	10,129	5,598	4,531
	Urban	482	2,622	1,608	1,014
Kupwara	Total	56	335	173	162
	Rural	56	335	173	162
	Urban	-	-	-	-
Baramula	Total	134	1,074	723	351
	Rural	114	942	651	291
	Urban	20	132	72	60
Srinagar	Total	232	1,613	901	712
	Rural	82	519	280	239
	Urban	150	1,094	621	473

Contd.

Contd.

(1)	(2)	(3)	(4)	(5)	(6)
Badgam	Total	47	390	279	111
	Rural	26	204	114	90
	Urban	21	186	165	21
Pulwama	Total	41	206	108	98
	Rural	35	170	89	81
	Urban	6	36	19	17
Anantnag	Total	256	1,681	916	765
	Rural	223	1,495	822	673
	Urban	33	186	94	92
Leh (Ladakh)	Total	28	66	40	26
	Rural	28	66	40	26
	Urban	-	-	-	-
Kargil	Total	7	18	10	8
	Rural	7	18	10	8
	Urban	-	-	-	-
Doda	Total	92	534	282	252
	Rural	72	430	224	206
	Urban	20	104	58	46
Udhampur	Total	184	1,157	639	518
	Rural	157	1,046	567	479
	Urban	27	111	72	39
Punch	Total	21	126	59	67
	Rural	21	126	59	67
	Urban	-	-	-	-
Rajauri	Total	103	612	336	276
	Rural	97	595	326	269
	Urban	6	17	10	7
Jammu	Total	363	1,701	978	723
	Rural	236	1,205	651	554
	Urban	127	496	327	169
Kathua	Total	559	3,238	1,762	1,476
	Rural	487	2,978	1,592	1,386
	Urban	72	260	170	90
HIMACHAL PRADESH	Total	1,634	8,364	5,580	2,784
	Rural	1,356	7,047	4,736	2,311
	Urban	278	1,317	844	473

Contd.

Contd.

(1)	*(2)*	*(3)*	*(4)*	*(5)*	*(6)*
Chamba	Total	54	275	198	77
	Rural	39	210	165	45
	Urban	15	65	33	32
Kangra	Total	494	2,394	1,624	770
	Rural	432	2,100	1,435	665
	Urban	62	294	189	105
Lahul & Spiti	Total	4	4	3	1
	Rural	4	4	3	1
	Urban	-	-	-	-
Kullu	Total	45	234	151	83
	Rural	14	57	41	16
	Urban	31	177	110	67
Mandi	Total	179	875	544	331
	Rural	120	617	397	220
	Urban	59	258	147	111
Hamirpur	Total	100	456	287	169
	Rural	96	446	281	165
	Urban	4	10	6	4
Una	Total	295	1,657	1,038	619
	Rural	292	1,616	1,004	612
	Urban	3	41	34	7
Bilaspur	Total	117	615	408	207
	Rural	105	570	367	203
	Urban	12	45	41	4
Solan	Total	159	896	678	218
	Rural	141	819	634	185
	Urban	18	77	44	33
Sirmaur	Total	72	419	270	149
	Rural	52	322	208	114
	Urban	20	97	62	35
Shimla	Total	115	539	379	160
	Rural	61	286	201	85
	Urban	54	253	178	75
Kinnaur	Total	-	-	-	-
	Rural	-	-	-	-
	Urban	-	-	-	-

Contd.

Contd.

(1)	(2)	(3)	(4)	(5)	(6)
PUNJAB	Total	8,579	46,958	28,251	18,707
	Rural	4,065	23,549	13,733	9,816
	Urban	4,514	23,409	14,518	8,891
Gurdaspur	Total	559	2,972	1,708	1,264
	Rural	373	2,173	1,243	930
	Urban	186	799	465	334
Amritsar	Total	885	7,246	4,739	2,507
	Rural	251	1,708	953	755
	Urban	634	5,538	3,786	1,752
Kapurthala	Total	381	2,180	1,183	997
	Rural	209	1,175	644	531
	Urban	172	1,005	539	466
Jalandhar	Total	553	2,785	1,632	1,153
	Rural	261	1,478	845	633
	Urban	292	1,307	787	520
Hoshiarpur	Total	517	3,063	1,863	1,200
	Rural	420	2,447	1,512	935
	Urban	97	616	351	265
Nawanshahr *	Total	299	1,485	872	613
	Rural	188	914	570	344
	Urban	111	571	302	269
Rupnagar	Total	585	3,134	1,913	1,221
	Rural	465	2,561	1,576	985
	Urban	120	573	337	236
Fatehgarh Sahib *	Total	348	2,396	1,510	886
	Rural	133	909	609	300
	Urban	215	1,487	901	586
Ludhiana	Total	1,629	7,442	4,788	2,654
	Rural	367	2,423	1,474	949
	Urban	1,262	5,019	3,314	1,705
Moga *	Total	210	1,074	608	466
	Rural	105	500	284	216
	Urban	105	574	324	250
Firozpur	Total	421	2,337	1,301	1,036
	Rural	224	1,428	763	665
	Urban	197	909	538	371

Contd.

Contd.

(1)	(2)	(3)	(4)	(5)	(6)
Muktsar *	Total	248	1,191	666	525
	Rural	103	499	302	197
	Urban	145	692	364	328
Faridkot	Total	139	641	377	264
	Rural	97	498	270	228
	Urban	42	143	107	36
Bathinda	Total	415	2,020	1,162	858
	Rural	176	962	558	404
	Urban	239	1,058	604	454
Mansa *	Total	289	1,609	860	749
	Rural	226	1,267	678	589
	Urban	63	342	182	160
Sangrur	Total	606	3,249	1,783	1,466
	Rural	297	1,689	910	779
	Urban	309	1,560	873	687
Patiala	Total	495	2,134	1,286	848
	Rural	170	918	542	376
	Urban	325	1,216	744	472
CHANDIGARH	Total	757	2,722	2,588	134
	Rural	32	41	38	3
	Urban	725	2,681	2,550	131
Chandigarh	Total	757	2,722	2,588	134
	Rural	32	41	38	3
	Urban	725	2,681	2,550	131
UTTARANCHAL	Total	2,940	14,703	10,496	4,207
	Rural	1,942	10,768	7,762	3,006
	Urban	998	3,935	2,734	1,201
Uttarkashi	Total	187	1,021	765	256
	Rural	173	913	673	240
	Urban	14	108	92	16
Chamoli	Total	209	1,001	794	207
	Rural	151	747	610	137
	Urban	58	254	184	70
Rudraprayag *	Total	70	475	406	69
	Rural	68	467	402	65
	Urban	2	8	4	4

Contd.

Contd.

(1)	(2)	(3)	(4)	(5)	(6)
Tehri Garhwal	Total	172	970	811	159
	Rural	111	622	527	95
	Urban	61	348	284	64
Dehradun	Total	689	3,640	2,233	1,407
	Rural	337	2,249	1,282	967
	Urban	352	1,391	951	440
Garhwal	Total	288	1,250	1,056	194
	Rural	264	1,180	992	188
	Urban	24	70	64	6
Pithoragarh	Total	66	357	264	93
	Rural	59	330	249	81
	Urban	7	27	15	12
Bageshwar	Total	159	937	892	45
	Rural	149	906	867	39
	Urban	10	31	25	6
Almora	Total	129	800	630	170
	Rural	113	714	573	141
	Urban	16	86	57	29
Champawat	Total	63	304	198	106
	Rural	40	189	134	55
	Urban	23	115	64	51
Nainital	Total	182	941	727	214
	Rural	105	617	483	134
	Urban	77	324	244	80
Udham Singh Nagar *	Total	152	573	339	234
	Rural	75	317	191	126
	Urban	77	256	148	108
Hardwar	Total	574	2,434	1,381	1,053
	Rural	297	1,517	779	738
	Urban	277	917	602	315
HARYANA	Total	11,860	59,360	34,751	24,609
	Rural	6,806	35,384	20,724	14,660
	Urban	5,054	23,976	14,027	9,949
Panchkula *	Total	454	2,148	1,255	893
	Rural	145	829	517	312
	Urban	309	1,319	738	581

Contd.

Contd.

(1)	(2)	(3)	(4)	(5)	(6)
Ambala	Total	446	1,926	1,187	739
	Rural	290	1,506	886	620
	Urban	156	420	301	119
Yamunanagar	Total	368	1,675	953	722
	Rural	139	674	395	279
	Urban	229	1,001	558	443
Kurukshetra	Total	440	2,473	1,704	769
	Rural	155	942	581	361
	Urban	285	1,531	1,123	408
Kaithal	Total	120	638	374	264
	Rural	83	433	250	183
	Urban	37	205	124	81
Karnal	Total	485	2,605	1,682	923
	Rural	321	1,841	1,199	642
	Urban	164	764	483	281
Panipat	Total	346	1,418	813	605
	Rural	148	715	410	305
	Urban	198	703	403	300
Sonipat	Total	1,144	6,139	3,616	2,523
	Rural	936	4,963	2,955	2,008
	Urban	208	1,176	661	515
Jind	Total	275	1,293	775	518
	Rural	138	693	418	275
	Urban	137	600	357	243
Fatehabad *	Total	633	3,178	1,798	1,380
	Rural	328	1,690	966	724
	Urban	305	1,488	832	656
Sirsa	Total	1,131	6,047	3,296	2,751
	Rural	723	3,834	2,124	1,710
	Urban	408	2,213	1,172	1,041
Hisar	Total	967	4,552	2,714	1,838
	Rural	581	2,880	1,697	1,183
	Urban	386	1,672	1,017	655
Bhiwani	Total	884	4,595	2,607	1,988
	Rural	582	3,065	1,756	1,309
	Urban	302	1,530	851	679

Contd.

Contd.

(1)	(2)	(3)	(4)	(5)	(6)
Rohtak	Total	285	1,401	855	546
	Rural	149	795	496	299
	Urban	136	606	359	247
Jhajjar *	Total	450	2,156	1,283	873
	Rural	196	914	565	349
	Urban	254	1,242	718	524
Mahendragarh	Total	880	4,401	2,400	2,001
	Rural	568	2,903	1,590	1,313
	Urban	312	1,498	810	688
Rewari	Total	978	4,725	2,826	1,899
	Rural	598	3,086	1,820	1,266
	Urban	380	1,639	1,006	633
Gurgaon	Total	1,074	5,318	3,068	2,250
	Rural	624	3,121	1,824	1,297
	Urban	450	2,197	1,244	953
Faridabad	Total	500	2,672	1,545	1,127
	Rural	102	500	275	225
	Urban	398	2,172	1,270	902
DELHI	Total	10,044	24,966	21,247	3,719
	Rural	235	1,063	684	379
	Urban	9,809	23,903	20,563	3,340
North West *	Total	1,178	2,763	2,102	661
	Rural	41	227	131	96
	Urban	1,137	2,536	1,971	565
North *	Total	2,721	7,087	6,652	435
	Rural	4	28	28	-
	Urban	2,717	7,059	6,624	435
North East *	Total	395	967	715	252
	Rural	28	64	44	20
	Urban	367	903	671	232
East*	Total	419	854	678	176
	Rural	2	19	7	12
	Urban	417	835	671	164
New Delhi	Total	217	709	518	191
	Rural	-	-	-	-
	Urban	217	709	518	191

Contd.

Contd.

(1)	(2)	(3)	(4)	(5)	(6)
Central *	Total	2,444	5,676	5,340	336
	Rural	-	-	-	-
	Urban	2,444	5,676	5,340	336
West *	Total	969	2,135	1,782	353
	Rural	30	150	119	31
	Urban	939	1,985	1,663	322
South West *	Total	553	1,954	1,302	652
	Rural	95	430	275	155
	Urban	458	1,524	1,027	497
South *	Total	1,148	2,821	2,158	663
	Rural	35	145	80	65
	Urban	1,113	2,676	2,078	598
RAJASTHAN	Total	27,196	143,497	80,283	63,214
	Rural	16,194	87,866	47,975	39,891
	Urban	11,002	55,631	32,308	23,323
Ganganagar	Total	972	5,087	2,830	2,257
	Rural	637	3,571	1,992	1,579
	Urban	335	1,516	838	678
Hanumangarh *	Total	474	2,753	1,459	1,294
	Rural	383	2,323	1,232	1,091
	Urban	91	430	227	203
Bikaner	Total	665	3,693	2,002	1,691
	Rural	319	1,874	1,017	857
	Urban	346	1,819	985	834
Churu	Total	378	2,139	1,151	988
	Rural	201	1,237	647	590
	Urban	177	902	504	398
Jhunjhunun	Total	780	4,465	2,391	2,074
	Rural	467	2,676	1,450	1,226
	Urban	313	1,789	941	848
Alwar	Total	1,090	5,488	3,031	2,457
	Rural	739	3,726	2,026	1,700
	Urban	351	1,762	1,005	757
Bharatpur	Total	324	1,675	933	742
	Rural	213	1,151	652	499
	Urban	111	524	281	243

Contd.

Contd.

(1)	(2)	(3)	(4)	(5)	(6)
Dhaulpur	Total	298	1,438	731	707
	Rural	250	1,200	596	604
	Urban	48	238	135	103
Karauli *	Total	208	1,202	656	546
	Rural	167	994	547	447
	Urban	41	208	109.	99
Sawai Madhopur	Total	419	2,049	1,133	916
	Rural	276	1,514	828	686
	Urban	143	535	305	230
Dausa *	Total	422	2,394	1,305	1,089
	Rural	324	1,934	1,060	874
	Urban	98	460	245	215
Jaipur	Total	3,090	15,047	8,540	6,507
	Rural	978	5,744	3,214	2,530
	Urban	2,112	9,303	5,326	3,977
Sikar	Total	1,083	6,558	3,650	2,908
	Rural	732	4,369	2,471	1,898
	Urban	351	2,189	1,179	1,010
Nagaur	Total	730	3,976	2,052	1,924
	Rural	471	2,658	1,313	1,345
	Urban	259	1,318	739	579
Jodhpur	Total	896	4,334	2,469	1,865
	Rural	413	2,125	1,242	883
	Urban	483	2,209	1,227	982
Jaisalmer	Total	195	1,103	620	483
	Rural	173	967	540	427
	Urban	22	136	80	56
Barmer	Total	458	2,749	1,500	1,249
	Rural	424	2,624	1,425	1,199
	Urban	34	125	75	50
Jalor	Total	665	3,759	2,091	1,668
	Rural	566	3,215	1,797	1,418
	Urban	99	544	294	250
Sirohi	Total	806	3,869	2,370	1,499
	Rural	522	2,779	1,767	1,012
	Urban	284	1,090	603	487

Contd.

Contd.

(1)	(2)	(3)	(4)	(5)	(6)
Pali	Total	878	4,585	2,520	2,065
	Rural	679	3,619	1,991	1,628
	Urban	199	966	529	437
Ajmer	Total	1,859	11,798	8,006	3,792
	Rural	621	3,124	1,686	1,438
	Urban	1,238	8,674	6,320	2,354
Tonk	Total	665	3,372	1,883	1,489
	Rural	460	2,363	1,329	1,034
	Urban	205	1,009	554	455
Bundi	Total	1,111	5,881	3,234	2,647
	Rural	866	4,619	2,568	2,051
	Urban	245	1,262	666	596
Bhilwara	Total	1,378	6,917	3,718	3,199
	Rural	794	4,090	2,172	1,918
	Urban	584	2,827	1,546	1,281
Rajsamand *	Total	575	2,915	1,531	1,384
	Rural	413	2,083	1,088	995
	Urban	162	832	443	389
Udaipur	Total	1,103	5,814	3,090	2,724
	Rural	864	4,541	2,354	2,187
	Urban	239	1,273	736	537
Dungarpur	Total	252	1,319	697	622
	Rural	203	1,021	522	499
	Urban	49	298	175	123
Banswara	Total	292	1,531	804	727
	Rural	138	648	347	301
	Urban	154	883	457	426
Chittaurgarh	Total	1,226	6,130	3,339	2,791
	Rural	845	4,344	2,350	1,994
	Urban	381	1,786	989	797
Kota	Total	2,396	11,403	6,258	5,145
	Rural	868	4,510	2,425	2,085
	Urban	1,528	6,893	3,833	3,060
Baran *	Total	837	4,669	2,480	2,189
	Rural	604	3,407	1,829	1,578
	Urban	233	1,262	651	611

Contd.

Contd.

(1)	(2)	(3)	(4)	(5)	(6)
Jhalawar	Total	671	3,385	1,809	1,576
	Rural	584	2,816	1,498	1,318
	Urban	87	569	311	258
UTTAR PRADESH	Total	43,033	201,029	128,278	72,751
	Rural	21,800	104,387	57,880	46,507
	Urban	21,233	96,642	70,398	26,244
Saharanpur	Total	358	1,375	839	536
	Rural	159	793	464	329
	Urban	199	582	375	207
Muzaffarnagar	Total	483	2,874	1,687	1,187
	Rural	276	1,709	967	742
	Urban	207	1,165	720	445
Bijnor	Total	261	1,437	794	643
	Rural	175	953	512	441
	Urban	86	484	282	202
Moradabad	Total	311	1,891	1,128	763
	Rural	145	751	445	306
	Urban	166	1,140	683	457
Rampur	Total	115	524	305	219
	Rural	68	332	207	125
	Urban	47	192	98	94
Jyotiba Phule Nagar *	Total	119	605	342	263
	Rural	37	260	153	107
	Urban	82	345	189	156
Meerut	Total	1,110	5,379	2,944	2,435
	Rural	209	1,193	662	531
	Urban	901	4,186	2,282	1,904
Baghpat *	Total	79	377	223	154
	Rural	40	217	128	89
	Urban	39	160	95	65
Ghaziabad	Total	1,691	6,612	4,212	2,400
	Rural	303	1,738	1,018	720
	Urban	1,388	4,874	3,194	1,680
Gautam Buddha Nagar *	Total	571	2,577	1,507	1,070
	Rural	113	581	354	227
	Urban	458	1,996	1,153	843

Contd.

Contd.

(1)	*(2)*	*(3)*	*(4)*	*(5)*	*(6)*
Bulandshahar	Total	291	1,553	882	671
	Rural	92	419	254	165
	Urban	199	1,134	628	506
Aligarh	Total	449	2,067	1,196	871
	Rural	211	1,047	609	438
	Urban	238	1,020	587	433
Hathras *	Total	204	1,013	565	448
	Rural	182	903	509	394
	Urban	22	110	56	54
Mathura	Total	657	3,017	1,840	1,177
	Rural	241	1,231	724	507
	Urban	416	1,786	1,116	670
Agra	Total	712	3,731	2,209	1,522
	Rural	276	1,494	796	698
	Urban	436	2,237	1,413	824
Firozabad	Total	426	1,718	1,027	691
	Rural	144	626	359	267
	Urban	282	1,092	668	424
Etah	Total	530	2,438	1,379	1,059
	Rural	429	1,927	1,079	848
	Urban	101	511	300	211
Mainpuri	Total	848	3,967	2,270	1,697
	Rural	720	3,344	1,920	1,424
	Urban	128	623	350	273
Budaun	Total	302	1,385	809	576
	Rural	234	1,131	668	463
	Urban	68	254	141	113
Bareilly	Total	552	2,610	1,500	1,110
	Rural	283	1,489	862	627
	Urban	269	1,121	638	483
Pilibhit	Total	176	929	538	391
	Rural	80	406	226	180
	Urban	96	523	312	211
Shahjahanpur	Total	334	1,531	861	670
	Rural	162	801	450	351
	Urban	172	730	411	319

Contd.

Contd.

(1)	(2)	(3)	(4)	(5)	(6)
Kheri	Total	291	1,442	815	627
	Rural	226	1,110	619	491
	Urban	65	332	196	136
Sitapur	Total	452	2,008	1,081	927
	Rural	343	1,556	830	726
	Urban	109	452	251	201
Hardoi	Total	467	2,182	1,248	934
	Rural	379	1,740	1,010	730
	Urban	88	442	238	204
Unnao	Total	747	3,276	1,861	1,415
	Rural	672	2,921	1,636	1,285
	Urban	75	355	225	130
Lucknow	Total	4,008	8,987	7,119	1,868
	Rural	283	1,225	698	527
	Urban	3,725	7,762	6,421	1,341
Rae Bareli	Total	1,446	6,115	3,199	2,916
	Rural	1,377	5,775	3,013	2,762
	Urban	69	340	186	154
Farrukhabad	Total	282	2,259	1,673	586
	Rural	191	1,758	1,357	401
	Urban	91	501	316	185
Kannauj *	Total	195	936	533	403
	Rural	129	615	373	242
	Urban	66	321	160	161
Etawah	Total	634	2,617	1,471	1,146
	Rural	526	2,085	1,169	916
	Urban	108	532	302	230
Auraiya *	Total	267	1,367	811	556
	Rural	187	932	550	382
	Urban	80	435	261	174
Kanpur Dehat	Total	333	1,628	856	772
	Rural	327	1,613	850	763
	Urban	6	15	6	9
Kanpur Nagar	Total	6,175	30,721	26,919	3,802
	Rural	311	1,343	771	572
	Urban	5,864	29,378	26,148	3,230

Contd.

Contd.

(1)	(2)	(3)	(4)	(5)	(6)
Jalaun	Total	169	963	580	383
	Rural	108	687	422	265
	Urban	61	276	158	118
Jhansi	Total	362	1,895	1,141	754
	Rural	94	442	242	200
	Urban	268	1,453	899	554
Lalitpur	Total	290	1,167	669	498
	Rural	251	1,027	585	442
	Urban	39	140	84	56
Hamirpur	Total	147	713	408	305
	Rural	131	650	373	277
	Urban	16	63	35	28
Mahoba *	Total	168	598	365	233
	Rural	110	378	234	144
	Urban	58	220	131	89
Banda	Total	325	1,684	953	731
	Rural	153	861	460	401
	Urban	172	823	493	330
Chitrakoot *	Total	73	363	202	161
	Rural	54	281	153	128
	Urban	19	82	49	33
Fatehpur	Total	526	2,631	1,449	1,182
	Rural	503	2,524	1,392	1,132
	Urban	23	107	57	50
Pratapgarh	Total	658	3,200	1,658	1,542
	Rural	624	3,027	1,562	1,465
	Urban	34	173	96	77
Kaushambi *	Total	174	850	489	361
	Rural	137	667	385	282
	Urban	37	183	104	79
Allahabad	Total	2,758	20,253	14,077	6,176
	Rural	1,034	5,023	2,645	2,378
	Urban	1,724	15,230	11,432	3,798
Barabanki	Total	600	2,497	1,369	1,128
	Rural	460	2,135	1,138	997
	Urban	140	362	231	131

Contd.

Contd.

(1)	(2)	(3)	(4)	(5)	(6)
Faizabad	Total	711	3,093	1,692	1,401
	Rural	610	2,789	1,504	1,285
	Urban	101	304	188	116
Ambedkar Nagar *	Total	265	1,219	644	575
	Rural	260	1,207	637	570
	Urban	5	12	7	5
Sultanpur	Total	999	5,810	3,085	2,725
	Rural	774	3,804	2,007	1,797
	Urban	225	2,006	1,078	928
Bahraich	Total	182	902	503	399
	Rural	162	844	469	375
	Urban	20	58	34	24
Shrawasti *	Total	170	865	476	389
	Rural	169	864	476	388
	Urban	1	1	-	1
Balrampur *	Total	92	441	258	183
	Rural	86	421	246	175
	Urban	6	20	12	8
Gonda	Total	410	1,869	1,101	768
	Rural	387	1,746	1,012	734
	Urban	23	123	89	34
Siddharthnagar	Total	460	2,023	1,164	859
	Rural	442	1,966	1,118	848
	Urban	18	57	46	11
Basti	Total	492	2,105	1,247	858
	Rural	459	2,024	1,198	826
	Urban	33	81	49	32
Sant Kabir Nagar *	Total	151	606	344	262
	Rural	138	542	314	228
	Urban	13	64	30	34
Mahrajganj	Total	404	1,855	979	876
	Rural	359	1,625	856	769
	Urban	45	230	123	107
Gorakhpur	Total	811	3,153	1,997	1,156
	Rural	256	1,205	665	540
	Urban	555	1,948	1,332	616

Contd.

Contd.

(1)	(2)	(3)	(4)	(5)	(6)
Kushinagar *	Total	361	1,486	760	726
	Rural	347	1,442	731	711
	Urban	14	44	29	15
Deoria	Total	627	2,908	1,582	1,326
	Rural	477	2,209	1,179	1,030
	Urban	150	699	403	296
Azamgarh	Total	742	4,031	2,209	1,822
	Rural	677	3,657	2,008	1,649
	Urban	65	374	201	173
Mau	Total	416	1,942	1,025	917
	Rural	293	1,262	639	623
	Urban	123	680	386	294
Ballia	Total	237	1,225	663	562
	Rural	216	1,152	616	536
	Urban	21	73	47	26
Jaunpur	Total	833	4,111	2,169	1,942
	Rural	798	3,946	2,082	1,864
	Urban	35	165	87	78
Ghazipur	Total	586	2,497	1,318	1,179
	Rural	515	2,260	1,200	1,060
	Urban	71	237	118	119
Chandauli *	Total	448	2,601	1,403	1,198
	Rural	362	1,848	971	877
	Urban	86	753	432	321
Varanasi	Total	781	3,209	1,898	1,311
	Rural	184	1,056	561	495
	Urban	597	2,153	1,337	816
Sant Ravidas	Total	201	882	508	374
Nagar Bhadohi *	Rural	198	863	494	369
	Urban	3	19	14	5
Mirzapur	Total	445	1,930	1,067	863
	Rural	370	1,654	892	762
	Urban	75	276	175	101
Sonbhadra	Total	83	304	183	121
	Rural	72	201	172	109
	Urban	11	23	11	12

Contd.

Contd.

(1)	(2)	(3)	(4)	(5)	(6)
BIHAR	Total	6,940	42,498	27,895	14,603
	Rural	4,235	29,768	19,951	9,817
	Urban	2,705	12,730	7,944	4,786
Pashchim Champaran	Total	77	334	178	156
	Rural	47	200	107	93
	Urban	30	134	71	63
Purba Champaran	Total	162	853	461	392
	Rural	121	641	351	290
	Urban	41	212	110	102
Sheohar *	Total	17	51	28	23
	Rural	17	51	28	23
	Urban	-	-	-	-
Sitamarhi	Total	123	443	213	230
	Rural	81	294	154	140
	Urban	42	149	59	90
Madhubani	Total	153	800	406	394
	Rural	120	620	316	304
	Urban	33	180	90	90
Supaul *	Total	42	185	97	88
	Rural	40	182	94	88
	Urban	2	3	3	-
Araria	Total	73	266	125	141
	Rural	69	246	116	130
	Urban	4	20	9	11
Kishanganj	Total	80	254	164	90
	Rural	47	122	75	47
	Urban	33	132	89	43
Purnia	Total	100	393	224	169
	Rural	53	185	101	84
	Urban	47	208	123	85
Katihar	Total	134	514	269	245
	Rural	94	439	221	218
	Urban	40	75	48	27
Madhepura	Total	47	223	120	103
	Rural	40	204	110	94
	Urban	7	19	10	9

Contd.

Contd.

(1)	(2)	(3)	(4)	(5)	(6)
Saharsa	Total	51	247	132	115
	Rural	33	154	72	82
	Urban	18	93	60	33
Darbhanga	Total	141	731	406	325
	Rural	120	637	349	288
	Urban	21	94	57	37
Muzaffarpur	Total	301	1,870	870	1,000
	Rural	260	1,705	770	935
	Urban	41	165	100	65
Gopalganj	Total	73	398	209	189
	Rural	66	378	198	180
	Urban	7	20	11	9
Siwan	Total	259	1,363	743	620
	Rural	210	1,097	567	530
	Urban	49	266	176	90
Saran	Total	276	1,637	909	728
	Rural	245	1,497	821	676
	Urban	31	140	88	52
Vaishali	Total	183	929	478	451
	Rural	171	854	431	423
	Urban	12	75	47	28
Samastipur	Total	470	10,628	9,969	659
	Rural	437	10,482	9,887	595
	Urban	33	146	82	64
Begusarai	Total	182	950	527	423
	Rural	94	409	241	168
	Urban	88	541	286	255
Khagaria	Total	57	255	130	125
	Rural	42	195	101	94
	Urban	15	60	29	31
Bhagalpur	Total	191	828	448	380
	Rural	113	514	279	235
	Urban	78	314	169	145
Banka *	Total	35	140	75	65
	Rural	35	140	75	65
	Urban	-	-	-	-

Contd.

Contd.

(1)	(2)	(3)	(4)	(5)	(6)
Munger	Total	43	219	115	104
	Rural	18	101	46	55
	Urban	25	118	69	49
Lakhisarai *	Total	170	1,563	840	723
	Rural	28	125	61	64
	Urban	142	1,438	779	659
Sheikhpura *	Total	42	216	107	109
	Rural	24	134	69	65
	Urban	18	82	38	44
Nalanda	Total	192	884	474	410
	Rural	134	612	337	275
	Urban	58	272	137	135
Patna	Total	1,609	7,016	4,790	2,226
	Rural	194	907	479	428
	Urban	1,415	6,109	4,311	1,798
Bhojpur	Total	176	757	422	335
	Rural	125	494	269	225
	Urban	51	263	153	110
Buxar *	Total	90	480	265	215
	Rural	75	421	239	182
	Urban	15	59	26	33
Kaimur (Bhabua) *	Total	137	718	387	331
	Rural	135	714	384	330
	Urban	2	4	3	1
Rohtas	Total	236	1,226	644	582
	Rural	189	1,009	534	475
	Urban	47	217	110	107
Jehanabad	Total	280	1,322	702	620
	Rural	254	1,170	627	543
	Urban	26	152	75	77
Aurangabad	Total	243	1,364	700	664
	Rural	180	1,038	513	525
	Urban	63	326	187	139
Gaya	Total	306	1,427	733	694
	Rural	156	846	428	418
	Urban	150	581	305	276

Contd.

Contd.

(1)	(2)	(3)	(4)	(5)	(6)
Nawada	Total	102	558	275	283
	Rural	90	519	255	264
	Urban	12	39	20	19
Jamui *	Total	87	456	260	196
	Rural	78	432	246	186
	Urban	9	24	14	10
SIKKIM	Total	80	286	173	113
	Rural	55	228	130	98
	Urban	25	58	43	15
North	Total	6	31	15	16
	Rural	3	13	5	8
	Urban	3	18	10	8
West	Total	19	82	44	38
	Rural	17	80	43	37
	Urban	2	2	1	1
South	Total	33	95	65	30
	Rural	24	85	55	30
	Urban	9	10	10	-
East	Total	22	78	49	29
	Rural	11	50	27	23
	Urban	11	28	22	6
ARUNACHAL PRADESH	Total	105	442	251	191
	Rural	82	360	208	152
	Urban	23	82	43	39
Tawang	Total	1	3	-	3
	Rural	-	-	-	-
	Urban	1	3	-	3
West Kameng	Total	6	16	10	6
	Rural	6	16	10	6
	Urban	-	-	-	-
East Kameng	Total	2	8	3	5
	Rural	1	3	2	1
	Urban	1	5	1	4
Papum Pare *	Total	16	78	48	30
	Rural	1	10	9	1
	Urban	15	68	39	29

Contd.

Contd.

(1)	*(2)*	*(3)*	*(4)*	*(5)*	*(6)*
Lower Subansiri	Total	25	116	65	51
	Rural	25	116	65	51
	Urban	-	-	-	-
Upper Subansiri	Total	-	-	-	-
	Rural	-	-	-	-
	Urban	-	-	-	-
West Siang	Total	5	43	27	16
	Rural	4	42	26	16
	Urban	1	1	1	-
East Siang	Total	4	18	10	8
	Rural	2	16	9	7
	Urban	2	2	1	1
Upper Siang *	Total	-	-	-	-
	Rural	-	-	-	-
	Urban	-	-	-	-
Dibang Valley	Total	2	4	3	1
	Rural	2	4	3	1
	Urban	-	-	-	-
Lohit	Total	12	12	10	2
	Rural	11	11	10	1
	Urban	1	1	-	1
Changlang	Total	31	138	72	66
	Rural	29	136	71	65
	Urban	2	2	1	1
Tirap	Total	1	6	3	3
	Rural	1	6	3	3
	Urban	-	-	-	-
NAGALAND	Total	452	2,002	1,165	837
	Rural	260	1,254	712	542
	Urban	192	748	453	295
Mon	Total	8	38	19	19
	Rural	8	38	19	19
	Urban	-	-	-	-
Tuensang	Total	54	350	212	138
	Rural	53	344	208	136
	Urban	1	6	4	2

Contd.

Contd.

(1)	(2)	(3)	(4)	(5)	(6)
Mokokchung	Total	24	112	47	65
	Rural	4	25	13	12
	Urban	20	87	34	53
Zunheboto	Total	43	218	113	105
	Rural	32	151	77	74
	Urban	11	67	36	31
Wokha	Total	48	214	120	94
	Rural	17	75	36	39
	Urban	31	139	84	55
Dimapur *	Total	134	473	317	156
	Rural	15	62	43	19
	Urban	119	411	274	137
Kohima	Total	132	567	318	249
	Rural	122	529	297	232
	Urban	10	38	21	17
Phek	Total	9	30	19	11
	Rural	9	30	19	11
	Urban	-	-	-	-
MANIPUR	Total	522	2,607	1,312	1,295
	Rural	429	2,235	1,095	1,140
	Urban	93	372	217	155
Senapati (Excl. 3 sub-distt.)	Total	15	96	49	47
	Rural	15	96	49	47
	Urban	-	-	-	-
Tamenglong	Total	6	25	15	10
	Rural	6	25	15	10
	Urban	-	-	-	-
Churachandpur	Total	142	741	366	375
	Rural	142	741	366	375
	Urban	-	-	-	-
Bishnupur	Total	47	239	118	121
	Rural	36	190	92	98
	Urban	11	49	26	23
Thoubal	Total	23	102	51	51
	Rural	17	73	36	37
	Urban	6	29	15	14

Contd.

Contd.

(1)	*(2)*	*(3)*	*(4)*	*(5)*	*(6)*
Imphal West	Total	77	286	165	121
	Rural	24	108	53	55
	Urban	53	178	112	66
Imphal East *	Total	56	269	140	129
	Rural	38	178	91	87
	Urban	18	91	49	42
Ukhrul	Total	19	70	35	35
	Rural	19	70	35	35
	Urban	-	-	-	-
Chandel	Total	137	779	373	406
	Rural	132	754	358	396
	Urban	5	25	15	10
MIZORAM	Total	72	336	182	154
	Rural	15	73	44	29
	Urban	57	263	138	125
Mamit *	Total	4	22	17	5
	Rural	4	22	17	5
	Urban	-	-	-	-
Kolasib *	Total	-	-	-	-
	Rural	-	-	-	-
	Urban	-	-	-	-
Aizawl	Total	59	274	142	132
	Rural	3	12	5	7
	Urban	56	262	137	125
Champhai *	Total	4	15	10	5
	Rural	3	14	9	5
	Urban	1	1	1	-
Serchhip *	Total	-	-	-	-
	Rural	-	-	-	-
	Urban	-	-	-	-
Lunglei	Total	-	-	-	-
	Rural	-	-	-	-
	Urban	-	-	-	-
Lawngtlai	Total	2	7	4	3
	Rural	2	7	4	3
	Urban	-	-	-	-

Contd.

Contd.

(1)	(2)	(3)	(4)	(5)	(6)
Saiha *	Total	3	18	9	9
	Rural	3	18	9	9
	Urban	-	-	-	-
TRIPURA	Total	246	857	483	374
	Rural	162	670	377	293
	Urban	84	187	106	81
West Tripura	Total	115	321	175	146
	Rural	51	179	94	85
	Urban	64	142	81	61
South Tripura	Total	54	209	132	77
	Rural	40	176	112	64
	Urban	14	33	20	13
Dhalai *	Total	20	82	39	43
	Rural	18	74	36	38
	Urban	2	8	3	5
North Tripura	Total	57	245	137	108
	Rural	53	241	135	106
	Urban	4	4	2	2
MEGHALAYA	Total	380	1,827	946	881
	Rural	333	1,644	850	794
	Urban	47	183	96	87
West Garo Hills	Total	32	143	80	63
	Rural	31	139	77	62
	Urban	1	4	3	1
East Garo Hills	Total	61	267	111	156
	Rural	45	199	81	118
	Urban	16	68	30	38
South Garo Hills *	Total	13	47	43	4
	Rural	10	39	35	4
	Urban	3	8	8	-
West Khasi Hills	Total	69	273	134	139
	Rural	64	246	122	124
	Urban	5	27	12	15
Ri Bhoi *	Total	35	147	77	70
	Rural	31	136	72	64
	Urban	4	11	5	6

Contd.

Contd.

(1)	(2)	(3)	(4)	(5)	(6)
East Khasi Hills	Total	65	266	142	124
	Rural	57	245	127	118
	Urban	8	21	15	6
Jaintia Hills	Total	105	684	359	325
	Rural	95	640	336	304
	Urban	10	44	23	21
ASSAM	Total	3,126	13,355	7,325	6,030
	Rural	2,571	10,989	5,728	5,261
	Urban	555	2,366	1,597	769
Kokrajhar	Total	533	2,456	1,229	1,227
	Rural	518	2,421	1,213	1,208
	Urban	15	35	16	19
Dhubri	Total	163	586	280	306
	Rural	142	561	265	296
	Urban	21	25	15	10
Goalpara	Total	38	145	71	74
	Rural	38	145	71	74
	Urban	-	-	-	-
Bongaigaon	Total	80	271	145	126
	Rural	55	207	105	102
	Urban	25	64	40	24
Barpeta	Total	94	361	180	181
	Rural	86	342	167	175
	Urban	8	19	13	6
Kamrup	Total	338	1,587	1,052	535
	Rural	161	568	306	262
	Urban	177	1,019	746	273
Nalbari	Total	74	303	155	148
	Rural	73	301	154	147
	Urban	1	2	1	1
Darrang	Total	107	382	186	196
	Rural	105	380	184	196
	Urban	2	2	2	-
Marigaon	Total	46	234	117	117
	Rural	41	214	108	106
	Urban	5	20	9	11

Contd.

Contd.

(1)	(2)	(3)	(4)	(5)	(6)
Nagaon	Total	185	714	380	334
	Rural	142	612	311	301
	Urban	43	102	69	33
Sonitpur	Total	487	2,183	1,205	978
	Rural	462	2,090	1,152	938
	Urban	25	93	53	40
Lakhimpur	Total	61	431	332	99
	Rural	50	236	188	48
	Urban	11	195	144	51
Dhemaji	Total	53	259	138	121
	Rural	48	242	131	111
	Urban	5	17	7	10
Tinsukia	Total	140	571	353	218
	Rural	77	311	172	139
	Urban	63	260	181	79
Dibrugarh	Total	96	409	210	199
	Rural	85	374	188	186
	Urban	11	35	22	13
Sibsagar	Total	52	170	108	62
	Rural	41	140	85	55
	Urban	11	30	23	7
Jorhat	Total	44	174	97	77
	Rural	27	89	45	44
	Urban	17	85	52	33
Golaghat	Total	50	187	98	89
	Rural	28	114	59	55
	Urban	22	73	39	34
Karbi Anglong	Total	235	955	532	423
	Rural	169	743	408	335
	Urban	66	212	124	88
North Cachar Hills	Total	9	40	20	20
	Rural	8	38	19	19
	Urban	1	2	1	1
Cachar	Total	84	353	166	187
	Rural	78	322	149	173
	Urban	6	31	17	14

Contd.

Contd.

(1)	(2)	(3)	(4)	(5)	(6)
Karimganj	Total	92	321	146	175
	Rural	79	303	138	165
	Urban	13	18	8	10
Hailakandi	Total	65	263	125	138
	Rural	58	236	110	126
	Urban	7	27	15	12
WEST BENGAL	Total	19,385	110,535	78,105	32,430
	Rural	5,337	19,726	10,506	9,220
	Urban	14,048	90,809	67,599	23,210
Darjiling	Total	542	3,431	2,564	867
	Rural	309	1,249	673	576
	Urban	233	2,182	1,891	291
Jalpaiguri	Total	510	2,637	1,887	750
	Rural	298	849	449	400
	Urban	212	1,788	1,438	350
Koch Bihar	Total	306	868	425	443
	Rural	252	658	314	344
	Urban	54	210	111	99
Uttar Dinajpur	Total	1,073	3,531	1,879	1,652
	Rural	282	993	504	489
	Urban	791	2,538	1,375	1,163
Dakshin	Total	136	617	443	174
Dinajpur *	Rural	88	271	165	106
	Urban	48	346	278	68
Maldah	Total	231	889	514	375
	Rural	214	779	413	366
	Urban	17	110	101	9
Murshidabad	Total	705	2,995	1,539	1,456
	Rural	542	2,278	1,142	1,136
	Urban	163	717	397	320
Birbhum	Total	361	1,272	656	616
	Rural	266	959	501	458
	Urban	95	313	155	158
Barddhaman	Total	1,253	4,300	2,468	1,832
	Rural	618	2,397	1,255	1,142
	Urban	635	1,903	1,213	690

Contd.

Contd.

(1)	(2)	(3)	(4)	(5)	(6)
Nadia	Total	353	1,173	702	471
	Rural	195	741	414	327
	Urban	158	432	288	144
North Twenty Four Parganas	Total	1,620	6,717	4,223	2,494
	Rural	352	1,445	774	671
	Urban	1,268	5,272	3,449	1,823
Hugli	Total	927	4,043	2,625	1,418
	Rural	466	1,842	984	858
	Urban	461	2,201	1,641	560
Bankura	Total	165	535	305	230
	Rural	136	459	253	206
	Urban	29	76	52	24
Puruliya	Total	288	1,126	614	512
	Rural	204	791	422	369
	Urban	84	335	192	143
Medinipur	Total	715	2,460	1,429	1,031
	Rural	503	1,727	950	777
	Urban	212	733	479	254
Haora	Total	890	4,404	3,257	1,147
	Rural	213	790	495	295
	Urban	677	3,614	2,762	852
Kolkata	Total	8,731	67,676	51,531	16,145
	Rural	-	-	-	-
	Urban	8,731	67,676	51,531	16,145
South Twenty Four Parganas	Total	579	1,861	1,044	817
	Rural	399	1,498	798	700
	Urban	180	363	246	117
JHARKHAND	Total	2,559	10,887	6,009	4,878
	Rural	1,585	6,998	3,650	3,348
	Urban	974	3,889	2,359	1,530
Garhwa *	Total	157	748	391	357
	Rural	131	613	320	293
	Urban	26	135	71	64
Palamu	Total	211	952	521	431
	Rural	189	821	430	391
	Urban	22	131	91	40

Contd.

Contd.

(1)	(2)	(3)	(4)	(5)	(6)
Chatra *	Total	26	96	46	50
	Rural	21	73	34	39
	Urban	5	23	12	11
Hazaribagh	Total	137	553	304	249
	Rural	84	355	190	165
	Urban	53	198	114	84
Kodarma *	Total	73	367	197	170
	Rural	32	204	104	100
	Urban	41	163	93	70
Giridih	Total	174	891	467	424
	Rural	158	815	426	389
	Urban	16	76	41	35
Deoghar	Total	56	328	176	152
	Rural	17	63	41	22
	Urban	39	265	135	130
Godda	Total	138	655	337	318
	Rural	124	593	310	283
	Urban	14	62	27	35
Sahibganj	Total	86	373	204	169
	Rural	63	289	160	129
	Urban	23	84	44	40
Pakaur *	Total	53	206	101	105
	Rural	42	159	82	77
	Urban	11	47	19	28
Dumka	Total	147	715	360	355
	Rural	133	686	341	345
	Urban	14	29	19	10
Dhanbad	Total	244	914	551	363
	Rural	82	299	167	132
	Urban	162	615	384	231
Bokaro *	Total	87	450	295	155
	Rural	24	125	71	54
	Urban	63	325	224	101
Ranchi	Total	259	1,044	605	439
	Rural	114	497	257	240
	Urban	145	547	348	199

Contd.

Contd.

(1)	(2)	(3)	(4)	(5)	(6)
Lohardaga	Total	8	53	32	21
	Rural	5	40	26	14
	Urban	3	13	6	7
Gumla	Total	150	630	312	318
	Rural	109	445	211	234
	Urban	41	185	101	84
Pashchimi Singhbhum	Total	233	894	500	394
	Rural	133	453	237	216
	Urban	100	441	263	178
Purbi Singhbhum	Total	320	1,018	610	408
	Rural	124	468	243	225
	Urban	196	550	367	183
ORISSA	Total	13,044	42,871	25,343	17,528
	Rural	7,998	31,039	16,609	14,430
	Urban	5,046	11,832	8,734	3,098
Bargarh *	Total	598	2,243	1,204	1,039
	Rural	534	1,980	1,036	944
	Urban	64	263	168	95
Jharsuguda *	Total	476	2,012	1,039	973
	Rural	416	1,805	930	875
	Urban	60	207	109	98
Sambalpur	Total	454	1,640	854	786
	Rural	392	1,441	741	700
	Urban	62	199	113	86
Debagarh *	Total	109	621	363	258
	Rural	72	362	197	165
	Urban	37	259	166	93
Sundargarh	Total	707	2,454	1,363	1,091
	Rural	538	1,905	1,041	864
	Urban	169	549	322	227
Kendujhar	Total	203	647	357	290
	Rural	136	426	233	193
	Urban	67	221	124	97
Mayurbhanj	Total	395	1,452	770	682
	Rural	332	1,168	603	565
	Urban	63	284	167	117

Contd.

Contd.

(1)	(2)	(3)	(4)	(5)	(6)
Baleshwar	Total	245	1,290	920	370
	Rural	196	1,121	830	291
	Urban	49	169	90	79
Bhadrak *	Total	160	541	271	270
	Rural	120	450	222	228
	Urban	40	91	49	42
Kendrapara *	Total	93	354	200	154
	Rural	89	347	195	152
	Urban	4	7	5	2
Jagatsinghapur *	Total	591	2,455	1,492	963
	Rural	518	2,207	1,305	902
	Urban	73	248	187	61
Cuttack	Total	559	2,132	1,523	609
	Rural	229	864	469	395
	Urban	330	1,268	1,054	214
Jajapur *	Total	254	984	540	444
	Rural	240	930	508	422
	Urban	14	54	32	22
Dhenkanal	Total	238	947	514	433
	Rural	224	859	463	396
	Urban	14	88	51	37
Anugul *	Total	1,152	4,889	2,433	2,456
	Rural	1,039	4,393	2,190	2,203
	Urban	113	496	243	253
Nayagarh *	Total	100	412	220	192
	Rural	92	396	210	186
	Urban	8	16	10	6
Khordha *	Total	3,516	6,242	5,026	1,216
	Rural	150	639	334	305
	Urban	3,366	5,603	4,692	911
Puri	Total	277	939	544	395
	Rural	183	703	379	324
	Urban	94	236	165	71
Ganjam	Total	960	3,740	2,039	1,701
	Rural	748	2,967	1,516	1,451
	Urban	212	773	523	250

Contd.

Contd.

(1)	(2)	(3)	(4)	(5)	(6)
Gajapati *	Total	182	694	435	259
	Rural	167	634	391	243
	Urban	15	60	44	16
Kandhamal	Total	134	479	275	204
	Rural	122	459	260	199
	Urban	12	20	15	5
Baudh *	Total	74	243	104	139
	Rural	64	220	93	127
	Urban	10	23	11	12
Sonapur *	Total	169	620	301	319
	Rural	161	600	293	307
	Urban	8	20	8	12
Balangir	Total	373	1,281	624	657
	Rural	331	1,110	528	582
	Urban	42	171	96	75
Nuapada *	Total	115	407	204	203
	Rural	109	374	179	195
	Urban	6	33	25	8
Kalahandi	Total	214	925	551	374
	Rural	173	708	430	278
	Urban	41	217	121	96
Rayagada *	Total	199	654	342	312
	Rural	176	579	298	281
	Urban	23	75	44	31
Nabarangapur *	Total	150	454	246	208
	Rural	124	366	199	167
	Urban	26	88	47	41
Koraput	Total	268	878	470	408
	Rural	248	791	421	370
	Urban	20	87	49	38
Malkangiri *	Total	79	242	119	123
	Rural	75	235	115	120
	Urban	4	7	4	3
CHHATTISGARH	Total	7,504	28,772	15,761	13,011
	Rural	5,611	22,558	12,141	10,417
	Urban	1,893	6,214	3,620	2,594

Contd.

Contd.

(1)	(2)	(3)	(4)	(5)	(6)
Koriya *	Total	341	1,212	651	561
	Rural	263	988	500	488
	Urban	78	224	151	73
Surguja	Total	566	2,409	1,321	1,088
	Rural	513	2,201	1,179	1,022
	Urban	53	208	142	66
Jashpur *	Total	89	292	207	85
	Rural	74	256	183	73
	Urban	15	36	24	12
Raigarh	Total	718	2,610	1,476	1,134
	Rural	625	2,430	1,343	1,087
	Urban	93	180	133	47
Korba *	Total	463	1,717	884	833
	Rural	276	1,059	553	506
	Urban	187	658	331	327
Janjgir - Champa*	Total	1,110	4,240	2,191	2,049
	Rural	995	3,788	1,930	1,858
	Urban	115	452	261	191
Bilaspur	Total	714	2,812	1,513	1,299
	Rural	570	2,449	1,317	1,132
	Urban	144	363	196	167
Kawardha *	Total	202	866	461	405
	Rural	174	769	407	362
	Urban	28	97	54	43
Rajnandgaon	Total	481	1,866	1,026	840
	Rural	327	1,404	761	643
	Urban	154	462	265	197
Durg	Total	460	1,764	962	802
	Rural	277	1,249	687	562
	Urban	183	515	275	240
Raipur	Total	1,113	4,224	2,373	1,851
	Rural	535	2,133	1,123	1,010
	Urban	578	2,091	1,250	841
Mahasamund *	Total	350	1,277	680	597
	Rural	293	1,090	572	518
	Urban	57	187	108	79

Contd.

Contd.

(1)	(2)	(3)	(4)	(5)	(6)
Dhamtari *	Total	156	636	326	310
	Rural	91	403	204	199
	Urban	65	233	122	111
Kanker *	Total	190	720	404	316
	Rural	169	642	365	277
	Urban	21	78	39	39
Bastar	Total	323	1,209	678	531
	Rural	271	1,003	553	450
	Urban	52	206	125	81
Dantewada*	Total	228	918	608	310
	Rural	158	694	464	230
	Urban	70	224	144	80
MADHYA PRADESH	Total	53,489	231,246	123,903	107,343
	Rural	37,827	169,376	88,581	80,795
	Urban	15,662	61,870	35,322	26,548
Sheopur *	Total	362	1,807	970	837
	Rural	244	1,312	698	614
	Urban	118	495	272	223
Morena	Total	232	974	541	433
	Rural	148	688	370	318
	Urban	84	286	171	115
Bhind	Total	193	923	506	417
	Rural	125	614	337	277
	Urban	68	309	169	140
Gwalior	Total	1,194	5,104	2,882	2,222
	Rural	301	1,420	760	660
	Urban	893	3,684	2,122	1,562
Datia	Total	766	3,424	1,841	1,583
	Rural	627	2,832	1,509	1,323
	Urban	139	592	332	260
Shivpuri	Total	644	2,980	1,672	1,308
	Rural	451	1,961	1,100	861
	Urban	193	1,019	572	447
Guna	Total	1,357	6,484	3,432	3,052
	Rural	1,156	5,555	2,925	2,630
	Urban	201	929	507	422

Contd.

Contd.

(1)	(2)	(3)	(4)	(5)	(6)
Tikamgarh	Total	172	856	457	399
	Rural	88	444	229	215
	Urban	84	412	228	184
Chhatarpur	Total	404	1,815	1,029	786
	Rural	230	1,047	562	485
	Urban	174	768	467	301
Panna	Total	223	1,030	569	461
	Rural	202	926	506	420
	Urban	21	104	63	41
Sagar	Total	4,185	17,924	9,023	8,901
	Rural	3,897	16,989	8,487	8,502
	Urban	288	935	536	399
Damoh	Total	1,012	3,601	1,953	1,648
	Rural	942	3,343	1,809	1,534
	Urban	70	258	144	114
Satna	Total	751	2,708	1,445	1,263
	Rural	416	1,653	858	795
	Urban	335	1,055	587	468
Rewa	Total	340	1,279	702	577
	Rural	151	688	373	315
	Urban	189	591	329	262
Umaria *	Total	170	715	375	340
	Rural	139	619	322	297
	Urban	31	96	53	43
Shahdol	Total	296	1,017	592	425
	Rural	129	467	263	204
	Urban	167	550	329	221
Sidhi	Total	238	817	482	335
	Rural	154	529	295	234
	Urban	84	288	187	101
Neemuch *	Total	1,106	5,501	2,927	2,574
	Rural	679	3,360	1,756	1,604
	Urban	427	2,141	1,171	970
Mandsaur	Total	1,654	8,380	4,455	3,925
	Rural	1,387	7,103	3,781	3,322
	Urban	267	1,277	674	603

Contd.

Contd.

(1)	(2)	(3)	(4)	(5)	(6)
Ratlam	Total	1,531	6,866	3,791	3,075
	Rural	904	4,301	2,333	1,968
	Urban	627	2,565	1,458	1,107
Ujjain	Total	2,890	13,298	7,176	6,122
	Rural	1,740	8,442	4,466	3,976
	Urban	1,150	4,856	2,710	2,146
Shajapur	Total	1,227	5,384	2,977	2,407
	Rural	921	4,158	2,261	1,897
	Urban	306	1,226	716	510
Dewas	Total	1,667	8,221	4,334	3,887
	Rural	1,312	6,619	3,477	3,142
	Urban	355	1,602	857	745
Jhabua	Total	241	1,159	676	483
	Rural	123	580	332	248
	Urban	118	579	344	235
Dhar	Total	2,256	10,392	5,344	5,048
	Rural	1,588	7,519	3,825	3,694
	Urban	668	2,873	1,519	1,354
Indore	Total	3,434	16,499	8,846	7,653
	Rural	1,615	8,518	4,405	4,113
	Urban	1,819	7,981	4,441	3,540
West Nimar	Total	1,324	5,293	2,871	2,422
	Rural	898	3,649	1,965	1,684
	Urban	426	1,644	906	738
Barwani *	Total	662	3,141	1,683	1,458
	Rural	466	2,227	1,173	1,054
	Urban	196	914	510	404
East Nimar	Total	1,310	5,629	3,042	2,587
	Rural	822	3,760	1,966	1,794
	Urban	488	1,869	1,076	793
Rajgarh	Total	642	3,056	1,724	1,332
	Rural	504	2,395	1,325	1,070
	Urban	138	661	399	262
Vidisha	Total	3,873	18,156	9,306	8,850
	Rural	3,610	17,037	8,680	8,357
	Urban	263	1,119	626	493

Contd.

Contd.

(1)	(2)	(3)	(4)	(5)	(6)
Bhopal	Total	2,349	8,989	5,169	3,820
	Rural	696	2,737	1,442	1,295
	Urban	1,653	6,252	3,727	2,525
Sehore	Total	1,102	4,473	2,419	2,054
	Rural	828	3,418	1,805	1,613
	Urban	274	1,055	614	441
Raisen	Total	2,686	13,427	6,864	6,563
	Rural	2,443	12,161	6,216	5,945
	Urban	243	1,266	648	618
Betul	Total	410	1,529	887	642
	Rural	270	1,174	678	496
	Urban	140	355	209	146
Harda *	Total	1,062	4,740	2,597	2,143
	Rural	942	4,309	2,337	1,972
	Urban	120	431	260	171
Hoshangabad	Total	1,422	5,214	3,006	2,208
	Rural	771	3,022	1,667	1,355
	Urban	651	2,192	1,339	853
Katni *	Total	562	2,189	1,204	985
	Rural	417	1,731	921	810
	Urban	145	458	283	175
Jabalpur	Total	3,299	11,112	5,756	5,356
	Rural	1,980	7,449	3,500	3,949
	Urban	1,319	3,663	2,256	1,407
Narsimhapur	Total	2,139	7,832	4,141	3,691
	Rural	1,895	7,075	3,716	3,359
	Urban	244	757	425	332
Dindori *	Total	225	812	482	330
	Rural	208	691	399	292
	Urban	17	121	83	38
Mandla	Total	400	1,248	743	505
	Rural	312	895	540	355
	Urban	88	353	203	150
Chhindwara	Total	602	2,051	1,218	833
	Rural	435	1,440	815	625
	Urban	167	611	403	208

Contd.

Contd.

(1)	(2)	(3)	(4)	(5)	(6)
Seoni	Total	368	1,180	681	499
	Rural	311	1,044	599	445
	Urban	57	136	82	54
Balaghat	Total	507	2,017	1,113	904
	Rural	350	1,475	798	677
	Urban	157	542	315	227
GUJARAT	Total	48,095	220,786	123,181	97,605
	Rural	31,409	148,691	79,241	69,450
	Urban	16,686	72,095	43,940	28,155
Kachchh	Total	382	1,621	914	707
	Rural	231	964	544	420
	Urban	151	657	370	287
Banas Kantha	Total	1,022	5,176	2,859	2,317
	Rural	891	4,712	2,595	2,117
	Urban	131	464	264	200
Patan *	Total	316	1,526	870	656
	Rural	251	1,339	758	581
	Urban	65	187	112	75
Mahesana	Total	1,223	6,608	3,649	2,959
	Rural	1,070	5,936	3,252	2,684
	Urban	153	672	397	275
Sabar Kantha	Total	1,211	6,155	3,442	2,713
	Rural	995	5,085	2,768	2,317
	Urban	216	1,070	674	396
Gandhinagar	Total	1,116	5,830	3,212	2,618
	Rural	563	2,969	1,588	1,381
	Urban	553	2,861	1,624	1,237
Ahmadabad	Total	3,443	12,471	7,426	5,045
	Rural	534	2,765	1,469	1,296
	Urban	2,909	9,706	5,957	3,749
Surendranagar	Total	523	2,774	1,480	1,294
	Rural	425	2,359	1,246	1,113
	Urban	98	415	234	181
Rajkot	Total	1,556	7,409	4,144	3,265
	Rural	860	4,531	2,505	2,026
	Urban	696	2,878	1,639	1,239

Contd.

Contd.

(1)	(2)	(3)	(4)	(5)	(6)
Jamnagar	Total	1,087	5,103	2,755	2,348
	Rural	641	3,459	1,816	1,643
	Urban	446	1,644	939	705
Porbandar *	Total	746	3,449	1,805	1,644
	Rural	594	2,958	1,522	1,436
	Urban	152	491	283	208
Junagadh	Total	1,199	6,082	3,223	2,859
	Rural	907	4,720	2,459	2,261
	Urban	292	1,362	764	598
Amreli	Total	422	2,097	1,171	926
	Rural	317	1,662	931	731
	Urban	105	435	240	195
Bhavnagar	Total	940	5,339	3,099	2,240
	Rural	446	2,521	1,495	1,026
	Urban	494	2,818	1,604	1,214
Anand *	Total	1,862	9,706	5,207	4,499
	Rural	1,376	7,296	3,879	3,417
	Urban	486	2,410	1,328	1,082
Kheda	Total	1,608	8,349	4,475	3,874
	Rural	1,470	7,727	4,127	3,600
	Urban	138	622	348	274
Panch Mahals	Total	765	3,758	2,068	1,690
	Rural	557	2,710	1,463	1,247
	Urban	208	1,048	605	443
Dohad *	Total	223	1,221	645	576
	Rural	99	479	247	232
	Urban	124	742	398	344
Vadodara	Total	4,943	23,653	13,209	10,444
	Rural	2,712	13,250	7,080	6,170
	Urban	2,231	10,403	6,129	4,274
Narmada *	Total	342	1,387	768	619
	Rural	292	1,227	687	540
	Urban	50	160	81	79
Bharuch	Total	3,293	14,753	8,106	6,647
	Rural	2,777	12,593	6,851	5,742
	Urban	516	2,160	1,255	905

Contd.

Contd.

(1)	(2)	(3)	(4)	(5)	(6)
Surat	Total	15,376	67,194	38,258	28,936
	Rural	9,742	41,828	21,654	20,174
	Urban	5,634	25,366	16,604	8,762
The Dangs	Total	189	846	476	370
	Rural	189	846	476	370
	Urban	-	-	-	-
Navsari *	Total	2,241	9,363	5,115	4,248
	Rural	1,774	7,424	3,981	3,443
	Urban	467	1,939	1,134	805
Valsad	Total	2,067	8,916	4,805	4,111
	Rural	1,696	7,331	3,848	3,483
	Urban	371	1,585	957	628
DAMAN & DIU	Total	227	1,071	682	389
	Rural	135	659	433	226
	Urban	92	412	249	163
Diu	Total	12	48	24	24
	Rural	5	13	7	6
	Urban	7	35	17	18
Daman	Total	215	1,023	658	365
	Rural	130	646	426	220
	Urban	85	377	232	145
DADRA & NAGAR HAVELI	Total	305	1,471	797	674
	Rural	255	1,261	665	596
	Urban	50	210	132	78
Dadra & Nagar Haveli	Total	305	1,471	797	674
	Rural	255	1,261	665	596
	Urban	50	210	132	78
MAHARASHTRA	Total	87,474	340,924	197,088	143,836
	Rural	56,880	236,412	127,406	109,006
	Urban	30,594	104,512	69,682	34,830
Nandurbar *	Total	826	4,044	2,150	1,894
	Rural	640	3,200	1,727	1,473
	Urban	186	844	423	421
Dhule	Total	862	3,620	1,926	1,694
	Rural	695	3,156	1,666	1,490
	Urban	167	464	260	204

Contd.

Contd.

(1)	(2)	(3)	(4)	(5)	(6)
Jalgaon	Total	3,531	16,879	8,981	7,898
	Rural	3,016	14,596	7,734	6,862
	Urban	515	2,283	1,247	1,036
Buldana	Total	1,322	5,340	2,874	2,466
	Rural	1,054	4,515	2,395	2,120
	Urban	268	825	479	346
Akola	Total	1,412	5,842	3,279	2,563
	Rural	1,071	4,636	2,551	2,085
	Urban	341	1,206	728	478
Washim *	Total	595	2,593	1,420	1,173
	Rural	532	2,322	1,270	1,052
	Urban	63	271	150	121
Amravati	Total	2,603	9,904	5,389	4,515
	Rural	2,159	8,429	4,545	3,884
	Urban	444	1,475	844	631
Wardha	Total	2,731	10,434	5,679	4,755
	Rural	2,383	9,376	5,037	4,339
	Urban	348	1,058	642	416
Nagpur	Total	2,959	8,995	5,321	3,674
	Rural	1,499	5,644	3,057	2,587
	Urban	1,460	3,351	2,264	1,087
Bhandara	Total	652	2,472	1,363	1,109
	Rural	584	2,201	1,220	981
	Urban	68	271	143	128
Gondiya *	Total	561	1,914	1,055	859
	Rural	499	1,754	950	804
	Urban	62	160	105	55
Gadchiroli	Total	935	3,476	2,084	1,392
	Rural	852	3,160	1,901	1,259
	Urban	83	316	183	133
Chandrapur	Total	2,118	8,139	4,407	3,732
	Rural	1,633	6,331	3,386	2,945
	Urban	485	1,808	1,021	787
Yavatmal	Total	2,466	9,581	5,231	4,350
	Rural	2,172	8,567	4,625	3,942
	Urban	294	1,014	606	408

Contd.

Contd.

(1)	(2)	(3)	(4)	(5)	(6)
Nanded	Total	1,280	5,600	2,953	2,647
	Rural	1,032	4,757	2,509	2,248
	Urban	248	843	444	399
Hingoli *	Total	286	1,286	669	617
	Rural	241	1,040	540	500
	Urban	45	246	129	117
Parbhani	Total	631	2,653	1,401	1,252
	Rural	538	2,273	1,181	1,092
	Urban	93	380	220	160
Jalna	Total	1,396	5,525	2,902	2,623
	Rural	1,261	5,069	2,648	2,421
	Urban	135	456	254	202
Aurangabad	Total	1,724	7,132	3,852	3,280
	Rural	1,265	5,334	2,822	2,512
	Urban	459	1,798	1,030	768
Nashik	Total	5,649	25,421	13,911	11,510
	Rural	4,480	21,179	11,315	9,864
	Urban	1,169	4,242	2,596	1,646
Thane	Total	13,080	51,888	30,191	21,697
	Rural	6,077	25,252	14,000	11,252
	Urban	7,003	26,636	16,191	10,445
Mumbai (Suburban) *	Total	4,591	15,074	10,407	4,667
	Rural	-	-	-	-
	Urban	4,591	15,074	10,407	4,667
Mumbai	Total	7,180	24,000	20,034	3,966
	Rural	-	-	-	-
	Urban	7,180	24,000	20,034	3,966
Raigarh	Total	3,648	14,607	8,021	6,586
	Rural	2,964	11,867	6,412	5,455
	Urban	684	2,740	1,609	1,131
Pune	Total	4,618	16,316	9,317	6,999
	Rural	2,816	11,615	6,350	5,265
	Urban	1,802	4,701	2,967	1,734
Ahmadnagar	Total	2,598	10,494	5,719	4,775
	Rural	2,181	8,954	4,784	4,170
	Urban	417	1,540	935	605

Contd.

Contd.

(1)	*(2)*	*(3)*	*(4)*	*(5)*	*(6)*
Bid	Total	1,435	5,811	3,105	2,706
	Rural	1,295	5,210	2,771	2,439
	Urban	140	601	334	267
Latur	Total	687	3,308	1,762	1,546
	Rural	508	2,282	1,224	1,058
	Urban	179	1,026	538	488
Osmanabad	Total	1,267	5,337	2,807	2,530
	Rural	1,108	4,577	2,406	2,171
	Urban	159	760	401	359
Solapur	Total	5,031	18,112	9,584	8,528
	Rural	4,522	17,032	8,873	8,159
	Urban	509	1,080	711	369
Satara	Total	2,143	8,843	4,670	4,173
	Rural	1,921	8,058	4,236	3,822
	Urban	222	785	434	351
Ratnagiri	Total	1,592	6,294	3,561	2,733
	Rural	1,452	5,756	3,253	2,503
	Urban	140	538	308	230
Sindhudurg	Total	1,391	6,172	3,680	2,492
	Rural	1,289	5,832	3,486	2,346
	Urban	102	340	194	146
Kolhapur	Total	1,945	7,416	3,954	3,462
	Rural	1,653	6,648	3,502	3,146
	Urban	292	768	452	316
Sangli	Total	1,729	6,402	3,429	2,973
	Rural	1,488	5,790	3,030	2,760
	Urban	241	612	399	213
ANDHRA PRADESH	Total	40,818	163,938	87,279	76,659
	Rural	24,167	97,101	49,791	47,310
	Urban	16,651	66,837	37,488	29,349
Adilabad	Total	1,560	6,453	3,397	3,056
	Rural	1,200	4,855	2,534	2,321
	Urban	360	1,598	863	735
Nizamabad	Total	1,489	6,822	3,506	3,316
	Rural	1,246	5,684	2,867	2,817
	Urban	243	1,138	639	499

Contd.

Contd.

(1)	(2)	(3)	(4)	(5)	(6)
Karimnagar	Total	3,423	14,662	7,751	6,911
	Rural	2,674	11,119	5,769	5,350
	Urban	749	3,543	1,982	1,561
Medak	Total	1,009	4,547	2,316	2,231
	Rural	871	3,885	1,973	1,912
	Urban	138	662	343	319
Hyderabad	Total	3,426	14,441	8,160	6,281
	Rural	-	-	-	-
	Urban	3,426	14,441	8,160	6,281
Rangareddi	Total	4,365	18,616	9,685	8,931
	Rural	1,142	4,997	2,538	2,459
	Urban	3,223	13,619	7,147	6,472
Mahbubnagar	Total	1,969	8,923	4,413	4,510
	Rural	1,691	7,647	3,755	3,892
	Urban	278	1,276	658	618
Nalgonda	Total	1,440	6,130	3,248	2,882
	Rural	1,100	4,522	2,332	2,190
	Urban	340	1,608	916	692
Warangal	Total	2,702	10,914	5,620	5,294
	Rural	2,053	8,296	4,213	4,083
	Urban	649	2,618	1,407	1,211
Khammam	Total	1,193	4,794	2,572	2,222
	Rural	959	4,003	2,137	1,866
	Urban	234	791	435	356
Srikakulam	Total	824	2,705	1,360	1,345
	Rural	622	2,045	1,004	1,041
	Urban	202	660	356	304
Vizianagaram	Total	503	1,531	774	757
	Rural	385	1,261	632	629
	Urban	118	270	142	128
Visakhapatnam	Total	1,642	6,181	3,398	2,783
	Rural	628	2,191	1,094	1,097
	Urban	1,014	3,990	2,304	1,686
East Godavari	Total	1,960	6,194	3,621	2,573
	Rural	1,013	3,607	1,870	1,737
	Urban	947	2,587	1,751	836

Contd.

Contd.

(1)	(2)	(3)	(4)	(5)	(6)
West Godavari	Total	1,628	6,641	3,610	3,031
	Rural	948	3,270	1,705	1,565
	Urban	680	3,371	1,905	1,466
Krishna	Total	2,124	8,824	4,942	3,882
	Rural	1,246	4,960	2,562	2,398
	Urban	878	3,864	2,380	1,484
Guntur	Total	1,920	6,932	3,739	3,193
	Rural	1,317	5,207	2,616	2,591
	Urban	603	1,725	1,123	602
Prakasam	Total	1,064	3,807	2,010	1,797
	Rural	641	2,314	1,219	1,095
	Urban	423	1,493	791	702
Nellore	Total	1,333	4,580	2,507	2,073
	Rural	959	3,420	1,816	1,604
	Urban	374	1,160	691	469
Cuddapah	Total	990	4,056	2,135	1,921
	Rural	797	3,344	1,756	1,588
	Urban	193	712	379	333
Kurnool	Total	1,348	5,775	2,938	2,837
	Rural	1,031	4,303	2,192	2,111
	Urban	317	1,472	746	726
Anantapur	Total	1,299	4,939	2,656	2,283
	Rural	740	2,845	1,481	1,364
	Urban	559	2,094	1,175	919
Chittoor	Total	1,607	5,471	2,921	2,550
	Rural	904	3,326	1,726	1,600
	Urban	703	2,145	1,195	950
KARNATAKA	Total	26,057	102,226	57,959	44,267
	Rural	14,690	61,898	33,962	27,936
	Urban	11,367	40,328	23,997	16,331
Belgaum	Total	2,627	10,826	5,796	5,030
	Rural	2,164	9,109	4,841	4,268
	Urban	463	1,717	955	762
Bagalkot *	Total	1,579	6,729	3,543	3,186
	Rural	1,431	6,069	3,162	2,907
	Urban	148	660	381	279

Contd.

Contd.

(1)	(2)	(3)	(4)	(5)	(6)
Bijapur	Total	573	2,646	1,375	1,271
	Rural	462	2,169	1,132	1,037
	Urban	111	477	243	234
Gulbarga	Total	789	3,715	2,074	1,641
	Rural	538	2,596	1,459	1,137
	Urban	251	1,119	615	504
Bidar	Total	936	4,565	2,411	2,154
	Rural	747	3,537	1,882	1,655
	Urban	189	1,028	529	499
Raichur	Total	725	3,240	1,773	1,467
	Rural	429	1,916	1,023	893
	Urban	296	1,324	750	574
Koppal	Total	314	1,399	722	677
	Rural	211	930	477	453
	Urban	103	469	245	224
Gadag *	Total	388	1,507	832	675
	Rural	212	874	470	404
	Urban	176	633	362	271
Dharwad	Total	544	2,238	1,221	1,017
	Rural	179	936	502	434
	Urban	365	1,302	719	583
Uttara Kannada	Total	1,108	4,229	2,526	1,703
	Rural	853	3,464	2,040	1,424
	Urban	255	765	486	279
Haveri *	Total	253	1,192	669	523
	Rural	164	808	448	360
	Urban	89	384	221	163
Bellary	Total	659	2,736	1,458	1,278
	Rural	386	1,748	905	843
	Urban	273	988	553	435
Chitradurga	Total	248	1,061	554	507
	Rural	152	623	298	325
	Urban	96	438	256	182
Davanagere	Total	555	2,490	1,352	1,138
	Rural	341	1,540	841	699
	Urban	214	950	511	439

Contd.

Contd.

(1)	(2)	(3)	(4)	(5)	(6)
Shimoga	Total	1,266	5,297	2,929	2,368
	Rural	990	4,266	2,347	1,919
	Urban	276	1,031	582	449
Udupi*	Total	649	2,311	1,599	712
	Rural	406	1,381	930	451
	Urban	243	930	669	261
Chikmagalur	Total	574	2,348	1,290	1,058
	Rural	431	1,763	938	825
	Urban	143	585	352	233
Tumkur	Total	1,143	4,553	2,531	2,022
	Rural	703	3,001	1,681	1,320
	Urban	440	1,552	850	702
Kolar	Total	781	3,146	1,676	1,470
	Rural	470	1,762	916	846
	Urban	311	1,384	760	624
Bangalore	Total	5,408	17,748	10,779	6,969
	Rural	388	1,561	870	691
	Urban	5,020	16,187	9,909	6,278
Bangalore Rural	Total	961	3,465	2,016	1,449
	Rural	753	2,816	1,634	1,182
	Urban	208	649	382	267
Mandya	Total	566	1,908	1,105	803
	Rural	468	1,610	920	690
	Urban	98	298	185	113
Hassan	Total	968	3,728	2,042	1,686
	Rural	678	2,750	1,487	1,263
	Urban	290	978	555	423
Dakshina Kannada	Total	1,243	4,365	2,887	1,478
	Rural	383	1,513	931	582
	Urban	860	2,852	1,956	896
Kodagu	Total	530	2,350	1,461	889
	Rural	389	1,683	1,031	652
	Urban	141	667	430	237
Mysore	Total	581	2,131	1,172	959
	Rural	306	1,300	704	596
	Urban	275	831	468	363

Contd.

Contd.

(1)	(2)	(3)	(4)	(5)	(6)
Chamaraja-	Total	89	303	166	137
nagar *	Rural	56	173	93	80
	Urban	33	130	73	57
GOA	Total	1,393	5,280	3,466	1,814
	Rural	701	2,991	1,844	1,147
	Urban	692	2,289	1,622	667
North Goa	Total	749	3,185	2,001	1,184
	Rural	459	2,011	1,222	789
	Urban	290	1,174	779	395
South Goa	Total	644	2,095	1,465	630
	Rural	242	980	622	358
	Urban	402	1,115	843	272
LAKSHADWEEP	Total	-	-	-	-
	Rural	-	-	-	-
	Urban	-	-	-	-
LAKSHADWEEP	Total	-	-	-	-
	Rural	-	-	-	-
	Urban	-	-	-	-
KERALA	Total	5,654	16,533	10,089	6,444
	Rural	2,885	9,096	5,279	3,817
	Urban	2,769	7,437	4,810	2,627
Kasaragod	Total	174	671	393	278
	Rural	102	390	220	170
	Urban	72	281	173	108
Kannur	Total	678	1,875	1,211	664
	Rural	201	686	419	267
	Urban	477	1,189	792	397
Wayanad	Total	168	727	476	251
	Rural	162	665	424	241
	Urban	6	62	52	10
Kozhikode	Total	487	1,672	1,036	636
	Rural	237	771	458	313
	Urban	250	901	578	323
Malappuram	Total	409	1,373	854	519
	Rural	328	1,173	723	450
	Urban	81	200	131	69

Contd.

Contd.

(1)	(2)	(3)	(4)	(5)	(6)
Palakkad	Total	389	1,379	749	630
	Rural	217	809	412	397
	Urban	172	570	337	233
Thrissur	Total	611	1,629	1,061	568
	Rural	220	652	406	246
	Urban	391	977	655	322
Ernakulam	Total	586	1,696	1,141	555
	Rural	161	390	255	135
	Urban	425	1,306	886	420
Idukki	Total	238	608	335	273
	Rural	212	577	312	265
	Urban	26	31	23	8
Kottayam	Total	410	1,034	640	394
	Rural	255	699	397	302
	Urban	155	335	243	92
Alappuzha	Total	231	644	357	287
	Rural	84	234	132	102
	Urban	147	410	225	185
Pathanamthitta	Total	250	640	391	249
	Rural	181	437	269	168
	Urban	69	203	122	81
Kollam	Total	425	1,177	682	495
	Rural	266	835	462	373
	Urban	159	342	220	122
Thiruvanantha-puram	Total	598	1,408	763	645
	Rural	259	778	390	388
	Urban	339	630	373	257
TAMIL NADU	Total	20,532	86,472	47,057	39,415
	Rural	7,913	29,344	15,454	13,890
	Urban	12,619	57,128	31,603	25,525
Thiruvallur	Total	1,220	4,789	2,505	2,284
	Rural	613	2,432	1,265	1,167
	Urban	607	2,357	1,240	1,117
Chennai	Total	5,019	27,329	14,705	12,624
	Rural	-	-	-	-
	Urban	5,019	27,329	14,705	12,624

Contd.

Contd.

(1)	(2)	(3)	(4)	(5)	(6)
Kancheepuram	Total	958	3,716	1,940	1,776
	Rural	270	1,044	537	507
	Urban	688	2,672	1,403	1,269
Vellore	Total	1,112	4,159	2,211	1,948
	Rural	588	2,251	1,183	1,068
	Urban	524	1,908	1,028	880
Dharmapuri	Total	810	3,242	1,668	1,574
	Rural	630	2,502	1,292	1,210
	Urban	180	740	376	364
Tiruvannamalai	Total	500	2,246	1,288	958
	Rural	286	995	526	469
	Urban	214	1,251	762	489
Viluppuram	Total	546	2,065	1,068	997
	Rural	397	1,516	788	728
	Urban	149	549	280	269
Salem	Total	473	1,736	932	804
	Rural	257	928	490	438
	Urban	216	808	442	366
Namakkal *	Total	513	2,041	1,047	994
	Rural	379	1,398	721	677
	Urban	134	643	326	317
Erode	Total	990	3,868	2,155	1,713
	Rural	385	1,333	696	637
	Urban	605	2,535	1,459	1,076
The Nilgiris	Total	283	1,094	576	518
	Rural	68	247	134	113
	Urban	215	847	442	405
Coimbatore	Total	1,044	4,516	2,541	1,975
	Rural	281	981	497	484
	Urban	763	3,535	2,044	1,491
Dindigul	Total	549	2,226	1,252	974
	Rural	306	1,061	568	493
	Urban	243	1,165	684	481
Karur *	Total	505	1,308	763	545
	Rural	80	262	144	118
	Urban	425	1,046	619	427

Contd.

Contd.

(1)	(2)	(3)	(4)	(5)	(6)
Tiruchirappalli	Total	677	2,023	1,130	893
	Rural	323	1,055	561	494
	Urban	354	968	569	399
Perambalur *	Total	151	534	295	239
	Rural	139	504	275	229
	Urban	12	30	20	10
Ariyalur *	Total	163	592	305	287
	Rural	119	433	229	204
	Urban	44	159	76	83
Cuddalore	Total	504	1,934	987	947
	Rural	310	1,175	642	533
	Urban	194	759	345	414
Nagapattinam *	Total	458	1,440	825	615
	Rural	221	699	417	282
	Urban	237	741	408	333
Thiruvarur	Total	388	1,813	1,037	776
	Rural	274	1,299	724	575
	Urban	114	514	313	201
Thanjavur	Total	633	2,875	1,761	1,114
	Rural	354	1,342	752	590
	Urban	279	1,533	1,009	524
Pudukkottai	Total	244	956	504	452
	Rural	195	748	388	360
	Urban	49	208	116	92
Sivaganga	Total	165	631	317	314
	Rural	151	560	281	279
	Urban	14	71	36	35
Madurai	Total	627	2,087	1,175	912
	Rural	285	1,047	574	473
	Urban	342	1,040	601	439
Theni *	Total	197	641	364	277
	Rural	77	244	128	116
	Urban	120	397	236	161
Virudhunagar	Total	345	1,191	613	578
	Rural	210	774	394	380
	Urban	135	417	219	198

Contd.

Contd.

(1)	(2)	(3)	(4)	(5)	(6)
Ramanatha-puram	Total	485	1,779	946	833
	Rural	310	1,171	578	593
	Urban	175	608	368	240
Thoothukkudi	Total	309	876	462	414
	Rural	145	464	237	227
	Urban	164	412	225	187
Tirunelveli	Total	368	1,551	1,032	519
	Rural	167	507	248	259
	Urban	201	1,044	784	260
Kanniyakumari	Total	296	1,214	653	561
	Rural	93	372	185	187
	Urban	203	842	468	374
PONDICHERRY	Total	710	1,662	956	706
	Rural	81	194	118	76
	Urban	629	1,468	838	630
Yanam	Total	24	50	34	16
	Rural	-	-	-	-
	Urban	24	50	34	16
Pondicherry	Total	551	1,339	746	593
	Rural	45	115	73	42
	Urban	506	1,224	673	551
Mahe	Total	17	30	27	3
	Rural	-	-	-	-
	Urban	17	30	27	3
Karaikal	Total	118	243	149	94
	Rural	36	79	45	34
	Urban	82	164	104	60
ANDAMAN and NICOBAR ISLANDS	Total	217	242	235	7
	Rural	55	78	73	5
	Urban	162	164	162	2
Andamans	Total	213	238	232	6
	Rural	51	74	70	4
	Urban	162	164	162	2
Nicobars	Total	4	4	3	1
	Rural	4	4	3	1
	Urban	-	-	-	-

Bibliography

Barfield, Thomas, *The Nomadic Alternative*, Prentice Hall, Englewood Cliffs, NJ, 1993

Clarke, G., "China's reforms of Tibet, and their Effects on Pastoralism", *IDS Discussion Paper* No. 237. Institute of Development Studies: Brighton, England, 1987.

Clarke, Graham (ed.), "Development, Society, and Environment in Tibet", *Papers Presented at a Panel of the 7th International Association for Tibetan Studies*, Graz 1995.

Cribb, R., *Nomads in Archaeology*, Cambridge University Press, Cambridge, 1991

Di Cosmo, N., "Ancient Inner Asian Nomads: Their Economic Basis and Its Significance", *In* Chinese History, *Journal of Asian Studies* 53:4: 1092-1126, 1994

Ekvall, Robert, "Fields on the Hoof: The Nexus of Tibetan Nomadic Pastoralism", Hold, Rinehart and Winston, New York, 1968.

Fletcher, J., "The Mongols: Ecological and Social Perspectives", *Harvard Journal of Asiatic Studies* 46:1:11-50, 1986

George Schaller, "Rangelands of the Chang Tang Wildlife Reserve", Tibet, Rangelands 18(3): 91-96, 1996

Humphrey, Caroline and David Sneath, *The End of Nomadism? Society, State and the Environment in Inner Asia*. Duke University Press, Durham, 1999

Humphrey, Caroline and David Sneath (eds.), *Culture and Environment in Inner Asia, vol I: The Pastoral Economy and The Environment*, White Horse Press, Cambridge, 1996

Jagchid, Sechin and Van Jay Symons, *Peace, War and Trade Along the Great Wall: Nomadic-Chinese Interaction Through Two Millennia*, Indiania University Press, Bloomington, 1989.

Roe, Emery, Lynn Huntsinger and Keith Labnow, "High reliability pastoralism", *Journal of Arid Environments* 39: 39-55.

Vainshtein, S.I., *Nomads of South Siberia: The Pastoral Economies of Tuva*, Cambridge University Press, Cambridge, 1980

Volkov, V.V., "Early Nomads of Mongolia", In, *Nomads of The Eurasian Steppes in the Early Iron Age*. J. Davis-Kimball, ed. pp. 319-333. Zinat Press, Berkeley, 1995.

Williams, Dee M., "The barbed walls of China: A contemporary grassland drama", *The Journal of Asian Studies*, 55(3): 665-691.

Index